SERVICE ENTERPRISE INTEGRATION

INTEGRATED SERIES IN INFORMATION SYSTEMS

Series Editors

Professor Ramesh Sharda
Oklahoma State University

Prof. Dr. Stefan Voß
Universität Hamburg

Other published titles in the series:

E-BUSINESS MANAGEMENT: *Integration of Web Technologies with Business Models*/ edited by Michael J. Shaw
VIRTUAL CORPORATE UNIVERSITIES: *A Matrix of Knowledge and Learning for the New Digital Dawn*/ Walter R.J. Baets & Gert Van der Linden
SCALABLE ENTERPRISE SYSTEMS: *An Introduction to Recent Advances*/ edited by Vittal Prabhu, Soundar Kumara, Manjunath Kamath
LEGAL PROGRAMMING: *Legal Compliance for RFID and Software Agent Ecosystems in Retail Processes and Beyond*/ Brian Subirana and Malcolm Bain
LOGICAL DATA MODELING: *What It Is and How To Do It*/ Alan Chmura and J. Mark Heumann
DESIGNING AND EVALUATING E-MANAGEMENT DECISION TOOLS: *The Integration of Decision and Negotiation Models into Internet-Multimedia Technologies*/ Giampiero E.G. Beroggi
INFORMATION AND MANAGEMENT SYSTEMS FOR PRODUCT CUSTOMIZATION/ Thorsten Blecker et al
MEDICAL INFORMATICS: *Knowledge Management and Data Mining in Biomedicine*/ edited by Hsinchun Chen et al
KNOWLEDGE MANAGEMENT AND MANAGEMENT LEARNING: *Extending the Horizons of Knowledge-Based Management*/ edited by Walter Baets
INTELLIGENCE AND SECURITY INFORMATICS FOR INTERNATIONAL SECURITY: *Information Sharing and Data Mining*/ Hsinchun Chen
ENTERPRISE COLLABORATION: *On-Demand Information Exchange for Extended Enterprises*/ David Levermore & Cheng Hsu
SEMANTIC WEB AND EDUCATION/ Vladan Devedžić
INFORMATION SYSTEMS ACTION RESEARCH: *An Applied View of Emerging Concepts and Methods*/ Ned Kock
ONTOLOGIES IN THE CONTEXT OF INFORMATION SYSTEMS/ edited by Raj Sharman, Rajiv Kishore, Ram Ramesh
METAGRAPHS AND THEIR APPLICATIONS/ *Amit Basu and Robert W. Blanning*

SERVICE ENTERPRISE INTEGRATION
An Enterprise Engineering Perspective

Edited by

Cheng Hsu
Rensselaer Polytechnic Institute

Springer

Cheng Hsu
Rensselaer Polytechnic Institute
Troy, NY, USA

Library of Congress Control Number: 2006933302

ISBN-10: 0-387-46361-5 (HB) ISBN-10: 0-387-46364-X (e-book)
ISBN-13: 978-0-387-46361-2 (HB) ISBN-13: 978-0-387-46364-3 (e-book)

Printed on acid-free paper.

9 8 7 6 5 4 3 2 1

springer.com

Dedication

Dedicated to our colleagues,

who made research rewarding

Contents

Contributing Authors

In the order of their appearance in the book:

Ananth Krishmamurthy, Ph.D.
Assistant Professor, Department of Decision Sciences and Engineering Systems, Rensselaer Polytechnic Institute, Troy, NY 12180-3590
krisha@rpi.edu http://www.rpi.edu/~krisha

James M. Tien, Ph.D.
Yamada Corporation Professor, Departments of Decision Sciences and Engineering Systems, and Electrical, Computer and Systems Engineering, Rensselaer Polytechnic Institute, Troy, NY 12180-3590
tienj@rpi.edu

Francois B. Vernadat, Ph.D.
IT Administrator, European Commission, DG Informatics (Unit for Interoperability, Architecture and Methodologies), JMO C2/103, L-2920 Luxemburg francois.vernadat@ec.europa.eu

Jian Chen, Ph.D.
Professor and Chair, Department of Management Science and Engineering, School of Economics and Management, and Director, Research Center for Contemporary Management, Key Research Institute of Humanities and Social Sciences at Universities, Tsinghua University, Beijing, 100084, PR China jchen@mail.tsinghua.edu.cn

Nan Zhang
Ph.D. candidate, Department of Management Science and Engineering, School of Economics and Management, Tsinghua University, Beijing, 100084, PR China

Juong-Sik Lee, MS
Ph.D. candidate, Department of Computer Science, Rensselaer Polytechnic Institute, Troy, NY 12180-3590 leej6@cs.rpi.edu and Optimaret Inc., Newtonville, NY 12128-0301 jslee@optimaret.com

Boleslaw K. Szymanski, Ph.D.
Professor, Department of Computer Science, and Founding Director, Center for Pervasive Computing and Networking, Rensselaer Polytechnic Institute szymab@rpi.edu and Optimaret Inc., Newtonville, NY 12128-0301 bks@optimaret.com

Mark E. Dausch, Ph.D.
Senior Computer Scientist, GE Global Research Center, One Research Circle, Niskayuna, NY 12309 dausch@crd.ge.com

Ming-Chuan Wu, Ph.D.
Associate Professor, Department of Information Management, Chang-Jung Christian University, Taiwan mikewu@mail.cju.edu.tw

Cheng Hsu, Ph.D.
Professor, Department of Decision Sciences and Engineering Systems and Faculty of Information Technology, Rensselaer Polytechnic Institute, Troy, NY 12180-3590 hsuc@rpi.edu http://viu.eng.rpi.edu

Preface

One could argue that service is ultimately based on knowledge, and knowledge on the interaction between human and information resources. A significant phenomenon is, information resources exhibit a propensity to connect with each other especially when they are digitized. Evidence is manifested in the evolution of enterprise databases, peer-to-peer applications on the Internet, and the Web world itself. One would be tempted to liken the connection to the formation of galaxies, stars, and planets from the basic elements of the universe. The "gravitational pull" in the case of digital integration seems to be the utility of connection, or, the economy of scale of digital resources. Therefore, service seems to be poised to not only reap the benefits of Information Technology as manufacturing does, but also to enjoy more economy of scale than manufacturing can, since the latter is constrained by physical materials when it comes to connection.

However, the service sector of the economy has long lagged behind manufacturing in productivity gains from computerization. This presents an unfortunate problem since our economy is increasingly based on services. The root cause is commonly attributed, ironically, to the lack of economy of scale for service (co-)production. Its justification seems to rest on the difficulty of standardization of knowledge workers and other production factors for services; as compared to what manufacturing has achieved since Industrial Revolution – e.g., standard parts, bills-of-materials, and machining processes. However, standardization does not have to be the only mode that allows for large scale production. For instance, we submit that connection gives scale and sharing yields economy. Therefore, services could possibly enjoy economy of scale by, e.g., exploring new modes of production.

In a general sense, many researchers believe that when service and manufacturing both rely on information technology for their production, then what happened to one due to IT should have a way to happen to the other. To explore this conviction, a common approach in the field is to identify the IT-enabled generic results of manufacturing enterprise engineering and apply them to service enterprises. Modifications and new results would then be figured out to accommodate the differences between these two genres. In addition, new thinking is possible and, perhaps, desirable.

The contributors of the book have developed their answers to the service productivity question. Some of the results analyze the field; some others propose new models and methods; and yet others represent new thinking and new approaches. They constitute a literature of service enterprise engineering. We briefly summarize these results below.

Chapter 1, by Ananth Krishnamurthy, analyzes the literature and thereby sets a corner stone to the book. The author reveals the scientific road from on-demand manufacturing to on-demand services. He examines Just-in-Time manufacturing and mass-customization, and shows that manufacturing shares some common problems with service, such as portfolio optimization, workflow optimization, and resource allocation. Strategies are suggested for engineering on-demand services from these established results.

Chapter 2, by Jim Tien, provides a bold step forward to analyze service innovation. The author establishes a comprehensive conceptual framework which promises to help an enterprise transforming itself in a growing knowledge economy. The model theorizes six decision-oriented attributes of service innovation and normalizes nine enablers and four drivers of innovations. The Decision Informatics paradigm is established to be a key enabler. Future spaces of innovation are suggested.

Chapter 3, by Francois Vernadat, presents a particular service enterprise engineering approach. The author, an expert in manufacturing, explores the combination of agile inter-operable enterprise systems with more traditional business processes as a way to re-engineer legacy organizations and thereby enhance an orientation in service. He also reduces the concept to practice in an actual case under the auspices of European Union, concerning especially the aspects of enterprise engineering and IT implementation.

Chapter 4, by Jian Chen and Nan Zhang, manages customer expectation on waiting time. The authors first review the customer incentive issues that are related to waiting time in services. A tutorial covering such basics as the micro-economic concepts of firms and a customer's utility function is offered. A detailed analysis of the technical literature is then presented as the main focus of the chapter. Finally, the authors discuss some new ideas toward the design of new optimal incentives.

Chapter 5, by Juong-Sik Lee and Bolek Szymanski, proposes a new pricing mechanism for e-services. The authors analyze that many e-service markets exhibit recurring auctions and other unique characteristics which make the prevailing methods of auction today unable to achieve the best efficiency for the market. Instead, they develop a novel Optimal Recurring Auction model and prove through simulation that the ORA model works better under certain market conditions.

Chapter 6, by Mark Dausch, develops strategic service products for manufacturers. The author shows a particular reference framework of service enterprise integration to help manufacturers transforming their traditional business of producing physical products. Traditional product services are developed into strategic products in and of themselves. A particular industrial case is analyzed to illustrate the methodology in action. The work also represents a link between traditional manufactures and service.

Chapter 7, by Ming-Chuan Mike Wu, evaluates information services. The author focuses on the evaluation of new Information Systems and Information Technology projects, and analyzes the issues that traditional methods such as Return on Investment fail to address properly. He develops a "Continuous Evaluation" model to facilitate the well-known problems of uncertainty; and employs a generic reference framework to comprehensively account for possible organizational benefits.

Chapter 8, by Cheng Hsu, explores productivity issues of knowledge economy. The author postulates that new cyber-infrastructure could provide optimization of value to person and economy-of-scale to enterprises. With the notion of an Output-Input Fusion paradigm, he suggests a framework of concurrent co-productions using concurrent virtual configurations of the new cyber-infrastructure. Computerized manufacturing and e-commerce/e-business are reviewed as harbingers, along with a research agenda.

On a personal note, as the editor of the book, I must confess my pride in these chapters. The contributors have presented some of the truly original and thoughtful works on the subjects addressed, which add to the scientific field. In my opinion, these results represent some of the best analyses available today. Interestingly, although all contributors developed their chapters completely in their own choice and control, their results nonetheless exhibit considerable mutual consistency. They show common philosophy towards service, compatible analyses of service, and complementary basic approaches to service enterprise engineering. Could we take this coherence as evidence of a scientific foundation to a discipline of services?

Cheng Hsu

Acknowledgments

Many colleagues have provided assistance to the book. Foremost are, naturally, the contributing authors. I wish to express my deep appreciation for their acceptance of my personal invitations to participate, and contribution of their quality works to the book. The book idea was originally inspired by a meeting between the Decision Sciences and Engineering Systems Department of Rensselaer Polytechnic Institute (led by Dr. Jim Tien, chairperson) and a team from the IBM (led by Ms. Linda Sanford, senior vice-president) in 2005, concerning on-demand business. Mr. Gary Folven, the senior publisher at Springer, and the reviewers of the book proposal helped solidify the book idea. I wish to express my sincere gratitude to all of these colleagues. Finally, I am indebted to Mr. Anuj Goel who provided expert assistance to compile the book.

Chapter 1

FROM JUST IN TIME MANUFACTURING TO ON-DEMAND SERVICES

Just in Time Manufacturing to On-Demand Services

Ananth Krishnamurthy
Department of Decision Sciences and Engineering Systems, Rensselaer Polytechnic Institute, Troy, New York 12180, USA.

Abstract: This survey examines the transformation of manufacturing industry to Just in Time (JIT) manufacturing and mass customization. The main objective is to identify strategies that will accelerate the realization of information technology enabled on-demand services. Manufacturing and service systems are compared in terms of the similarities and differences with respect to issues related to their design, planning, and performance evaluation. These comparisons show that problems related to portfolio optimization, workforce optimization, and resources allocation are important in both manufacturing and service systems, suggesting that the similarities be exploited to develop strategies for on-demand services. This study also identifies several unique characteristics of services that need to be accounted for while developing specific strategies for the service industry.

Key words: Manufacturing Systems, Just in Time, On-demand Services, Healthcare, Education, Business Consulting

1. INTRODUCTION

Over the last two decades, the major economies have seen a shift in emphasis from traditional manufacturing to service sectors. Recent studies indicate that in this period nations such as United States, Japan, France and Italy have witnessed over 20% growth in their service sectors. In the United States alone, currently the service sector employs over 80% of the workforce, while other economic sectors such as manufacturing, construction, agriculture, and mining together employ the remaining 20% of the workforce. Within the service sector, healthcare, education and business consulting (excluding government) constitute the three major components, and account for about 30% of the total employment (Tien and Cahn, 1981; Tien and Berg, 2003). These numbers underscore why service sector is an important focus area.

Despite the significant employment that the service sector provides, the service sector is not efficiently run. Across the different industries that constitute the service sector, such as healthcare, education, financial services, and transportation there is increased pressure to deliver better *quality* of customized service, at *lower* costs. The popular phrase often used to summarize these expectations is on-demand services. On-demand services is a heavily loaded phrase and a closer examination of the customer expectations with respect to a few industries in the service sector, will enable us to better understand what on-demand services really means.

1. In the context of healthcare services, on-demand healthcare service means access to the best possible healthcare facilities, with a guarantee of getting a high quality of treatment (with minimal side-effects and long term health benefits), at a reasonable cost. It also means customized diagnosis aimed at disease prevention rather than post infection cure. Where disease cannot be prevented, on-demand healthcare services should result in minimal stay at hospitals, individualized patient care, customized medicines and treatment regimens. To meet these expectations, this 1 trillion dollar industry (in US alone) comprised of doctors, group practices, public health departments, government research institutes, integrated health systems, and hospitals must develop appropriate facilities, technologies, workforce, and systems. More importantly, they must be designed, engineered, and managed so as to be able to meet each the expectations of each patient.
2. In the context of education services, on-demand implies high quality of customized learning experiences for each individual. This implies that students and professionals are provided enrollment in the right kind of institution, exposed to the appropriate curriculum, and individual learning takes place in an environment (using appropriate facilities, methodology, and evaluation methods) that maximizes ones learning abilities. To meet these expectations, the education system comprised of high schools, technical colleges, community colleges, professional institutes, and universities need to be designed, engineered, and managed so as to be able to meet each the expectations of each student.
3. In terms of the business consulting services, on-demand implies that clients receive customized solutions (that possibly span strategy, operations, information technology and financial planning aspects of a business) with sufficient detail that would enable quick implementation with a reasonable guarantee of measurable improvements. To provide

such services, the consulting industry must not only develop the required skilled workforce, technology and infrastructure, but also develop systems and engineering principles that would enable the analysis and redesign of business operations to yield the desired improvements.

The expectations associated with on-demand services are similar in other industries as well. Across industries, the service sector is under increasing pressure (or threat) to provide on-demand services. There are three main reasons for this phenomenon. First, there is a pressing need for on-demand services. The service sector has a direct influence on the quality of lives and in many situations, one could argue that on-demand healthcare and educational services should be the basic right of each citizen. Second, trends in other economic sectors such as manufacturing indicate that expectations of on-demand services are not futuristic. In fact, in the manufacturing sector, Just In Time (JIT) manufacturing and mass customization is a reality. Customers are increasingly demanding a high variety of custom products at better quality, and reduced costs and lead times. The manufacturing industry has over the years, transformed itself by identifying systems, principles, theories, technologies, and best practices that now enable it to meet these seemingly irrational demands of customers. These trends in manufacturing sector have raised expectations of the service sector. Third, increased globalization catalyzed by the growth of the internet and Information Technology (IT) have led to an enormous increase in the computing capabilities. These advances have broken international barriers and increased competition in all sectors, manufacturing as well as service. This implies that if US service sector does not transform itself to meet the needs of on-demand service, it is likely that services might be off-shored to other nations resulting in significant impact on nation's economy. One only needs to see the impact of globalization on US manufacturing to understand the threat being posed by economies such as China, and India with respect to the expectations of on-demand services.

Under pressure to improve service operations, the service industries have looked to the manufacturing sector to identify a roadmap for transition to on-demand customer centric services. The idea is to exploit the similarities between manufacturing and services and adapt principles and practices that would enable service industries undertake the transition to on-demand services much quicker. It should be noted that this transition took the manufacturing industry over two centuries, and is still far from being complete. In order to understand the extent to which service sector could "learn" from the manufacturing sector one needs to (i) understand the similarity and differences between manufacturing and services, and (ii) the generality and limitations of manufacturing principles and practices in the context of services. Providing a service can be very different from manufacturing a product. Services have some unique and distinguishing features. Unlike manufacturing in the service sector the primary "product" is (i) intangible, (ii) generally consumed at the time it is produced, (iii) provides added value in different forms, and probably most importantly, it is (iv) co-produced. Co-production implies that the customer and provider are communication constantly reevaluating the need of the customer and the manner in which it is being satisfied (Tien and Berg, 2003). Given these differences, it is not clear to what extent manufacturing principles and practices can be adapted to provide on-demand services.

This survey critically examines the possibilities and identifies opportunities and challenges in this regard. The discussion is structured at three levels, first in terms of the *design and engineering* of manufacturing ands service systems, second in terms of the *planning and control* of manufacturing and service operations, and third in terms of the *measurement and performance evaluation* of manufacturing and service systems. The outline of the remainder of this chapter is as follows. In Section 2, the transformation of manufacturing industry is traced with emphasis on the evolution of fundamental principles and practices that guided manufacturing systems design and operations. Subsequently, the state of three key service sectors namely, healthcare, education and business consulting is examined. It is argued that there are significant similarities between the issues that plague the service sector today, with the issues that plagued manufacturing industries in the past. In Section 3, the critical role of IT in the transformation of manufacturing to JIT is recognized, to underscore the fact that IT is expected to play an even greater role in the transition of services to on-demand services. In Section 4, an attempt to provide a detailed roadmap toward on demand services is made. The discussion addresses four key issues in manufacturing and services, namely (i) *portfolio optimization*, (ii) *workforce optimization*, (iii) *resource planning and allocation*, and (iv) *operations analysis*. With respect to each of these issues, the discussion compares the similarities and differences between manufacturing and services. References to key literature are made with the intention of identifying research issues that require further exploration. In Section 5 it is argued that the metrics of cost, quality, speed, customization, and impact are relevant for on-demand services. While these metrics have enabled transformation of manufacturing systems in significant ways, they could similarly influence the evolution of on-demand services as well. In Section 6, a summary of the main conclusions from this survey are provided.

2. EVOLUTION AND CURRENT STATE OF MANUFACTURING AND SERVICE SYSTEMS

In this section, we examine the transformation of manufacturing industry through the last two centuries in order to better understand the evolution of fundamental principles and practices that guided manufacturing systems design and operations. Such a study would help understand how service sector would need to transform in order to provide on-demand services. Subsequently, the state of three key service sectors namely, healthcare, education and business consulting is examined in Sections 2.2 through 2.4. The objective is to identify the similarities in the issues faced by the service and manufacturing sectors.

2.1 Evolution of Manufacturing Processes and Systems

Prior to the first industrial revolution, manufacturing in the United States was on a small scale typically composed of locally organized, family owned labor intensive operations. Subsequently, American manufacturing systems emphasized concepts of mass production and this resulted in several large vertically integrated factories. The era of mass production also saw the origins of one of the most fundamental principles of manufacturing, namely, the need to *design manufacturing products and processes so that they are composed of interchangeable parts*. The idea was to transform manufacturing from a "craft" to a "science" that enabled production of many similar parts, each of which could perform the same function. This enabled manufacturers to stock inventory of parts in advance and better respond to demand or production uncertainties. This concept grew into inventory theory – a fundamental aspect of manufacturing systems engineering. The concept of inter-changeable parts was followed by efforts to split complex manufacturing processes into simple tasks that could be performed by people with minimum training or expertise. These concepts led to the *theory of time and motion studies*, an integral part of modern industrial engineering. These concepts were further extended to enable the design of manufacturing processes into a sequence of steps, each simple enough that they could be automated and performed by machines. This reduced the dependency on worker skills and resulted in the growth of mechanization and *the modern field of production automation*.

The subsequent major change in manufacturing was spurred by availability of new energy sources (in the form of coal) and better transportation infrastructure (in the form of railroads). US manufacturers typically built large factories and transported finished products using rail and waterways to different parts of the nation. Having mastered the techniques of mass production and distribution, the US manufacturing industry advanced to a level where it could produce and distribute goods to the rest of the world at a pace and scale that was greater than anywhere else. The mass production factories led to concepts that now form the fundamental principles of the *theory of production planning and distribution.*

The advent of the 1980s brought the first post-war paradigm shift in manufacturing. Japanese manufacturing re-emerged from the devastation of the war and introduced new manufacturing concepts such as *Just in Time and Toyota Production System.* It emphasized that product cost reductions did not require a compromise on product quality. Improved quality would lead to reduced costs as well. The Japanese firms also brought about revolutionary concepts such as cellular manufacturing, small batch production supported by quick production changeovers, kanban controlled inventory replenishments, just in time supplies, cross trained operators, and total quality management. A lot these concepts were fundamentally different from those followed by mass production factories in US. This led to new *theory of facility design, production and inventory control, and total quality management.* American manufacturers learned these lessons the hard way – at the expense of significant loss of market shares. The 1990s and subsequent years have led to an emphasis on speed and mass customization. Advances in information technology have shrunk geographical distances and erased political boundaries, resulting in *global supply chains* and theories related to *Lean Manufacturing* (Womack and Jones, 1996) and *Quick Response Manufacturing* (Suri, 1998) are enabling manufacturers anywhere in the world to produce an increased variety of customized products at reduced costs and shorter delivery lead times to customers anywhere in the world. (Table 1-1 summarizes these key principles).

Table 1-1: Theories and Principles of Manufacturing Systems

Inter-changeable parts
Time and motion studies
Production automation
Production planning and distribution
Just in Time or Toyota Production System
Facility design
Production and inventory control
Total quality management
Global supply chain management
Lean and Quick Response Manufacturing

Having examined the transformation of manufacturing services, next we examine the current state of three key service sectors, namely, *healthcare, education* and *business consulting*. As mentioned before, these sectors correspond to about 30% of the total employment.

2.2 Current State of Healthcare Services

History of healthcare in United States: During the early 1900s, like manufacturing, the healthcare industry was primarily a local industry. Healthcare in a local area was managed by doctors, surgeons, and pharmacists living in the area. They managed the entire set of activities ranging from diagnosis, treatment, surgery, patient care, therapy, and rehabilitation. Although, healthcare costs were low, several people had no access to healthcare and even if they did, the quality varied significantly and desired much improvement. Over the years, the healthcare industry has grown considerably in size and complexity. The modern healthcare industry is made of doctors, group practices, public health departments, government research institutes, integrated health systems, and hospitals. The hospitals themselves might be public or private, for-profit and not-for-profit, university-connected, general or specialized. The healthcare industry is funded by patients, employers, health maintenance organizations, the government, and a plethora of insurance companies, and pension programs. In the United States, healthcare has grown into a $1 trillion industry accounting for nearly 15 percent of its economy.

Despite the size of the industry, the statistics for such benchmarks as infant mortality and longevity in the United States consistently fall behind those of many other industrialized nations. It is estimated that some 40 million residents lack health insurance. Studies have shown that mismanagement is the cause for the current state of healthcare. The fact is that, *there are a lot of inefficient practices in the current healthcare system.* Unfortunately, many of the features of the current health care system make it operate as though patient health were a commodity, when in fact; it should be viewed as a customized service. Furthermore, an enormous amount of money – possibly as much as 25 cents of every healthcare dollar – is spent in documentation of transactions and litigation (Flower, 1996). *There is an increasing pressure to redesign healthcare systems and develop new practices and controls that will ensure increased access to high quality healthcare at lower costs.* By high quality it is expected that each individual will have (i) access to the best available diagnosis and treatment for his/her health problems; (ii) treatment regimens with minimal side effects; and (iii) opportunities for better health in the long term.

Table 1-2: Evolution of Manufacturing and Services

	Manufacturing	**Services**		
		Health Services	*Educational Services*	*Business Services*
Value chain	From local markets to global supply chains	From local providers to global systems	From local citizens to global responders	From accounting to global enterprise processes
Technology	From craft to IT-based automation	From craft to IT- supported service	From rote memorization to e-learning	From manual to IT- based automation
Workforce	From single skilled to multi-skilled	From single skilled to multi-skilled	From single skilled to multi-skilled	From single skilled to multi-skilled
Performance Metrics	From cost to speed and customization	From availability to cost and quality	From availability to cost and customization	From availability to speed and impact

2.3 Current State of Educational Services

History of education in United States: The first American schools opened during the colonial era. The school system remained largely private and unorganized until the 1840s and early efforts focused primarily on elementary education Secondary education infrastructure developed much later, and it was only in the late 1800s that several colleges were set up. This trend improved through the 1900s and was assisted by philanthropists who endowed several private institutions. Further the Morrill Land-Grant Colleges Acts of 1862 and 1890 led to the establishment of American public universities that have subsequently evolved to offer education in engineering, law, and business disciplines. The modern education system is made up of universities, government research labs, technical colleges, community colleges, professional institutes, and schools providing pre-college education all the way down to the primary school level.

The two major issues influencing educational services in United States are the costs and the quality of the education. The federal budget allocates roughly 70 billion dollars each year toward education. These Federal funding accounts for little of the overall money schools receive and the vast majority comes from the state government and from local property taxes. Unfortunately, college costs are rising at the same time that state appropriations for aid are shrinking. From 2002 to 2004 alone, tuition rates at public schools increased by just over 14 percent, largely due to dwindling state funding (http://nces.ed.gov). Furthermore, the *curriculum quality in the United States varies from district to district, and it has been questioned whether the mode of instruction, instructional media, academic environment, and learning mechanisms are providing effective education to the unique needs of different individuals.* The national results in international comparisons have often been below the average of developed countries. In OECD's Program for International Student Assessment 2003, 15 year olds ranked 24th of 38 in mathematics, 19th of 38 in science, 12th of 38 in reading, and 26th of 38 in problem solving (*http://nces.ed.gov*). In addition, many business leaders have expressed concerns that the quality of education given in the country is generally below acceptable standards, and should be adapted in order to conform to the needs of an evolving world.

2.4 Current State of Business Consulting Services

History of business consulting in United States: Business consulting (sometimes also called strategy consulting) refers to both the practice of helping companies to improve performance through the analysis of existing business problems and development of future plans, as well as to the firms that specialize in providing these services. Management consulting may involve the identification and cross-fertilization of best practices, analytical techniques, change management, technology implementations, strategy development or even the simple advantage of an outsider's perspective. Business consulting is a relatively new field, and grew with the rise of management as a unique field of study. The first management consulting firm was Arthur D. Little, founded in the late 1890s by the MIT professor of the same name. Subsequently, several consulting firms such as Booz Allen, McKinsey, Boston Consulting Group (BCG) were established. The subsequent development of consulting arms by both accounting firms (such as Arthur Andersen) and global IT services companies (such as IBM) enhanced the scope of business consulting. The late 1900s have challenged corporations with unprecedented new global competition, and IT advances and new concepts about organizational structure. Business consultants help to bring IT solutions and ideas to firms and play a vital role in integrating diverse economies such as China, Brazil, and India. Consequently, management consulting has grown rapidly, with growth rates of the industry exceeding 20% in the 1980s and 1990s. In 2004, revenues were up 3% over the previous year, yielding a market size of just under $125 billion.

Currently, there are three main types of consulting firms. First, there are the large, diversified organizations, such as IBM's Global Services that offer a range of services, including IT consulting, in addition to a management consulting practice. Second, there are the large management and strategic consulting specialists that offer purely management consulting, but are not specialized in any specific industry, like the McKinsey & Company. Finally, there are the small firms that have focused areas of consulting expertise in specific industries or technologies. Knowledge in areas like logistics management, knowledge management, data warehousing, multimedia, client-server development, sales force automation, electronic commerce, brand management, and value management are becoming increasingly important aspects of business consulting.

One of the major issues facing business consulting is the criticism that consulting forms are unable to develop executable plans that can be followed through. A major reason for this is that each client's operating environments and constraints are unique and it is extremely challenging and often very hard. Furthermore, the pressure to deliver solutions fast, typically leads to providing "standard and packaged solutions" to solve the unique problems of a client. This leads to customer dissatisfaction sometimes in substantial damages to existing businesses. *Business consulting firms are looking for new ways to design and engineer there service offerings so that they could provide better quality consulting service more efficiently and cost effectively.*

Having examined the transformation of manufacturing sector and the evolution of three critical service industries, in the next section, we examine the vital role information technology in these transformations.

3. INFORMATION TECHNOLOGY: THE ENABLER OF JIT MANUFACTURING AND ON-DEMAND SERVICES

There is no doubt that the advances in information technology (IT) have played a vital role in the evolution of manufacturing from mass production to just in time and mass customization. Computer automation enabled manufacturing enterprises to manage the massive amounts of data collected from their operations and incorporate them into planning and decision making. These advances also led to process automation and automatic controls. More recently, IT has enabled the creation of global manufacturing enterprises. Supply chains are no longer restricted by inter-national boundaries and the global market has been transformed into a level playing field. This has made manufacturing more competitive, leading to better quality of customized products at shorter delivery times. Advances in RFID technology in the future are poised to lead to further information explosion. New database integration systems and networking technologies are being developed to support systems engineering approaches to translate massive data available to useful information for the decision maker. The access to unprecedented amount of data and information to support decision making needs to be supported by systems engineering approaches that can help identify how best US manufacturers can respond to the emerging challenges of manufacturing.

Similarly, there is no doubt that IT would play an important role in the delivery of on-demand services. IT will influence (i) the type of service provided to customers, (ii) the structure of the enterprise providing this service, and (iii) the business processes being adopted to deliver a customized services on demand at the best possible quality and lowest cost. Most of the emerging services have a significant portion of electronic component. For instance, in healthcare, information systems provide new repositories and databases that allow patients and doctors to obtain better quality treatment and care. Similarly, e-learning is poised to transform the manner in which education is delivered and increasingly, business consulting project involve the use of IT to streamline and automate business processes. IT is also enabling service providers break geographical barriers and globalize their operations. This has allowed them to take advantage of the economies of outsourcing and provide better service to customers.

Therefore, there is no doubt that IT would continue to play a central role in the transformation of manufacturing and service sectors. However, what is not clear is how IT should be used as a catalyst to steer the transformation of manufacturing and service sectors in the desired direction. In the next section, we examine design, planning and operations issues in manufacturing and service systems to obtain the specifics related to the desired transformation.

4. DESIGN, PLANNING AND OPERATIONAL ISSUES IN MANUFACTURING AND SERVICE SYSTEMS

As mentioned before, the transformation of manufacturing industry into the modern global supply chains required significant design and engineering of manufacturing systems. In addition, the planning and execution strategies used to manage production operations also underwent significant change. All these led to the development of new theories that were tested and validated over the years, resulting in the discover of fundamental laws that govern manufacturing operations and established best practices that enable customers to receive the best product that satisfies their individual needs. It should therefore be expected that several design, planning and operational issues would need to be solved before on-demand services becomes a reality. In the following sections, four key problems will be explored in further detail namely *(i) portfolio optimization, (ii) workforce optimization, (iii) resource planning, and (iv) operations analysis.* The portfolio optimization and workforce optimization problems address issues related to the design manufacturing and service enterprises in terms of capital and human resources to fulfill long term objectives, while the resource planning deals with the planning and control of production and service operations at a medium or short term level. Operations analysis focuses on critical evaluation of manufacturing and service operations to understand the underlying scientific principles. This discussion in the following sections will elaborate on these issues in relation to manufacturing as well as service industries and identify similarities and distinctions between the two sectors with respect to several design, planning and operational issues.

4.1 Portfolio Optimization (PO)

The portfolio optimization problem determines the product/service portfolio of a manufacturing facility or service provider. The product/service portfolio determines the target customer market segments for the operations. The expectations of customer with respect to costs, quality and responsiveness in these markets directly influence long term decisions with respect to capital investment and locations of operating facilities, and short term operating strategies to balance risk and revenue streams. The following paragraphs address issues related to static the optimization of portfolio composition and the dynamic evolution of portfolios over time. The similarities and differences between manufacturing and service operations are highlighted to better understand the research required to provide on-demand services.

4.1.1 Portfolio Scope, Scale and Composition

With respect to the manufacturing sector, the portfolio refers to the spectrum of potential customers and their demands. The scope of the portfolio in turn influences the types of products being offered by a manufacturing enterprise. Determining the scope, scale, and composition of the portfolio addresses several questions such as: what customer/industry segment (such as automobile, hi-tech, aerospace) should a manufacturing facility supply to, and should the mix of products offered be composed of high volume, low variety products or low volume, high mix, customized products? What would be the scale of the business operations and how should the supply chain be set up (facility location and investments in plant and machinery) in order to best support a given portfolio? How should portfolios be constituted so as to provide financial stability, growth, and revenue?

Table 1-3: Issues in Portfolio Optimization of Manufacturing and Service Systems

	Manufacturing	**Services**		
		Health Services	Education Services	Business Services
Portfolio Scope, Scale, Composition	What products (high volume low mix product, or high mix low volume products) Local versus global market	What services (specialized long term care or primary care) Local versus regional population	What services (standard curriculum, or professional degrees) Local versus global population	What services (strategy, or financial, or IT) Local versus global market
Portfolio Evolution	Next generation products and markets	Next generation technologies and remedies	Next generation professionals and entrepreneurs	Next generation business models

Similar questions are relevant in the service sector. Healthcare providers need to determine what kind of customers segments they would like to serve? Will the focus be on primary care, acute care, or on specialized long term care? Should healthcare service provided by an institution be restricted to a particular geographic region? In the education sector too, such questions are relevant. Should a college be research oriented, or oriented towards the teaching undergraduate and educating working professionals? How should course and curriculum be designed so as to best prepare students for their future careers? How should students optimize their curriculum and plans so as to obtain the education that best suits their unique and individual requirements? What kind of investments should institutions make in terms of infrastructure and facilities to deliver these services? Similarly, issues related to portfolio optimization are relevant in business consulting too. Should business strategies and solutions be focused on relatively small/local industry sector? Where should a service enterprise locate its key facilities and what kind of services should it offer (strategy consulting, IT consulting, financial consulting)? How should the portfolio of services offered by structured so as to provide financial stability, growth and revenue?

4.1.2 Portfolio Evolution

Probably the hardest of the portfolio related problems is to determine how these demand portfolios should evolve over time. In the manufacturing sector this issue is becoming increasingly complex as product life cycles get shorter and technologies, skills and core competencies get out dated relatively very quickly. Firms need to constantly innovate and be prepared for disruptive technologies that might restructure existing market balance. New products and technologies are constantly being developed that improve the form and functionality of products requiring manufacturing firms to constantly work towards the customer requirements of tomorrow. Even in healthcare, consulting and education sectors, existing portfolio of service offerings (whether it be treatment technologies or software services, or curriculum content) are undergoing constant evaluation in terms of their long term viability and profitability.

4.1.3 State of the Art and Research Challenges

One of the simplest versions of the portfolio optimization problem in the manufacturing context is the product mix optimization problem analyzed in the context of production facilities (See references in Nahmias, 2004). More recently, there have been several studies related to pricing and risk management of portfolios in manufacturing industry. However, in the context of service sector the portfolio optimization problem is hard to define quantitatively. Manufacturing involves physical, tangible, products which permits the estimation of costs and revenues fairly accurately. In service, the "product" is less tangible and could evolve while being delivered to the customer. Hence evaluation of cost of service and associated revenues is much harder. An area of recent research that captures these features to some extent is the problem of optimizing portfolio of R&D projects. The related literature addresses portfolio optimization using (i) scoring models, where each portfolio component is assigned a score by experts (ii) mathematical programming models, where an objective is maximized over a set of constraints using linear programming, integer programming, dynamic programming, goal programming or other optimization techniques; and (iii) economics or financial models, relying on cost/benefit analysis, payback period, or NPV methods. Examples of relevant literature include Baker and Freeland (1975), Schmidt and Freeland (1992), Heidenberger (1996), and Tavares (1990) but much work remains to be done. Further, most portfolio optimization models typically involve more than a single criterion and often these criteria are non-quantifiable and highly subjective, for example criterion such as long term strategic fit and corporate image. Recent work by Gandforoush et al. (1992), and Lai and Li, (1999) and Oral et al. (1991) try to integrate multiple criteria via an IT based Decision Support System.

This brief survey of literature in this are indicates that there is significant work that remains to be done in terms of being able to characterize the optimum portfolios for a particular service provider. Next, we examine the issue of workforce optimization.

4.2 Workforce Optimization (WO)

Workforce optimization deals with long term and short term strategies related to the multi-skilled workforce involved in manufacturing goods and delivering services. Both manufacturing and service sectors depend significantly on the workforce in order to meet customer expectations of cost, quality, customization and speed. In both industries, workforce level and composition need to be optimized. In addition, workforce assignment into specific activities plays an important role in terms of the quality of resulting product/service. The following paragraphs address these issues, pointing out the similarities and difference between manufacturing and service sectors.

Table 1-4: Issues in Workforce Optimization of Manufacturing and Service Systems

	Manufacturing	**Services**		
		Health Services	Education Services	Business Services
Workforce Level and Composition	Staffing level and plan How many line operators, engineers, designers, material handlers	Staffing level and plan How many doctors, nurses, experts, surgeons, pharmacists	Staffing level and plan How many teachers, professors, technicians, research staff	Staffing level and plan How many programmers, application developers domain experts
Workforce Assignment	Cross training strategies	Specialists versus generalists	Specialists versus generalists	Specialists versus generalists
Workforce Evolution	Learning and problem solving	Career evolution and experience	Career evolution and experience	Career evolution and experience

4.2.1 Workforce Level and Composition

In the manufacturing sector, the problem of workforce composition has received significant attention. It essentially addresses the issue of the labor capacity investment required to satisfy production objectives set forth by a particular product portfolio. Workforce requirements are typically classified into different types. In manufacturing, workforce is classified into shop floor operators, design engineers, shop floor supervisors, technicians, assembly line operators, material handlers etc. The level of investment required in these areas and the composition of the workforce required in different areas bears a strong relation to the product portfolio of the manufacturing enterprise. In the healthcare sector, delivery of high quality of on-demand healthcare will require local, regional and national authorities to constantly assess the workforce in terms of the available number of doctors, nurses, experts, surgeons, therapists, pharmacist, and emergency responders. In the education sector, institutions will need to assess whether the availability of teachers, professors, technicians, and research staff is consistent with the portfolio of customized educational services that are to be provided to its customers. In the business consulting industry, consultant workforce or human capital is the prime investment. The workforce is classified into programmers, project managers, application developers and domain experts and the required staffing levels vary with project complexity, and composition of project portfolios.

One of the key issues is to determine what investments to make in which types of workforce skills and how these influence the ability to provide on-demand services. In the manufacturing sector, the underlying design principles and planning strategies have evolved over the years. The early emphasis on low costs products, resulted in strategies that simplified manufacturing processes so that only a workforce with minimal skills was required. Subsequent emphases on quality, quick response and customization have argued the need for cross trained operators with multiple skills. Cross trained operators have been shown to improve responsiveness and manufacturing lead times as well. While these concepts bear relevance to service industries, there are some unanswered questions. For instance, is the workforce composition that guarantees least cost service, the same as that which guarantees best quality of service? How does work force composition influence the ability to be responsive in providing customized service? Are these workforce compositions that motivate service innovations? These questions need to be answered in the context of particular service industries if on-demand services are to become a reality.

4.2.2 Workforce Assignment

Workforce assignment has been extensively studied in manufacturing. As mentioned earlier, cross trained operators on a shop floor have been shown to improve manufacturing quality and responsiveness. While it is no surprise that as the workforce acquires more skills, such flexibility increases, what is interesting is that most of the benefits of complete flexibility can be achieved by adopting a suitable chaining strategy and training the workforce to acquire a small subset of available skills. Workforce assignment issues in the service sector lead to similar questions. How should consultants, programmers, project managers be assigned across different consulting engagements? What influence does simultaneous assignment of personnel to multiple engagements influence overall costs, quality and project completion times? Consultants typically vary in skills and expertise. How should skill and expertise be considered while assigning personnel to consultant teams? While manufacturing products and processes can be designed so as to make their efficiencies fairly independent of the people running the operations, the same cannot be said about services. The co-production element of services makes the quality and effectiveness of the service delivery process highly dependent people involved. How should multi-skilled teams be composed to improve their efficiency, effectiveness and productivity? The above workforce assignments issues raised with respect to business consulting services find relevance in healthcare as well as education sectors as well.

4.2.3 Workforce Evolution

Workforce evolution addresses issues of dynamics of the workforce over time. Manufacturing research has studied the difference of level and chase strategies of workforce planning and it has been argued that such strategies fail to capture the advantages of worker learning and experience in terms of improved quality and productivity. However, in the service sector, workforce evolution raises several new issues. While individuals in the manufacturing workforce have a relatively stable career path, the same cannot be said about the highly skilled workforce providing business consulting, healthcare or educational services. Individual career paths could lead to workforce attrition reading to significant variability in capability and expertise of available workforce. How should retention strategies be designed to maintain the workforce profile required to match the needs specified by evolution of the product portfolio? It is not clear how workforce must be determined in order to ensure individual objectives are met while yet guaranteeing high quality low cost customized services on-demand.

4.2.4 State of the Art and Research Challenges

In the context of manufacturing operations workforce issues have been studied extensively. Milner and Pinker (2001) and Pinker and Larson (2003) and Sumukadas and Sawhney (2002) report the influence of adjusting workforce levels using contingent and temporary workers and suitable cross-trained workers. Hopp and Van Oyen (2004) argue that workforce agility via cross-training results in *flexible capacity* that can be shifted dynamically to where they are needed when they are needed. Hence, cross-trained workers should yield higher productivity. For service industries such as the call center industry, cross-training is a critical decision for both service quality and profit (Stuller 1999, Gans and Zhou, 2000). Bartholdi et al. (1999a, 2001) Bartholdi and Eisenstein (1996), Hopp and Spearman (2000), McClain et al. (2000, 1992), Ostolaza et al. (1990), Schultz et al. (1998), and Treleven (1989) provide quantitative models that analyze various control/management architectures and policies for making use of cross-trained workers. The impact of learning and experience on workforce performance has been investigated by Blake et al. (1964), Bordoloi and Matsuo (2001), Goldstein (2002), Nembhard (2000), Shafer et al. (2001), Smunt (1987), and Misra et al. (2004). Buzacott (2004) uses quantitative models to provide insights into cross-training may facilitate problem solving (for example, finding better work methods, diagnosing causes of quality problems and improving team-based kaizen initiatives). The influence of motivation on workforce performance has been studied by Hackman et al. (1978), Ichniowski and Shaw (1999), and Paul et al. (1969). Gans and Zhou (2000) analyze retention issues related to workforce and Pinker and Shumsky (2000) emphasize the dimension of learning based on experience and its impact on a quality-based performance measure in the context of service sector. Despite the extensive issue several issues still remain to be addressed. In service industries with significant knowledge workforce component such as healthcare and business consulting it is common for worker to have multiple overlapping skill levels. Worked routinely multi-task and switch between different jobs and collaborate between peers to improve efficiencies. However there are very few systematic studies that provide design principles in these areas.

Both portfolio and workforce optimization have led to evolution in the principles that govern the design of manufacturing systems and planning of operations. As manufacturing transformed from mass production to mass customization, manufacturing facilities have transformed from large factories with job shop layouts into smaller factories with cellular layouts. Factory designs are more tuned to adapt to future market upswings and downfalls and investment in flexible workforce seems vital for mass customization. It remains to be seen how the needs of on-demand, high quality, low cost service will influence the design and operation of service enterprises. In the next section, we examine the issue of resource planning and allocation in manufacturing and service industries.

4.3 Resource Planning and Allocation

Resource planning and allocation refers to short and medium term decisions related to matching requirements of resources to meet anticipated demands of products and services with the available pool of resources. The first step in this process is to obtain estimates of the requirements of specific resources needed to provide a service or manufacture a product. Subsequently, the requirements are matched against supply over time and necessary allocation decisions are made accounting for uncertainties and stochastic dynamics of manufacturing and service operations. Any excesses or shortfalls indicated by the allocation must be addressed by acquiring or disposing resources optimally. All these issues are addressed in the paragraphs below and challenges of applying some of the concepts routinely applied in the manufacturing sector to provide on-demand services are highlighted.

4.3.1 Resource Requirements and Allocation

This relates to the prediction of resource requirements need to meet a given forecast or demand for products/services. In the manufacturing sector, resources required to meet demand or forecasts are typically determined using an MRP (Orlicky, 1975) framework based on bill of materials and routing information for the particular product. Given these information, it is fairly straightforward to estimate the time required at a machine to process a part and the overall resource *requirement* is calculated by summing up the requirements at each step in the manufacturing process. As we shall see in the next paragraph the issue of resource allocation is far more complex. However, in a service industry, resource requirement estimation is also complex. For instance, in the healthcare or consulting service industry, service to a client or a patient requires time commitment of people with different skills. However, the same task might be done much quicker by an expert, or by someone with multiple skills, or by someone with significant experience. Each individuals experience and other commitments at a given time influences the time taken to perform a particular task and this makes the estimation of resources required to meet a given demand of services much more complex in the service sector. Unlike the manufacturing sector, the co-production nature of healthcare or consulting services implies that the so called "routing" of a service being provided would evolved with time complicating the estimation of resource requirements.

Table1- 5: Issues in Resource Planning and Allocation of Manufacturing and Service Systems

	Manufacturing	**Services**		
		Health Services	Education Services	Business Services
Resource Requirements and Allocation	Materials and Capacity Requirements Planning	Allocation of skilled personnel to teams to address service needs	Allocation of professionals, students to address special needs	Allocation of consulting personnel to engagements
Resource Acquisition and Disposition	Capital investment in machines, outsourcing labor requirements	Subcontracting services to other healthcare providing organizations	Subcontracting educational services to other institutions, organizations	Subcontracting software development to other organizations, countries
Scheduling and Optimization	Advanced Planning Systems	Optimizing availability of skilled personnel	Optimizing availability of educational professionals	Optimizing bench strength of consultants
	Material control strategies, Pricing strategies	Capacity planning and real time scheduling	Capacity planning and real time scheduling	Capacity planning and real time scheduling
Efficiency	How efficient was the plan/schedule?	How efficient was the treatment experience?	How efficient was the education experience?	How efficient was the engagement experience?

The second issue of efficient allocation of production resources to existing demand continues to be a challenging problem in the manufacturing sector. Most of these problems are very complex stochastic optimization problems and extremely hard. Computationally solving these problems might require extensive resources and the resulting solutions are often too complex to implement in practice. Consequently there has been extensive research on these issues and the most recent trend is to use (i) advanced planning systems (APS), or (ii) advanced control strategies such as Kanban, CONWIP (Hopp and Spearman, 2000) and POLCA (Suri,1998) or (iii) pricing and revenue management strategies (Bernstein and Federgruen, 2002). The APS address issues related to mid term and short term planning

(Fleischmann and Meyr, 2003). The advanced control strategies use simple congestion control concepts and leverage of IT developments that have resulted in increased collaboration and information sharing across supply chains. Pricing and revenue management strategies have been used to address tradeoffs related to capacity allocations among different products. Some of these concepts could be applied to allocate resources to service assignments as well. However, the issues related to forecasting of demand and resource requirements mentioned earlier, make the allocation problem more complex. Additionally, healthcare and consulting services are provided by teams. Therefore team dynamics and group efficiency can have a significant impact on efficient resource allocations, but these are hard to model and quantify.

4.3.2 Resource Acquisition and Disposition

Resource acquisition in the context of the manufacturing sector can be addressed in terms of (i) investment or disinvestment in capital equipment and/or (ii) recruiting or "laying-off" personnel. Both these problems have been addressed extensively using concepts of cost/benefit analysis, payback period, or NPV methods for the former and economics or financial models for the latter. More recently issues related to outsourcing labor intensive manufacturing to other low labor cost countries has been adopted by several manufacturing organizations. However, resource acquisition and disposition are more complex in the service industry. For instance, business consulting, it is routine practice to fill gaps in resource requirements by outsourcing part of the consulting assignment to other countries or partner organizations. While such outsourcing might be cost beneficial in the short run, it is not clear what impact it has on the quality of service provided. The co-production nature of services requires constant interaction between customer and service provider and outsourcing operations might make such interactions ineffective. New organizational structures need to be investigated that enable co-production of services in a global setting. Furthermore, outsourcing might lead to attrition of workforce skills, expertise and experience that might be required for future business growth. These tradeoffs are hard to model.

4.3.3 Scheduling and Optimization

Resource scheduling and production optimization problems in manufacturing have been subject of intensive research for several years. For instance, even the classic problem of allocating inventory buffers for different products in a manufacturing setting is hard to solve. In the service sector, some of these problems become harder to formulate. For instance, unlike manufacturing where future capacity shortfalls can be buffered by building inventory, in the business consulting environment, one cannot work on engagements in advance. Capacity shortfall must be addressed by investing in "excess people capacity" than "inventory". This is often referred to as the *bench strength*. However, having excess workforce on the bench is not the same as having excess inventory. People are not parts: inventory has its unique identity; it depreciates over time, and could become obsolete. A consultant on a bench or healthcare professional has multiple skills and could perform multiple activities serving different clients simultaneously, and his/her value appreciates with time and experience.

4.3.4 Efficiency of Resource Allocation

In manufacturing it is common practice to compare the resource allocated to a given customer order to the original plan and evaluate the efficiency of the allocation. Such evaluations provide better understanding of operations and help improve quality and costs of product offered to customers. In the service sector, it is very hard to determine whether the treatment procedure followed for a particular patient or the consulting solution govern to a client, or the educational service provided to a student was the best. While there are measures of service efficiency, since service is highly customized, they cannot be generalized to develop standards that estimate resource requirements or determine resource allocations.

4.3.5 State of the Art and Research Challenges

Extensive references on models for production, capacity and inventory planning issues related to manufacturing are available in Axsater (2000), Buzacott and Shanthikumar (1993), and Zipkin (2000). The issue of material requirement planning and rough cut planning of production capacities are discussed in Orlicky (1975) and Vollman et al. (1991). Some of these concepts could be adapted to the service industry as well. As mentioned earlier there are strong similarities and differences with inventory planning in manufacturing and optimization of bench strength in service industry. Axsater and Rosling (1993), Buzacott and Shanthikumar (1994), Federgruen (1993), and Hu et al. (2003), and the references therein provide quantitative models related to tradeoffs in inventory. It is possible that these techniques could be adapted to obtain insights on strategies to optimize investment in resources that enable services to be more efficient and cost effective. Pricing and product variety related issues in manufacturing have been discussed by

Benjafar et al (2004), Swaminathan and Tayur (1999), Chen et al. (2004), and Bernstein and Federgruen (2002). Scheduling and optimization of production has been addressed in Fleishmann and Meyr (2003), Kapuscinski and Tayur (1999), Lambrecht et al., (1998). Other works such as Cachon and Netessine (2004), Chen (2003) Karaesman et al (2003) provide additional references on resource planning and scheduling issues related to manufacturing. Models for resource allocation and planning in the service sector will need to address the unique aspects of service operations. These operations involve knowledge workforce, and specialized models will need to be formulated for optimizing the capacity of skilled personnel. Furthermore, skilled workforce provides opportunities for flexible sequencing, splitting and combination of tasks. While these features provide additional flexibility in resource planning and allocation, they could also raise issues related to synchronization. Stylized models will be required to understand the cost, quality and lead time implications resource allocation and planning in these settings.

While the portfolio optimization, workforce optimization and resource allocation problems focus on design and operational aspects of operations that affect individual customers and clients, the issues related to operations analysis affect clients and customers collectively. The issues related to the analysis of manufacturing and service operations are discussed in the next section.

4.4 Operations Analysis (OA)

One of the reasons why manufacturing systems evolved from mass production to mass customization was because there was a constant effort to analyze manufacturing operations and identify fundamental tradeoffs in operations, modeling and implementation. Like physical sciences where, theory has and experimentation have worked in parallel, manufacturing science has also evolved by evaluating theoretical results against practice. The following paragraphs address several issues related manufacturing and service industries.

4.4.1 Fundamental Laws

Over the years, manufacturing research has identified several fundamental laws governing factory operations (Hopp and Spearman, 2000). These fundamental laws serve as guiding principles for manufacturing systems design, in the same way laws of physics guide design of physical and mechanical systems. In addition, the fundamental laws of manufacturing enable managers and practitioners set realistic goals and plans. For instance, the Economic Order Quantity model and Newsvendor Model (see references in Nahmias, 2004) of classical inventory theory addresses fundamental cost tradeoffs in manufacturing and provide key insights. Little's Law on the other hand is invaluable in terms of understanding the tradeoffs between, capacity, lead times and inventories. The Bullwhip Effect (Lee et al. 1997) is a fundamental reality of supply chain dynamics. It is important to identify such fundamental laws that govern service operations. Given the similarities with manufacturing, one can expect that the fundamental laws should have some similarity. However, it is also clear that the fundamental laws need not be identical since, service operations involve co-production of intangible entities and the requirements of customers and resources evolve with time. It will be necessary to understand the science governing service operations, if on-demand service is to be a reality.

Table 1-6: Issues in Operations Analysis of Manufacturing and Service Systems

	Manufacturing	**Services**		
		Health Services	Education Services	Business Services
Fundamental Laws	Economic Order Quantity, Little's Law, Bullwhip Effect	Are there fundamental laws?	Are there fundamental laws?	Are there fundamental laws?
Analysis Complexity	NP hard, robust optimization Meta-heuristics	New models for uncertainty Which problems are tractable?	New models for uncertainty Which problems are tractable?	New models for uncertainty Which problems are tractable?
Best Practices	Benchmarking and best practices publicized	Need to benchmarking and publicize best practices	Need to benchmarking and publicize best practices	Need to benchmarking and publicize best practices

4.4.2 Analysis and Complexity

Manufacturing operations involve complex dynamics and significant amount of uncertainty. Even in the absence of uncertainty, analysis of manufacturing operations involves solutions to complex mathematical programming problems. Many of the problems in production scheduling and planning have been shown to be NP-hard. The solutions to the tractable versions of these problems have provided guidelines to devise meta-heuristics based on techniques such as simulated annealing, tabu search, and genetic algorithms. Based on the descriptions of the associated problems in the service sector, it appears that the problems would be equally if not more complex. In addition the nature of uncertainty prevalent in service operations is distinct from that in manufacturing. The unique nature of each service, whether it is healthcare provided to a patient or consulting service to a client, makes it hard to fit standard probabilistic models to evaluate effect of uncertainties. It appears that new modeling methodologies will be necessary. Further more, it is not clear which of these problems would be analytically tractable and also whether one could formulate efficient meta-heuristics to provide reasonable solutions to problems of practical dimensions.

4.4.3 Best Practices

Manufacturing sector has significantly benefited from benchmarking operations of similar firms. Although no two manufacturing operations are similar, benchmarking allows the industry to assess the state of operations and identify needs of individual firms. Several manufacturing firms have been proactive and taken the lead in developing strategies that have improved operations. Strategies such as Just in Time systems, Toyota Production System, Lean Manufacturing, Six Sigma that have enhanced manufacturing productivity have all stemmed from industry practice and not academic research. Subsequent academic research has investigated the detailed aspects of these strategies, but the origins have been from the industry itself. Similarly, if the service sector needs to be efficient, they would need to participate in benchmarking studies and identifying strategies that will enable the delivery of customized service on- demand

5. ROLE OF METRICS IN THE TRANSFORMATION OF MANUFACTURING AND SERVICE SYSTEMS

In this section, we continue to build on the analogy between manufacturing and service systems to build a road map towards on demand services. Recall that while the evolution of manufacturing from mass production to mass customization was enabled by IT, but it was also grounded in fundamental principles of manufacturing systems and industrial engineering with a strong emphasis on metrics to evaluate and motivate change. Similarly, for service systems to provide user centric on-demand services, similar focus on metrics to drive and measure change are essential. Lord Kelvin said "When you can measure what you are speaking about, and express it in numbers, you know something about it; but when you cannot measure it, when you cannot express it in numbers, your knowledge is of a meager and unsatisfactory kind: it may be the beginning of knowledge, but you have scarcely, in your thoughts, advanced to the state of science." The following paragraphs discuss how key performance metrics of manufacturing systems have evolved over the years, and how these have led to better understanding of the physics of factory operations and the science of manufacturing enabling the transition from mass production to Just in Time customization of products. An argument is made for a similar focus on metrics to enable on-demand services.

5.1 Role of Metrics in the Transformation of Manufacturing Systems

The Table 1-7 lists the key metrics for evaluating manufacturing systems. These are (i) cost, (ii) quality, (iii) speed, (v) customization, and (v) innovation. The subsequent paragraphs provide discussion on the role of these metrics in the transformation of manufacturing systems. It is not hard to see that the above metrics are relevant to service operations as well. In subsequent section, we will explore the implications of these metrics with respect to healthcare, education and business consulting services and elaborate on the role these could play in the development of on-demand services.

5.1.1 Manufacturing Cost

In terms of the manufacturing sector, cost was the main metric used measure efficiency of production in the era of mass production. The concept of economies of scale was one of the main drivers during those years. The focus on cost led to research on product cost estimation. For several years, cost estimation implied determining in the most accurate way the cost of materials, labor and overhead involved in the production. Extensive systems were devised to track material (material requisition sheets and purchase orders) and labor costs (time sheets and labor reports) and variances in these costs motivated improvements towards parts interchangeability and standardizing manufacturing processes. Costs reductions strategies led to focus on economic order quantities and job shop layouts. As material procurements became more efficient and automation reduced amount of labor content in manufacturing, the overhead costs (which typically included costs of all activities that supported manufacturing such as design, engineering, product development, aftermarket service) became a significant component of overall costs. Manufacturers soon realized that traditional means of estimating and allocating overhead could significantly miscalculate product costs. This led to the phenomena of the death spiral were several manufacturing companies withdrew products from the market under the assumption that they were not cost effective. As quality, speed and customization became more relevant metrics for manufacturing, cost estimation mechanisms have evolved from those measuring costs of quality to Time Based Costing, Activity Based Costing and Balanced Scorecard Mechanisms.

Table1- 7: Metrics in Manufacturing Systems and Resulting Principles

Metric	Time	Manufacturing System Principles
Cost	1960-1975	Economic Order Quantity, Interchangeable parts, Inventory theory
Quality	1975-1990	Reliability Theory, Quality Control
Speed	1990-2000	Cross Training, Cellular Manufacturing, Just in Time
Customization	2000-2010	ETO, CTO, MTO, Modular designs, Delayed Differentiation
Innovation	2010-2020	Niche product markets

5.1.2 Manufacturing Quality

In the mid 1970s, quality became the key metric for evaluating manufacturing systems. It was then believed that there was an inherent trade-off between costs and quality, in that better quality meant a more costly product. The Japanese manufacturing systems typified by the Toyota Production System through Just in Time concepts emphasized that cost reductions are not necessarily achieved by sacrificing on quality. Instead, improved quality could result in reduced costs. The focus on manufacturing quality has evolved from statistical process control techniques such as X and R charts, process capability assessment techniques, sampling theory, and total quality management to the modern day Six-Sigma concepts. The role of quality and Six Sigma has evolved into one that takes a systems engineering perspective of manufacturing as compared to the narrow process oriented view during the initial years.

5.1.3 Manufacturing Speed

However, in the mid 1990s with the advent of internet, the focus shifted into manufacturing or supply chain lead time. Time Based Competition, Quick Response, Lean and Agile Manufacturing began to emphasize the need to shift the focus from reduction of operation times to the reduction of lead times (the time from order receipt to shipment). This involved time taken for product design, prototype, process planning, marketing, production, distribution and service. The focus on time enhanced the scope of manufacturing improvements to beyond the shop-floor, and the key was to eliminate non-value added activities leading in the lead time. Several companies began to investigate and implement whole new ways of making products that led to significant lead time reduction (in the order of 50-90%) some times from months to days. This implied transition from job shop layouts to product focused cells, cross trained flexible operators, and small batch production with quick changeovers. A focus on lead time has been shown to reduce costs and improve quality, since unless one did it right the first time, you would not be able to reduce lead times.

5.1.4 Custom Manufacturing

In recent years, costs, quality and lead times are considered as a given and manufacturing competitiveness hinges on the ability to provide customized products that satisfy unique requirements of individuals. Manufacturers are now under increasing pressure to offer a wide variety of unique, customized products at shorter lead times, cost and better quality. Customization has redefined the role of inventory management and make to stock production is gradually being replaced by configured to order (CTO), engineered to order (ETO) and make to order concepts (MTO). CTO provides a customer to configure their product from a pre-defined set of available options (as in the on-line ordering of computers from Dell). In comparison, in ETO provides the ability to customize the product design to suit their particular needs, while in MTO the customer is able to influence the entire process from design through manufacturing. Strategies such as transformation of engineering and design functions into customer focused cells, delayed product differentiation and modular product designs have been investigated in order to enable manufactures respond to customized demands with shortest possible lead times.

5.1.5 Innovative Manufacturing

The future of manufacturing lies in innovative manufacturing, wherein manufacturers proactively create new markets for custom products. Product innovation would build on lean and quick response practices and would take customization to the next level. Innovative manufacturing leads to new market niches enabling to limit competition. New business models are being offered wherein products are bundles with services (for example, personal computers come packaged with software and service contracts) with the idea being to extend the business relationship between the customer and manufacturer from beyond the time of sale to the entire life cycle of the product.

5.2 Role of Metrics in the Transformation of Service Systems

It is obvious from the above discussion that cost, quality, speed, customization and innovation are an important aspect of next generation manufacturing. The discussion in this section will elaborate on how these same metrics are relevant in the design of services and their transformation into on-demand services. While the discussion below is supported by examples from healthcare, education, and business consulting services, it is not hard to see that the discussion can be extended to other service industries as well.

5.2.1 Service Costs

As with manufacturing costs of service bear a direct relation to the price a customer pays for a service. In healthcare, it relates to the cost of health insurance, primary, acute and long term care of individuals. In education, costs are related to the tuition fees while in business consulting, the costs are directly related to price charges by operations, financial or software consultants for the services rendered. While the premise that services should be rendered at low costs is universally true for manufacturing and service, it is not clear what the costs components are: what are the fundamental elements of service costs, i.e. are there equivalents of material, labor and overhead costs of manufacturing? For instant, should the cost of time spent by software programmers on an IT implementation be considered overhead costs or labor costs? Is there a distinction between direct labor and supporting overhead when it comes to healthcare or educational services? What is the design and engineering principle that will drive cost reduction efforts in the service industry. Are there equivalents of work standardization, economic order quantities and job shop layouts that can be applied to design service operations to reduce costs?

Table 1-8: Metrics in Service Systems

Metric	Service Systems Interpretation	Year	Service System Principles
Cost	Service with lowest fee	All are equally relevant currently	Principles are being developed
Quality	Service yielding most satisfaction		
Speed	Shortest delivery lead time		
Customization	Personalized service		
Innovation	Niche service areas		

5.2.2 Service Quality

One might argue that since, most customers are willing to pay a premium price for high quality of healthcare and education, the primary metric for services is the quality. Quality of consulting services has a direct bearing on reputation of service provider and has strong correlations with repeat businesses. It is also believed that designing systems to provide high quality of service (be it healthcare or education) will in the long run reduce the costs for the consumers, in terms of better health and fewer hospital visits in the case of healthcare, or better jobs and careers in the case of education. While quality of service is important, the specific metrics to measure service quality is still in its infancy. For instance, how do we extend control chart concepts to measure quality of healthcare, education or consulting? What are the underlying principles that allow us to identify whether the process of delivering the service is under control. Given that services are inherently customized, can we derive meaningful sampling procedures to analyze quality of service systems? Flexible cross trained operators were shown to improve manufacturing quality. However, is it possible that flexible operators, multi-tasking among services required by different customers could adversely affect service quality? If so, what kind of cross training strategies would help improve service quality?

5.2.3 Service Speed

While the importance of speed, automation and quick response in manufacturing took years to develop and evolve, advances in IT are making automation of services very much a reality. Information sharing has allowed patients and healthcare professionals to communicate quicker and provide better long term and emergency care. Business consulting routinely relies on automating business process (Enterprise Resource Planning Systems) in an attempt to provide faster service.

However, the lesson taught by Quick response and Lean manufacturing is that significant manufacturing lead time reduction is achieved not by merely automating existing procedures, but fundamentally redesigning the system with a customer centric focus. This led manufacturing to evolve from large scale job shops with large batched operations to cellular manufacturing relying on small batch size and quick change over tactics. Are their similar strategies in services? Can one fundamentally redesign how educational, consulting and healthcare services are provided so that one is better prepared to respond to the requirements of the customer? Should the focus be on service process optimization rather than on service process automation?

5.2.4 Service Customization

As mentioned earlier, service is in inherently customized. Emerging services are strongly IT-centric and have a significant element of co-production, wherein customer is constantly involved in the process of defining, evaluating, and redefining the service required from the provider. Healthcare treatment provided to patients has a significant amount of co-production. Education is increasingly becoming personalized with IT enabling students and professions to precisely learn the topics of their interest and in a manner of their choice (traditional classroom setting, on-line). No doubt consulting services are in response to specific problems of the client. Can concepts of ETO, CTO, and MTO be applied in the delivery of services? How does one apply concepts of delayed product differentiation, and modular designs to design service operations so as to be able to quickly provide customized service of high quality to customers? Some instances of these concepts are already being used today, but further understanding is required. For instance, medical diagnosis for a patient begins by conducting tests from a pre-defined set of possibilities. Software consultants are increasingly trying to identify modules (accounting modules, procurement management systems) that are common part of multiple assignments. These modules then formed "canned" components or suites of services offered.

5.2.5 Service Innovation

Regardless of whether service industry has identified metrics and systems to measure costs, quality, speed and customization, service innovation is already present. New business paradigms are constantly evolving offering new types of bundled services. On line auctions provided by E-bay, search services provided by Google, professional development services provided by Monster.com are prime examples of new business models that created new markets. Even in healthcare, education and consulting, innovative models are being constantly developed.

5.3 Prioritization of Metrics

A comment needs to be made about the time period when the different metrics were most relevant in the manufacturing and service industries. While it in the case of manufacturing, one can associate specific time periods when the different metrics were perceived as the key to competitive strength, the same cannot be said about services. Manufacturing practice underwent significant stress, before the importance of quality, speed, customization and innovation were understood. Even to date, top level managers in supply chains struggle with assigning priorities to these different metrics. A case and point here is the experience of John Deere that used to evaluate its supplier base based on all the metrics mentioned above, but till the early 1990s used cost as the primary metric in their supplier evaluation process. Unfortunately, setting cost as the primary metric did not result in the desired improvements in terms of quality and speed. In the mid 1990s, John Deere adopted the Time Based Supply Management strategies and Quick Response and began to measure supplier lead times as their primary metric. Interestingly enough, setting lead times as their primary metric automatically reduced the costs, improved their quality and delivery performance of their key suppliers. This reasons for this phenomenon behavior has been discussed extensively in Erickson and Suri (2001) and Suri (1998).

In contrast, with respect to services, there is no obvious precedence relationship among the different metrics – they are all relevant today. It is not clear whether one metric is likely to dominate the other. Service providers such as IBM feel that the innovation based on advances in IT might provide opportunities for reducing costs and guaranteeing better service quality. As we discuss specifics of transforming enterprises to provide on-demand services, we will address issues related to each of these metrics.

6. CONCLUSIONS

This study provides a comparison of manufacturing and service industries. It is evident from the study that there are significant similarities between manufacturing and services to warrant a combined effort identifying the underlying principles and practices that would enable the delivery of customized high quality products at low cost. It could be argued that as products become more customized; the distinction between products and services diminishes, with a product and a service both satisfying a unique need of a customer (Tien et al. 2004). Towards that eventuality one needs to identify design, manage, control and evaluate manufacturing and service systems. It is evident from the discussion that a system engineering perspective that leverages of the advances in IT is the key to making on-demand services a reality. However, the unique characteristics must be kept in mind while developing new systems engineering approaches that enable on demand services. An attempt has been made at establishing a roadmap towards transformation to on-demand services by identifying 4 issues that are common to manufacturing and service sectors, namely portfolio optimization, workforce optimization, resource planning and allocation, and operations analysis. There is significant overlap to enable synergistic efforts between researchers working in manufacturing and service sectors. However, such efforts must caution themselves against the temptation to directly apply best practices from manufacturing into service sectors. In the discussion above, several key aspects of service operations have been identified related to these issues with the objective of motivating new research in those areas.

REFERENCES

1. Aviv, Y., 2004, "Collaborative Forecasting and its Impact on Supply Chain Performance," in *Handbook of Quantitative Supply Chain Analysis–Modeling in the E-Business Era,* David Simchi-Levi, S. David Wu, and Zuo-Jun Shen (Editors), Kluwer International Series in Operations Research and Management Science, pp. 393-443.
2. Axsater, S., 2000, *Inventory Control,* Kluwer Academic Publishers, Norwell, MA.
3. Axsater, S., and Rosling, K., 1993, "Installation vs Echelon Stock Policies for Multilevel Inventory Control," *Management Science*, Vol. 39, pp. 1274-1280.
4. Baker, J. R. and J. R. Freeland, 1975, "Recent advances in R&D benefit measurement and project selection methods," *Management Science,* Vol. 21, No. 6, pp. 1164-1175.
5. Bartholdi, J.J., L.A. Bunimovich, and D.D. Eisenstein, 1999, "Dynamics of 2- and 3-worker bucket brigade production lines," *Operations Research*, Vol. 47, No. 13, pp. 488-491.
6. Bartholdi, J.J., and D.D. Eisenstein, 1996, "A production line that balances itself," *Operations Research*, Vol. 44, No.1, pp. 21-34.
7. Bartholdi, J.J., D.D. Eisenstein, and R.D. Foley, 2001, "Performance of bucket brigades when work is stochastic," *Operations Research*, Vol. 49, No. 5, pp. 710-719.

8. Benjaafar, S., Elhafsi, M., and de Vericourt, F., 2004, "Demand Allocation in Multi-Product, Multi-Facility Make-to-Stock Systems," *Management Science* (to appear).
9. Bernstein, F., and Federgruen, A., 2002, "Dynamic Inventory and Pricing Models for Competing Retailers," *Naval Research Logistic Quarterly*, Vol. 45, No. 3, pp. 397-412.
10. Blake, R.R., J.S. Mouton, L.B. Barnes, and L.E. Greiner, L.E., 1964, "Breakthrough in organization development," *Harvard Business Review*, Nov.-Dec.
11. Bordoloi, S.K., and H. Matsuo, 2001, "Human resource planning in knowledge-intensive operations: A model for learning with stochastic turnover," *European Journal of Operational Research*, Vol. 130, 169-189.
12. Buzacott, J.A. 2004, "Modelling teams and workgroups in manufacturing," *Annals of Operations Research*, Vol. 126, No. 1-4, pp. 215-230.
13. Buzacott, J.A., and Shanthikumar, J.G., 1993, *Stochastic Models of Manufacturing Systems*, Prentice Hall, Englewood Cliffs, NJ.
14. Buzacott, J.A., and Shanthikumar, J.G., 1994, "Safety Stock Versus Safety Times in MRP Controlled Production Systems," *Management Science*, Vol. 40, No. 12, pp. 1678-1689.
15. Cachon, G. and Netessine S., 2004, "Game Theory in Supply Chain Analysis," in *Handbook of Quantitative Supply Chain Analysis–Modeling in the E-Business Era*, David Simchi-Levi, S. David Wu, and Zuo-Jun Shen (Editors), Kluwer International Series in Operations Research and Management Science, pp. 13-57.
16. Chan, L.M.A., Shen, Z-J, Simchi-Lei, D., and Swann, J., 2004, "Coordination of Pricing and Inventory Decisions-A Survey and Classification," in *Handbook of Quantitative Supply Chain Analysis–Modeling in the E-Business Era*, David Simchi-Levi, S. David Wu, and Zuo-Jun Shen (Editors), Kluwer International Series in Operations Research and Management Science, pp. 335-392.
17. Chen, F., 2003, "Information Sharing and Supply Chain Coordination," in *Handbooks of OR and MS, Vol. 11: Supply Chain Management: Design , Coordination and Operation*, A. G. de Kok and S.C. Graves, (Editors) , Elsevier, New York, NY, pp. 341-413.
18. Ericksen, P.D. and Suri, R., 2001, "Managing the Extended Enterprise," *Purchasing Today*, Vol.12, No.2, pp. 58-63.
19. Federgruen, A., 1993, "Centralized Planning Models for Multi-echelon Inventory Systems Under Uncertainty," in *Handbooks of OR and MS, Vol. 4: Logistics of Production and Inventory*, S.C. Graves, A.H.G.R. Kan, and P.H. Zipkin (Editors) , North-Holland, New York, NY, pp. 133-173.
20. Fleischmann, B., and Meyr, H., 2003, Planning Hierarchy, Modeling and Advanced Planning Systems, in Supply Chain Management: Design, Coordination and Operation: *Handbooks in operations Research and Management Science*, Vol 11,A.G. de Kok and S.C. Graves (Editors), pp. 457-524.
21. Flower, J., 1996, "The Future of Healthcare," in *Encyclopedia of the Future*, Macmillan and Company.
22. Gandforoush, P., P. Y. Huang and L. J. Moore (1992) "Multi-project, multi-criteria evaluation and selection model for R&D management," *Management of R&D and Engineering*, D. F. Kocaoglu (Ed.) Elsevier Science Publishers, pp. 89-100.
23. Gans, N. and Y.-P., Zhou, 2000, Managing Learning and Turnover in Employee Staffing, Working Paper, OPIM Dept., Wharton School, University of Pennsylvania, Philadelphia, PA.

24. Goldstein, I. L. 2002. *Training in Organizations: Needs Assessment, Development, and Evaluation.* Wadsworth, Belmont, CA.
25. Hu, X., Duenyas, I., and Kapuscinski, R., 2003, "Advance Demand Information and Safety Capacity as a Hedge Against Demand and Capacity Uncertainty," *Manufacturing and Service Operations Management*, Vol. 5, No.1, pp. 55-58.
26. Hackman, J.R., J.L., Pearce, and J.C., Wolfe, 1978. "Effects of changes in job characteristics on work attitudes and behaviors: A naturally occurring quasi-experiment," *Organizational Behavior and Human Performance*, Vol. 21, No. 3, pp. 289-304.
27. Heidenberger, K., 1996, "Dynamic project selection and funding under risk: A decision tree based MILP approach," *European Journal of Operations Research*, Vol. 95, pp. 284-298.
28. Hopp, W.J. and M.L. Spearman, 2000 *Factory Physics: Foundations of Manufacturing Management*, Second Edition, Irwin/McGraw-Hill: Burr Ridge, IL.
29. Hopp, W.J. and M. van Oyen, 2004, "Agile workforce evaluation: a framework for cross-training and coordination," *IIE Transactions*, Vol. 36, no. 10, pp 919-940.
30. Ichniowski, C. and K., Shaw, 1999, "The effects of human resource management systems on economic performance: An international comparison of U.S. and Japanese plants," *Management Science*, Vol.45, No. 5, pp. 704-721.
31. Kapuscinski, R., and Tayur, S., 1999, "Optimal Policies and Simulation Based Optimization for Capacitated Production Inventory Systems," in *Quantitative Models for Supply Chain Management*, S. Tayur, R. Ganeshan and M. Magazine (Editors), International Series in Operations Research and Management Science, Kluwer Academic Publishers, pp. 7-40.
32. Karaesmen, F., Liberopoulos, G. and Dallery, Y., 2003, "Production/Inventory Control with Advance Demand Information," in *Stochastic Modeling and Optimization of Manufacturing Systems and Supply Chains*, J.G. Shanthikumar, D.D. Yao and W.H.M. Zijm (Editors), International Series in Operations Research and Management Science, Kluwer Academic Publishers, pp. 243-270.
33. Lai, K. K. and L. Li, 1999, "A dynamic approach to multiple-objective resource allocation problem," *European Journal of Operations Research*, Vol. 117, pp. 293-309.
34. Lambrecht, M., Ivens P. and Vandaele N., 1998, "ACLIPS: A Capacity and Lead Time Integrated Procedure for Scheduling," *Management Science*, Vol. 44 No. 11, pp. 1548-1561
35. Lee, H.L, V. Padmanabhan, S. Whang, 1997, "Information distortion in a supply chain: the bullwhip effect," *Management Science*, Vol. 43, No. 4, pp. 546-558.
36. McClain, J.O., K.L. Schultz and L.J. Thomas, 2000 Management of Worksharing Systems, *Manufacturing & Service Operations Management (M&SOM)*, Vol. 2 No.1, 49-67.
37. Milner, J.M., and Pinker, E.J. 2001, Contingent Labor Contracting Under Demand and Supply Uncertainty, *Management Science*, Vol. 47, No. 8, 1046-1062.
38. Misra, S., Pinker, E., and R., Shumsky, 2004, "Salesforce Design with Experience-based Learning," *IIE Transactions*, Vol. 36.
39. Nahmias, S., 2004, *Production and Operations Analysis* McGraw Hill Irwin, New York, NY.

40. Nembhard, D. A., 2000, "The effects of task complexity and experience on learning and forgetting: a field study," *Human Factors,* Vol. 42, 272-286.
41. Oral, M, O. Kettani and P. Lang, 1991, "A methodology for collective evaluation and selection of industrial R&D projects," *Management Science* Vol. 37, No. 7, pp. 971-885.
42. Orlicky, J., 1975, *Materials Requirement Planning*, McGraw Hill, New York, NY
43. Ostolaza, J., J., T.J., McClain, 1990, "The use of dynamic (state-dependent) assembly-line balancing to improve throughput," *Journal of Manufacturing Operations Management*, Vol. 3, pp. 105-133.
44. Paul, W.J. Jr., K.B., Robertson, and F. Herzberg, 1969, "Job enrichment pays off," *Harvard Business Review,* Mar.-Apr.
45. Pinker, E.J. and R.A. Shumsky, 2000." "The Efficiency-Quality Tradeoff of Crosstrained Workers. *Manufacturing and Service Operations Management (M&SOM),* Vol. 2, No. 1, 32-48.
46. Schmidt, R. L. and J. Freeland, 1992, "Recent progress in modeling R&D project selection processes," *IEEE Transactions on Engineering Management*, Vol. 39, No. 2, pp. 189-201.
47. Schultz, K.L., Juran, D.C., Boudreau, J.W., McClain, J.O., and Thomas, L.J, 1998 Modeling and worker motivation in Just In Time production systems, *Management Science*, Vol. 44, No.12, Part 1, pp. I595-I607.
48. Schultz, K.L., J.O. McClain, and L.J., Thomas, 2003, "Overcoming the Dark Side of Worker Flexibility," *Journal of Operations Management,* Vol. 21, pp. 81-92.
49. Shafer, S.M., D.A. Nembhard, M.V. Uzumeri, 2001, "The effects of worker learning, forgetting, and heterogeneity on assembly line productivity," *Management Science*, Vol.47, No. 12, pp. 1639-1653.
50. Smunt, T. L., 1987, "The impact of worker forgetting on production scheduling," *International Journal of Production Research*, Vol. 25, pp. 689-701.
51. Stuller, J. 1999, "Making call-center voices smile: A business case for better training," *Training,* April, pp. 26-32.
52. Sumukadas, N., Sawhney, R. 2002 Workforce agility through employee involvement, *IIE Transactions*, Vol. 36.
53. Suri, R., 1998, *Quick Response Manufacturing: A Companywide Approach to Reducing Lead Times*, Productivity Press, Portland, OR.
54. Swaminathan, J.S., and Tayur, S., 1999, "Stochastic Programming Models for Managing Product Variety," in *Quantitative Models for Supply Chain Management*, S. Tayur, R. Ganeshan and M. Magazine (Editors), International Series in Operations Research and Management Science, Kluwer Academic Publishers, pp. 585-624.
55. Tavares, L. V., 1990 "A multi-stage non-deterministic model for project scheduling under resource constraints," *European Journal of Operations Research*, Vol. 64, pp. 312- 325.
56. Tien, J. M. and D. Berg, 2003, "A Case for Service Systems Engineering," *International Journal of Systems Engineering,* Vol. 12, No. 1, pp. 13-39.
57. Tien, J. M. and M.F. Cahn, 1981, *An Evaluation of the Wilmington Management of Demand Program*, Washington, DC: National Institute of Justice.
58. Tien, J. M., A. Krishnamurthy, and A.Yasar, 2004, "Towards Real-Time Customized Management of Supply and Demand Chains," *Journal of Systems Science and Systems Engineering*, Vol. 13, No. 3, pp. 129-151.

59. Treleven, M. 1989, "A review of the dual resource constrained system research," *IIE Transactions*, Vol. 21, No. 3, pp. 279–287.
60. Vollmann, T.E., Berry, W.L. and Whybark, D.C., 1991, *Manufacturing Planning and Control Systems*, Dow Jones-Irwin, Homewood, IL.
61. Womack, J.P. and D.T. Jones, 1996, *Lean Thinking: Banish Waste and Create Wealth in your Corporation*, Simon and Schuster, New York, NY.
62. Zipkin, P.H., 2000, *Foundations of Inventory Management*, McGraw Hill, Boston, MA.

Chapter 2

SERVICES INNOVATION: DECISION ATTRIBUTES, INNOVATION ENABLERS, AND INNOVATION DRIVERS

James M. Tien
Rensselaer Polytechnic Institute, Troy, New York, USA

Abstract: Innovation in the services area – especially in the electronic services (e-services) domain – can be characterized by six decision-oriented attributes: decision-driven, information-based, real-time, continuously-adaptive, customer-centric and computationally-intensive. These attributes constitute the decision informatics paradigm. In turn, decision informatics is supported by information and decision technologies and based on the disciplines of data fusion/analysis, decision modeling and systems engineering. Out of the nine major innovation enablers in the services area (i.e., decision informatics, software algorithms, automation, telecommunication, collaboration, standardization, customization, organization, and globalization), decision informatics is shown to be a necessary enabler. Furthermore, four innovation drivers (i.e., collaboration, customization, integration and adaptation) are identified; all four are directed at empowering the individual – that is, at recognizing that the individual can, respectively, contribute in a collaborative situation, receive customized or personalized attention, access an integrated system or process, and obtain adaptive real-time or just-in-time input. In addition to expanding on current innovations in services and experiences, white spaces are identified for possible future innovations; they include those that can mitigate the unforeseen consequences or abuses of earlier innovations, safeguard our rights to privacy, protect us from the always-on, interconnected world, provide us with an authoritative search engine, and generate a GDP metric that can adequately measure the growing knowledge economy, one driven by intangible ideas and services innovation.

Key words: Services; innovation; decision informatics; software algorithms; automation; globalization; collaboration; customization; integration; adaptation; standardization; telecommunication; organization.

1. INTRODUCTION

Sometimes invention or discovery is mistaken for innovation. Robert Metcalfe, the inventor of the Ethernet protocol and the founder of 3Com, observes that "invention is a flower, innovation is a weed; that is, an original idea can be brilliant, profound and compelling – but what ultimately gives it power and influence is that it spreads [like a weed]". Thus, while inventions are to be celebrated, businesses must rely on innovations to survive and grow; in this regard, successful innovations are those that spread in terms of reach, impact, and/or commercial success. Although ingenuity, talent, analytical skills, focus, and perseverance are required to achieve either, an innovation does not necessarily depend on an invention (e.g., witness the thousands of commercial successes that are not based on any invention); likewise, an invention does not necessarily result in an innovation (e.g., witness the thousands of patents that have never been commercialized).

Automation underpins most of the innovations in the past century. In the first two-thirds of the 20th Century, electrification was the engine of automation, while in the latter third it has been the computer chip which – together with electrification and digitization – has made automation a flexible and intelligent mechanism. Indeed, as listed in Table 2-1, electrification is first among the top 20 achievements in the 20th Century, as compiled by the National Academy of Engineering (NAE) [2000]; it can be credited with spawning most, if not all, of the remaining 19 achievements, including the Internet and the continuous upgrading of the automobile, the airplane, the telephone, etc.

Table 2-1. Technological Innovations

• **National Academy of Engineering's Top 20 Engineering Achievements in the 20th Century:**	
1. Electrification	11. Highways
2. Automobile	12. Spacecraft
3. Airplane	13. Internet
4. Water Supply and Distribution	14. Imaging
5. Electronics	15. Household Appliances
6. Radio and Television	16. Health Technologies
7. Agricultural Mechanization	17. Petroleum and Petrochemical Technologies
8. Computers	18. Laser and Fiber Optics
9. Telephone	19. Nuclear Technologies
10. Air Conditioning and Refrigeration	20. High-Performance Materials
• **Possible Additional Achievements in the Early 21st Century:**	
21. Information Technology	
22. Nanotechnology (Nanomaterials, Nanotubes, Nanoelectronics)	
23. "Technobiology" (New Drugs, DNA Chips, Bionic Parts)	

Source: *National Academy of Engineering*, 2000

While Table 2-1 lists NAE's top 20 for the last century, we have also added three possible additional achievements for the early 21st Century: information technology, nanotechnology, and, what we define as, "technobiology." (Technobiology emphasizes the contribution of engineering or technology to biological issues, including the development of new drugs, DNA chips, and bionic parts; in contrast, biotechnology emphasizes the contribution of biology to technological issues, including the development of molecular computers, cognitive ergonomics, and neural networks.)

Returning to information technology, it should be noted that its key underpinning – the computer chip – has only been in existence for five decades; the first commercially available computer – the Universal Automatic Computer or Univac I – was built in 1951. Nevertheless, computers have already evolved through several generations. As indicated in Table 2-2, Intel's first chip – the 4004, introduced in 1971 – had only 2200 transistors per chip; today, there are several hundred million transistors per chip. Indeed, Gordon Moore [1965], co-founder – with Robert Noyce – of Intel, conjectured that the number of transistors per square inch of an integrated circuit would double every year, as it had up to 1965. In subsequent years, however, the pace has slowed down, with the data density doubling approximately every 18 months; this is now the current definition of Moore's Law, with which Moore himself has concurred.

Table 2-2. Computer Chip: The New Engine of Automation

Year	Intel Chip	Transistors Per Chip	Milestone
1971	4004	0.002M	Transformational beginning.
1972	8008	0.003M	--
1974	8080	0.005M	Inside first personal computer (Altair 8800).
1978	8086	0.029M	--
1982	286	0.120M	--
1985	386	0.275M	--
1989	486DX	1.180M	Introduction of a math coprocessor.
1993	Pentium	3.1M	Powers 85% of world's desktops.
1997	Pentium II	7.5M	--
1999	Pentium III	24.0M	--
2000	Pentium 4	42.0M	Powers portable computers and mobile devices.
2001	Ithanium	25.0M	--
2003	Ithanium 2	220.0M	--

Source: *Intel Corporation*, 2004

Today, the G5 processor chip – jointly developed by IBM and Apple – is based on a 64-bit architecture and possesses a speed of one gigahertz. Additionally, Advanced Micro Devices Inc. is producing multicore chips that may well become the industry standard. Most experts expect Moore's Law for smaller, better, faster and cheaper chips to hold for at least another two decades, although flexible plastics may well replace silicon as the material of choice for computer chips. In fact, a plastic screen was recently used on a digital camera from Kodak, which in 1979 discovered the first organic light-emitting diodes (OLEDs). In contrast to the liquid crystal displays (LCDs) in cell phones and computers, OLEDs do not break when dropped, save energy (since they generate their own light), and possess more vibrant colors.

An essential and complementary technology to the computer chip is, of course, software. Software contains the programs, routines, and procedures that control the functioning of the hardware (i.e., computer chips) and direct their operation. The two major categories of software are "system software" and "application software." System or platform software includes the basic input-output system (often described as firmware rather than software), the device drivers, an operating system, a database management system, and typically a graphical user interface which, altogether, allow a user to interact with the computer and its associated equipment or peripherals. Application software is any program that processes data for the user (e.g., inventory, payroll, spreadsheet, word processor, etc.); it is usually independent from the operating system, even though it is often tailored for a specific platform. An algorithm is a special application software; it refers to a set of ordered steps for solving a complex problem, such as a mathematical formula. As a consequence, software algorithms provide the means for automating innovations in modern, electronic-based goods and services (including experiences). Automating a services process, for example, through a carefully developed algorithm is, of course, a crucial step in enhancing productivity. Otherwise, extensive manpower is required to manually co-produce the services, a situation which would contribute to "Baumol's Disease". Baumol et al. [1989] recognized the connection between slow productivity growth and rising costs in certain stagnant industries within the services sector. Although automation has certainly improved productivity and decreased costs in some services (e.g., telecommunications, Internet commerce, etc.), it has not yet had a similar impact on other labor-intensive services (e.g., health care, education, etc.). In regard to software development itself, there is unfortunately no comparable Moore's Law in effect; however, standardization and supporting tools have improved software productivity.

Another critical underpinning of information technology is telecommunication. Although computers (i.e., mainframes) tended to centralize data and – data-based – decision making in the 1960s and 1970s, the advent of computer networks, together with personal computers (PCs), have been a decentralizing (i.e., less hierarchical) force. The most important and indispensable network is, of course, the Internet; it is becoming a platform for commerce (i.e., Web 2.0), whereby trillions of computers and sensors will be interconnected and will, in essence, diminish distance as an impediment for collaboration and commerce [Cairncross, 1997]. Companies like Wikipedia, Flickr and MySpace are leading the way to making Web 2.0 style of interconnection and collaboration a reality. Furthermore, new wireless telecommunication advances will soon make mobile devices a multi-purpose services instrument, with more memory and better screens and where traditional voice and data (i.e., Internet and email) services will converge with digital music, video clips, video conferencing, satellite radio, location tracking, traffic reporting, and other personal needs (e.g., credit checks, online education, etc.). All of these technological innovations – which are based on real-time computing – have ushered in a range of real-time or on-demand enterprises, which claim that critical business information is always up-to-date and available and that decisions can be promptly made; that is, the detection of an event, the reporting of that event, and the response decision can all occur within a very short time frame or near real-time. Clearly, as examples, the slow and inadequate responses to recent urban disruptions (e.g., 2001 9/11 tragedy, 2002 SARS – Severe Acute Respiratory Syndrome – epidemic, 2004 South Asia Tsunami, and 2005 Hurricane Katrina) demonstrate that although real-time actions are desirable, they are not a pervasive reality. On the other hand, Amazon does employ real-time information technology and automated decision making to suggest alternative reading material for its customers. Thus, real-time decision making is not only about real-time computing but also about developing the tools or algorithms to support real-time actions and activities.

Interestingly, economists claim that because of the astounding growth in information technology, the U. S. and other developed countries are now a part of the global "knowledge economy". Although information technology has transformed large-scale information systems from being the "glue" that holds the various units of an organization together to being the strategic asset that provides the organization with its competitive advantage, we are far from being in a knowledge economy. In a continuum of data, information, and knowledge, we are, at best, at the beginning of a data rich, information poor (DRIP) conundrum. The fact remains that data – both quantitative and qualitative – need to be effectively and efficiently fused and analyzed in order to yield appropriate information for intelligent decision making in regard to the design, production and delivery of goods and services. Today, retailers complain, "We are awash in data but starved for information." Thus, in order to overcome the somewhat embarrassing DRIP problem that Tien [1986] forewarned, it is critical to develop more sophisticated data fusers and data analyzers – as a part of what Tien [2003] calls "decision informatics" – that could yield the information or knowledge required for making smart choices [Hammond et al., 1999] or for developing new, and possibly disruptive, innovations. Indeed, we augur in Section 3 that decision informatics should be considered to be a critical enabler of services innovation.

In sum, although information technology facilitates robust and timely decision making; a necessary condition is one based on decision informatics or real-time, information-based decision making. Clearly, information, telecommunication, software and real-time decision making technologies, together, provide for a supportive environment within which innovations in goods and services can continue to flourish. This has been strikingly demonstrated by Wal-Mart with its point-of-sale information system, which is at the heart of its services value chain; the system has had a significant impact on the company's productivity gains, cost controls, services quality, and ultimately growth.

In the remainder of this paper, innovation enablers, services sector and decision informatics are, respectively, discussed in Sections 2, 3 and 4; they provide the framework for identifying past and future services innovation in Section 5. Some concluding remarks are made in Section 6.

2. INNOVATION ENABLERS

Given the importance of innovation to the economies of the world, it is not surprising that it is a topic of intense interest in both the popular and academic presses. Moreover, governments are also getting involved in helping their enterprises succeed in developing high-value innovation in services [OECD, 2005; NMIT, 2006]. For example, in response to the recommendations made by the Council on Competitiveness, the U. S. Congress [2005] is considering a National Innovation Act. This legislation focuses on three primary areas of importance to maintaining and improving U. S. innovation in the 21st Century: a) research investment, b) increasing science and technology talent, and c) developing an innovation infrastructure. The legislation also establishes a President's Council on Innovation, with responsibility for developing a comprehensive agenda that can promote innovation in the public and private sectors. In consultation with the Office of Management and Budget, the Council is to identify and employ metrics to assess the impact of existing and proposed laws that affect U. S. innovation. In addition, the Council is to coordinate and assess the performance of various Federal innovation programs, and an annual assessment report is to be submitted to the President and to the Congress.

Innovation requires changes or recombination of processes, products and businesses, including people, technologies, systems, attitudes, values, cultures and organizational structures. For each of the past two years, *BusinessWeek* and The Boston Consulting Group have surveyed about 1,000 senior managers from around the globe to ascertain the 25 most innovative companies. Table 2-3 summarizes the two annual surveys; it is seen that 20 of the top 25 companies in 2006 undertook product innovations, 14 undertook business model innovations, and 13 undertook process innovations. It is also seen that these 25 innovative companies had an average annualized 1995-2005 stock return of 14.3 percent, suggesting that innovation does pay off, at least in comparison with the Standard and Poor's 1200 Global Index, which had an 11.1 percent annualized stock return over the same decade. In examining the 25 companies' primary focus of innovation, it can be determined, to the best of our judgment, that 16 of them (i.e., 64%) are focused on services innovation and 9 (i.e., 36%) on goods innovation. This observation is consistent with Berg and Einspruch's [2006] findings. Of course, some innovations can be considered to impact both goods and services; thus, for example, we classify Apple's iPod and iTunes as primarily a services innovation, inasmuch as these goods have served to promulgate a major new service – indeed, a new experience.

In trying to identify innovation enablers, it should be noted that the enablers may differ between those for goods and those for services, and may further differ over time. For example, in the latter part of the 20th Century, innovation was about technology and control of quality and cost for goods; in the beginning of this 21st Century, the focus is on rewiring the processes, products and business models in order to achieve efficiency and growth in the services sector, especially since goods have become more and more commoditized. Our focus is, of course on those enablers that can enhance services innovation. In general, there are at least nine major innovation enablers in the services area: 1) decision informatics, 2) software algorithms, 3) automation, 4) telecommunication, 5) collaboration, 6) standardization, 7) customization, 8) organization, and 9) globalization. The first four have been addressed in Section 1, although decision informatics is further discussed in Section 4. The remainder of this section considers the remaining five enablers: collaboration, standardization, customization, organization, and globalization.

Table 2-3. Most Innovative Companies in 2006

Survey Rank		Company	Innovation Areas			Annualized 1995-2005 Stock Return	Innovation Focus Goods (G), Services (S)
2006	2005		Process	Product	Business		
1	1	Apple		✔	✔	24%	S: iPod, iTunes, Experience
2	8	Google		✔	✔	--	S: Search Ad Clicks, Mash-Ups
3	2	3M		✔		11.2%	G: Post-It Pictures, Research
4	14	Toyota	✔	✔		11.8%	G: Manufacturing, Value Chain
5	3	Microsoft		✔	✔	18.5%	S: Integration, Live
6	3	General Electric	✔	✔		13.4%	S: Imagination, Courage
7	9	Procter & Gamble	✔	✔	✔	12.6%	G: Intra-Collaboration
8	9	Nokia	✔	✔	✔	34.6%	S: Emerging Markets
9	19	Starbucks		✔	✔	27.6%	S: Media Bars, Experience
10	7	IBM	✔	✔	✔	14.4%	S: Open Invention Network
11	11	Virgin Group			✔	Private	S: Lifestyle
12	12	Samsung	✔	✔		22.7%	G: Speedy Product Cycles
13	5	Sony		✔		5.1%	G: High-Definition
14	6	Dell	✔		✔	39.4%	S: Supply Chain, Sales Channels
15	18	IDEO	✔	✔		Private	S: Palm V, Leap Chair
16	20	BMW	✔	✔		14.2%	G: Competitive Designs
17	16	Intel		✔	✔	13.8%	G: New Products
18	15	eBay			✔	--	S: Online Market, Fixed-Price

19	--	IKEA	✔	✔	✔	Private	G: Affordable Designs
20	13	Wal-Mart	✔			16.2%	S: Supply Chain
21	16	Amazon	✔	✔		--	S: Web Services
22	--	Target		✔	✔	25.2%	S: Discount Marketing
23	23	Honda		✔		12.9%	G: Engineering, Beyond Auto
24	--	Research In Motion		✔		--	S: Black Berry, Wireless Email
25	21	Southwest Airlines	✔		✔	13.9%	S: Operations, Low-Cost
Overall						14.3%	G: 9 (36%); S: 16 (64%)
Standard and Poor's 1200 Global Index						11.1%	

Source: *BusinessWeek*, April 24, 2006

Collaboration – especially inter-company collaboration – is perhaps the most surprising enabler. After all, patents were established to protect intellectual property, long enough for the inventors to recoup a good return on their creative investment. However, since services are, by necessity, co-created or co-produced, collaboration is essential. Indeed, von Hippel [2005] found that 40 percent of a company's customers modify its products in some way so as to better suit their needs. Moreover, as noted by Palmisano [2004], the innovation challenges are too complex; they require collaboration across disciplines, specialties, organizations and cultures. Additionally, the easy access to information through search engines (e.g., Google, AOL, Yahoo, Microsoft Network, etc.), the proliferation of collaborative software (e.g., Microsoft Office Live Meeting, MySpace), and the open source software movement (e.g., Linux, Open Invention Network) have all combined to facilitate collaboration. (In 2005, IBM gave – royalty free – 500 software patents to the Open Invention Network.) Chesbrough [2003] lauds IBM's open innovation outlook (especially as compared with Xerox PARC's closed approach); Govindarajan and Trimble [2005] recommend that past assumptions, mindsets, and biases must be forgotten (especially in regard to collaboration); and Sanford and Taylor [2005] further underscore this point by suggesting that companies must "let go to grow".

The National Science Foundation [2006] recently initiated the Partnerships for Innovation program that seeks to bring together researchers from academe, the private sector, and government for the purpose of exploring new innovation partnerships. Amazon has taken a giant step in collaboration; through the Amazon Web Services effort, it has, in essence, given its software (including personalization functions) and a good portion of its actual sales to thousands of software developers, who are finding – for a fee – innovative ways of connecting Web surfers to Amazon merchandise. Obviously, companies are collaborating not because they wish to give away their business, but because they wish to grow the business. On the other hand, a large number of individuals are collaborating – for free – to enhance an open source software (e.g., Apache), to network, including meeting new friends, sharing photos, or emailing internally (e.g., MySpace), to play a global game with guilds and imaginary gold (e.g., World of Warcraft), or even to live in a virtual world with individualized avatars and Linden dollars (e.g., Second Life), all to satisfy their creative, if not altruistic, and competitive needs. There is much to learn about collaboration, organization, and other real-time business applications from the always-on virtual world. In fact, the real-world is using Second Life type of environments to introduce and test new ads, to train new hires, and to design and market new products. Of course, the two worlds are becoming more intertwined when virtual land development companies act in a very realistic manner and when 300 Linden dollars can be exchanged for one U. S. dollar.

A critical by-product of collaboration is standardization. Standards establish clear boundaries of function and operation, eliminate data interface problems, define interchangeable components and platforms, and assure a high level of performance. Even with standards, there can be misunderstandings. A case in point is the difference between two wireless technologies: Wi-Fi (IEEE 802.11 standard) and WiMax (IEEE 802.16 standard). Wi-Fi is designed to be used indoors at close range, to connect a group of computers in an office or home to each other and to the Internet; on the other hand, WiMax allows devices atop buildings and towers to feed Internet service to appropriately equipped computers at broadband speeds and up to 50 kilometers away. In time, a high-end mobile device could have both capabilities, so that one can seamlessly move from a Starbucks Wi-Fi hotspot to an automobile with a WiMax capability. New wireless standards will have to be established as more sophisticated wireless technologies are introduced, including smart antennas (which, instead of sending a weak omni-directional signal, can adaptively focus its signal for maximum distance), mesh networks (which employ the ongoing connections among users as a part of its own adhoc network), and agile radios (which can communicate among a number of frequency bands, depending on which parts of the spectrum are free). Another area of standardization is at the interfaces of these technologies. For example, when cellular networks and Wi-Fi become seamless, cell phones will become an omnipresent device, capable of functioning in open space where cellular networks abound and within buildings where Wi-Fi dominates.

A cornerstone of standardization has been the ubiquitous bar code – called the Universal Product Code (UPC) – that has been uniquely associated with almost every good or service. The UPC is making way for the Electronic Product Code (EPC) which is stored in a radio frequency identification (RFID) tag or computer chip with a transmitter. The tags are being placed on pallets or individual items passing through the supply chain. When activated by a reader, the tags can send or receive information. Wal-Mart and the U. S. Department of Defense are beginning to mandate the use of RFID in the supply chain. The real question is how companies can go beyond compliance and derive real value from RFID. Suppliers implementing RFID face two sets of considerations: "before the beep" and "after the beep", where the "beep" refers to the point at which an RFID tag is read by a reader. Before the beep includes technical considerations to ensure that tags are properly encoded, affixed to pallets or cartoons, and positioned so that readers can obtain and interpret the data, while knowledge gleaned after the beep includes issues related to data management and abstracted information that could appropriately support or inform critical decision making. Early indications suggest that RFID can result in labor savings (as readers can replace employees by obtaining data from tags within 30 feet), revenue enhancement (as better inventory management can reduce inventory shrinkage), and more informed choices (as, for example, the elimination of unnecessary handling by automatically forwarding a product to the customer without having to go through a warehousing phase). Another benefit of employing RFID is speed; thus, whereas conveyor belts in a typical distribution center operate at about 20 to 30 feet per minute, the Wal-Mart mandate of 600 feet per minute is well within RFID's capabilities. Additionally, RFID can help suppliers take full responsibility for ensuring that the retailer's inventory is replenished on an as-needed basis, thereby eliminating lost sales due to out-of-stock merchandise. In essence, RFID serves to make the supply chains more visible in real-time, and as the price of tags decreases, RFID will become ever more popular and critical to the efficient functioning of any supply chain, including the distribution and shipping of goods.

In actuality, an RFID tag is just a digital sensor. Like all (including environmental and biological) sensors, standardization – which, in the RFID case, is the EPC – is required in order to understand the sensor's output. Depending on the type of sensor, other standards or protocols are required. As another example, IEEE 1451.4 is being promulgated to calibrate the output of analog sensors (e.g., temperature gauge) to digital signals.

Additionally, as with collaboration, standardization (based usually on best practices) allows a business to grow by reassembling itself – with interchangeable blocks of technologies, processes, expertise, assets, capital and information – as the customers or circumstances require. Paradoxically, although standardization facilitates and enables innovation in both goods and services, it also facilitates and enables commoditization (where fierce competition and price erosion are the norm). Thus, the cycle of life in innovation includes innovation, best practices, standardization, commoditization, and (new) innovation.

Another critical by-product of collaboration is customization. Tien et al. [2004] have identified several levels of customization. Partial customization occurs in an assemble-to-order environment; that is, upon the arrival of a customer order, the stocked components are assembled into a finished product. As examples, in addition to computer assemblers like Dell and Gateway, Nike offers a program called NikeiD that allows customers to choose the color, material, cushioning, and other attributes of their athletic shoe order, and Procter & Gamble allows women to create and order custom personal-care products such as cosmetics, fragrances, and shampoos. Another form of partial customization occurs when the customer market is partitioned into an appropriate number of segments, each with similar needs. For example, Amazon targets their marketing of a new book to an entire market segment if several members of the segment act to acquire the book, although its approach is neither massive nor timely at this time. Mass customization occurs when the customer market is partitioned into a very large number of segments, with each segment being a single individual. Customization of clothing, car seats, and other body-fitted products is being advanced through laser-based, 3-D body scanners that not only capture a "point cloud" of the targeted body surface (e.g., some 150,000 points are required to create a digital skin of the entire body) but also the software algorithms that integrate the points and extract the needed size measurements. For example, European shoe makers recently initiated a project called EUROShoE (*www.euro-shoe.net*), in which an individual's feet are laser scanned and the data are forwarded to a CAD/CAM computer that controls the manufacturing process. Likewise, electronics giant Toshiba wants to give Web surfers and walk-in customers new tools to view digital versions of themselves trying on clothes, accessories and make-up. Real-time mass customization occurs when the needs of an individualized customer market are met on a real-time basis (e.g., a tailor who laser scans an individual's upper torso and then delivers a uniquely fitted jacket within a reasonable period, while the individual is waiting). Tien et al. [2004] also suggest that goods and services will become indistinguishable when real-time mass customization becomes a reality.

The people, technologies, systems, attitudes, values, cultures and structures of an organization must likewise be flexibly aligned in order to facilitate and enable innovation, especially collaborative or open innovation. The CIO (Chief Information Officer) of yesteryear remains the CIO of today, except for the fact that the "I" now stands for Innovation and typically includes authority over the research and development activities of the organization. In fact, many research and development groups (e.g., Lucent's Bell Labs, Xerox's Palo Alto Research Center, IBM's T. J. Watson Research Center, and GE's Global Research) are being both redirected to focus on innovation and partitioned, with new locations in Europe, India, and China. Moreover, the qualifications for the new CIO position require not only an idea person but, more importantly, a persuasive individual who can adroitly navigate new, high-risk products and processes through the organization. Similar to the promulgation of total quality management in the 1990s, the Chief Executive Officer (CEO) is also getting personally behind the innovation initiative. Clearly, there is an organizational sea change occurring, one that reflects the reality of globalization, another innovation enabler that is considered next.

Friedman [2005] has captured the globalization phenomenon in a catchy phrase: the world is flat, implying that the competitive playing field has been flattened so that anyone can innovate without having to emigrate to the U. S. He astutely recognizes 10 events or forces that all came together in the 1990s and converged around the year 2000. They include: 1) 11/9/89, the day the Berlin Wall came down and the world became one; 2) 8/9/95, the day Netscape went public and ushered in the global potential of the Internet with a concomitant over-investment (and subsequent dot-com bubble and crash) in optic fibers, an investment which greatly benefited India's weak infrastructure; 3) out-sourcing, whereby support work – especially software-writing – can be digitized, disaggregated and shifted to any place in the world (e.g., India) where it could be done cheaper, better and faster; 4) off-shoring, whereby entire factories are shipped overseas (e.g., to China) because of cost considerations; 5) open-sourcing, whereby software source codes are shared and improved by interested users; 6) in-sourcing, whereby one company allows another company (e.g., United Parcel Service) to take over, for example, its logistics operation; 7) supply-chaining, whereby an efficient global supply chain links, for example, Wal-Mart to all its suppliers in real-time; 8) informing, whereby anyone can access data and information through the various search engines; 9) wireless access, whereby anyone can be reached at anytime and from anyplace; and 10) Voice over Internet Protocol (VoIP), whereby telephony is carried out over the Internet. It should be noted that flatteners 3 through 8 are actually different forms of collaboration. In order to counter the adverse impacts of a flat world on the U. S., he recommends that three U.S. versus China/India gaps have to be addressed: an ambition gap among our workers, a production gap of graduating engineers and scientists, and an education gap in our K-12 grades.

There is also a serious age gap between the so called developed (i.e., Europe and North America) and developing (i.e., Asia and Latin America) countries of the world. As summarized in Table 2-4, while all the world's population (except for Africa) is aging at an alarming rate, by 2050 the developed countries will only have about 2 working age persons per age 65 or older person and the comparable figure for the developing countries is almost 4. Additionally and barring large-scale immigration and dramatic changes in retirement policies, the demand for services by the retired and the elderly will be particularly acute in Europe and North America, where coincidentally the economies are primarily services-oriented. Thus, it is critical that services innovation be significantly enhanced so that the quality of life will not diminish in today's economically advanced, services-oriented nations (including Japan where only about 1.5 workers will support a retiree in 2050). However, Dychtwald et al. [2006] suggest that companies can mitigate the impact of boomer generation retirement by redefining retirement and transforming management and human resource practices to attract, accommodate, and retain skilled workers of all ages and backgrounds.

Table 2-4. Global Demographics

Regions	Percent of Population Aged 60 or Older		Working Age Persons Per Age 65 or Older Person	
	2002	2050	2002	2050
Europe	20.0%	37.0%	3.9	1.8
North America	15.7%	27.1%	5.0	2.8
Asia	8.6%	22.9%	11.1	3.9
Latin America	7.9%	22.1%	11.0	3.8
Africa	5.0%	10.0%	16.8	8.9

Source: *United Nations*, 2002 Population Data

Another interesting consequence of the flat world is the emergence of a "stateless", 24/7 (i.e., always-on) transnational enterprise. For example, Trend Micro, an antivirus software company with executives and laboratories spread out in seven locations throughout the world from Munich to Tokyo, has been able to react and respond to viruses faster than Symantec, the market leader. With dual headquarters in Switzerland and Silicon Valley and its manufacturing center in low-cost Taiwan and China, Logitech is able to compete effectively with Microsoft in the area of computer peripherals. Wipro, a technical services supplier with headquarters in both India and Silicon Valley, is becoming a vendor of choice because it can adaptively deploy its 20,000 India-based software engineers and consultants, as needed. To mitigate the differences in time zones and cultures, transnational companies communicate in real-time over the Internet, via e-mail, through instant messenger or by Web videoconferencing.

3. SERVICES SECTOR

The importance of the services sector can not be overstated; it employs a large and growing proportion of workers in the industrialized nations. As reflected in Table 2-5, the services sector includes a number of large industries; indeed, services employment in the U.S. is at 82.1 percent, while the remaining four economic sectors (i.e., manufacturing, construction, agriculture, and mining), which together can be considered to be the "goods" sector, employ the remaining 21.4 percent. In practice, the delineation between the different economic sectors are blurred; this is especially true between the manufacturing and services sectors, which are highly interdependent [Tien and Berg, 1995; Berg et al., 2001].

Clearly, the manufacturing sector provides critical products (e.g., autos, computers, aircrafts, telecommunications equipment, etc.) that enable the delivery of efficient and high-quality services; equally clear, the services sector provides critical services (e.g., financial, transportation, design, supply chain, etc.) that enable the production, distribution and consumption of effective and high-quality products. Moreover, such traditional manufacturing powerhouses like GE and IBM have become more vertically integrated and are now earning an increasingly larger share of their income and profit through their services operation. For example, in 2005, IBM's pre-tax income was $12.2B (based on a total revenue stream of $91.1B) and it was divided into three parts: 28 percent from computer systems, 37 percent from software, and 35 percent from information technology services and consulting. Thus, IBM earned 28 and 72 percent of its profits from goods and services, respectively; as a result, IBM no longer considers itself a computer company anymore – instead, it offers itself as a globally integrated innovation partner, one which is able to integrate expertise across industries, business processes and technologies.

Table 2-5. Scope and Size of U.S. Employment

Industries	Employment (M)	Percent
Trade, Transportation & Utilities	26.1M	19.0%
Professional & Business	17.2	12.6
Health Care	14.8	10.8
Leisure & Hospitality	13.0	9.5
Education	13.0	9.5
Government (Except Education)	11.7	8.5
Finance, Insurance & Real Estate	8.3	6.1
Information & Telecommunication	3.1	2.2
Other	5.4	3.9
SERVICES SECTOR	**112.6**	**82.1**
Manufacturing	14.3	10.3
Construction	7.5	5.5
Agriculture	2.2	1.6
Mining	0.7	0.5
GOODS SECTOR	**24.7**	**17.9**
TOTAL	**137.3**	**100.0**

Source: *Bureau of Labor Statistics,* April 2006

What constitutes the services sector? It can be considered "to include all economic activities whose output is not a physical product or construction, is generally consumed at the time it is produced and provides added value in forms (such as convenience, amusement, timeliness, comfort or health) that are essentially intangible..." [Quinn et al., 1987]. Implicit in this definition is the recognition that services production and services delivery are so integrated that they can be considered to be a single, combined stage in the services value chain, whereas the goods sector has a value chain that includes supplier, manufacturer, assembler, retailer, and customer. More specifically, as indicated in Section 2, services are co-produced, whereas goods have traditionally been pre-produced; this and other differences between services and goods are explored in Section 5 to identify possible innovations in services. Tien and Berg [2003] provide a comparison between the goods and services sectors. The goods sector requires material as input, is physical in nature, involves the customer at the design stage, and employs mostly quantitative measures to assess its performance. On the other hand, the services sector requires information as input, is virtual in nature, involves the customer at the production/delivery stage, and employs mostly qualitative measures to assess its performance. Since services are to a large extent subject to customer satisfaction and since, as Tien and Cahn [1981] postulated and validated, "satisfaction is a function of expectation," service performance or satisfaction can be enhanced through the effective "management" of expectation. Parasuraman et al. [1998] employed the gap between expectation and actual service to evaluate service quality, as defined by reliability, tangibles, assurance, responsiveness and empathy.

Tien and Berg [2003] also call for viewing services as systems that require integration with other systems and processes, over both time and space; in fact, they make a case for further developing a branch of systems engineering that focuses on problems and issues which arise in the services sector. In this manner, they demonstrate how the traditional systems approach to analysis, control and optimization can be applied to a system of systems that are each within the province of a distinct service provider. They underscore this special focus not only because of the size and importance of the services sector but also because of the unique opportunities that systems engineering can exploit in the design and joint production and delivery of services. In particular, a number of service systems engineering methods are identified to enhance the design and production/delivery of services, especially taking advantage of the unique features that characterize services – namely, services, especially emerging e(lectronic)-services, are decision-driven, information-based, customer-centric, computationally-intensive, and productivity-focused.

As we consider the future, it is perhaps more appropriate to focus on emerging e-services. E-services are, of course, totally dependent on information technology; they include, as examples, financial services, banking, airline reservation systems, and customer goods marketing. The introduction of the Universal Product Code (UPC) and the optical scanning of these codes have not only, for example, shortened checkout times but also yielded critical data for undertaking marketing research. Furthermore, the UPC has been critical to the coupling of the production and logistics stages in the supply chain. Additional e-services are based on the Global Positioning System (GPS), which is bringing significant productivity improvements to the world's transportation and emergency service (i.e., police, ambulance and fire) agencies, as well as to other dispatch-oriented industries (e.g., taxicab companies, delivery services, and maintenance services). Of course, the Internet is the world's data superhighway in which businesses can interact with their far-flung offices, or with other businesses; customers can buy goods and services; and individuals can exchange e-mails or surf for information. Despite the "dot-com bubble" burst in the early 2000s, the Internet is flourishing and e-services or e-commerce is continuing to grow.

As indicated in Table 2-6, the electronic service enterprises interact or "co-produce" with their customers in a digital (including voice mail, e-mail, and Internet) medium, as compared to the physical environment in which the traditional or bricks-and-mortar service enterprises interact with their customers. Similarly, in comparison to traditional services which include low-wage jobs, the electronic services typically employ high-wage earners – and they are more demanding in their requirements for self-service, transaction speed, and computation.

Table 2-6. Comparison of Traditional and Electronic Services

	SERVICE ENTERPRISES	
ISSUE	**TRADITIONAL**	**ELECTRONIC**
Co-Production Medium	Physical	Electronic
Labor Requirement	High	Low
Wage Level	Low	High
Self-Service Requirement	Low	High
Transaction Speed Requirement	Low	High
Computation Requirement	Medium	High
Data Sources	Multiple Homogeneous	Multiple Non-Homogeneous
Driver	Data-Driven	Information-Driven
Data Availability/Accuracy	Poor	Rich
Information Availability/Accuracy	Poor	Poor
Size	Economies of Scale	Economies of Expertise
Service Flexibility	Standard	Adaptive
Focus	Mass Production	Mass Customization
Decision Time Frame	Predetermined	Real-Time

In regard to data sources that could be used to help make appropriate service decisions, both sets of services rely on multiple data sources; however, the traditional services are primarily based on homogeneous (mostly quantitative) data, while the electronic services could require non-homogeneous (i.e., both quantitative and qualitative) data. Paradoxically, the traditional service enterprises have been driven by data, although data availability and accuracy have been limited (especially before the pervasive use of the UPC); likewise, the emerging e-service enterprises have been driven by information (i.e., processed data), although information availability and accuracy have been limited, again due to the aforementioned data rich, information poor (DRIP) conundrum. Consequently, while traditional services – like traditional manufacturing – are based on economies of scale and a standardized approach, electronic services – like electronic manufacturing – emphasize economies of expertise or knowledge and an adaptive approach. The result is a shift in focus from mass production to mass customization (whereby a service is produced and delivered in response to a customer's stated or imputed needs); it is intended to provide superior value to customers by meeting their unique needs. It is in this area of customization – where customer involvement is not only at the goods design stage but also at the manufacturing or production stage – that services and manufacturing are merging in concept. Another critical distinction between traditional and electronic services is that, although all services require decisions to be made, the former services are primarily based on predetermined decision rules, while the latter could require more real-time, adaptive decisions; that is why Tien [2003] has advanced a decision informatics paradigm that relies on both information and decision technologies from a real-time perspective.

Increasingly, customers want more than just traditional or electronic services; they are seeking experiences [Pine and Gilmore, 1999]. Customers walk around with their iPods, drink their coffee at Starbucks while listening to and downloading music, dine at such theme restaurants as the Hard Rock Cafe or Planet Hollywood, shop at such experiential destinations as Universal CityWalk in Los Angeles or Beursplien in Rotterdam, lose themselves in such virtual worlds as Second Life or World of Warcraft, and vacation at such theme parks as Disney World or the Dubai Ski Dome, all venues that stage a feast of engaging sensations that are provided by an integrated set of services and products or goods. There is, nevertheless, a distinction between services and experiences; a service includes a set of intangible activities carried out for the customer, whereas an experience engages the customer in a personal, memorable and holistic manner, one that tries to engage all of the customer's senses. Obviously, experiences have always been at the heart of entertainment, from plays and concerts to movies and television shows; however, the number of entertainment options has exploded with digitization and the Internet. Today, there is a vast array of new experiences, including interactive games, World Wide Web sites, motion-based simulators, 3D movies and virtual reality. Interestingly, the question may be asked: just as electronic services have accelerated the commoditization of goods, will experiences accelerate the commoditization of services?

In the previous section, we consider innovation enablers; in this section we consider services, in particular electronic services. It is now helpful to consider services innovation in terms of the pertinent enablers, the underpinning technologies and the underlying decision attributes. In particular, Table 2-7 lists seven of the nine enablers (all except decision informatics and software algorithms) and identifies chips, software, and information technologies as being able to facilitate, if not effect, the enablers of automation, telecommunication, collaboration, standardization, customization, organization, and globalization; in addition, sensor, Internet, wireless, cognition, visualization, collaboration, telecommunication and management technologies are required for some of these enablers. In regard to decision attributes, it is seen that all except two service innovation enablers (i.e., standardization and organization) require a i) decision-driven, ii) information-based, iii) real-time, iv) continuously-adaptive, v) customer-centric and vi) computationally-intensive approach; for obvious reasons, standardization and organization do not require a real-time focus. All six decision attributes are within the decision informatics paradigm that is considered next.

Table 2-7. Services Innovation: Enablers, Technologies and Decision Attributes

Enablers	**Underpinning Technologies**	**Underlying Decision Attributes***					
		DD	**IB**	**RT**	**CA**	**CC**	**CI**
Automation	Chips; Software; Information; Sensor	✔	✔	✔	✔	✔	✔
Telecommuni-cation	Chips; Software; Information; Internet; Wireless; Sensor	✔	✔	✔	✔	✔	✔
Collaboration	Chips; Software; Information; Cognition; Visualization	✔	✔	✔	✔	✔	✔
Standardization	Chips; Software; Information; Collaboration	✔	✔		✔	✔	✔
Customization	Chips; Software; Information; Telecommunication	✔	✔	✔	✔	✔	✔
Organization	Chips; Software; Information; Telecommunication; Management	✔	✔		✔	✔	✔
Globalization	Chips; Software; Information; Telecommunication; Collaboration	✔	✔	✔	✔	✔	✔

*DD (Decision-Driven), IB (Information-Based), RT (Real-Time), CA (Continuously-Adaptive), CC (Customer-Centric), CI (Computationally-Intensive)

4. DECISION INFORMATICS

Before discussing decision informatics [Tien, 2003], it is helpful to highlight the difference between data and information, especially from a decision making perspective. As shown in Table 2-8, data represent basic transactions captured during operations, while information represents processed data (e.g., derivations, groupings, patterns, etc.). Clearly, except for simple operational decisions, decision making at the tactical or higher levels requires, at a minimum, appropriate information or processed data.

Table 2-8. Decision Making Framework

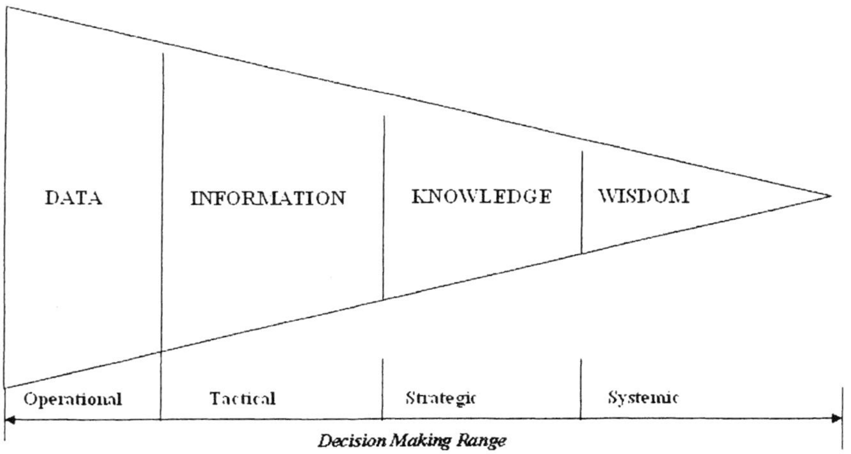

(a) Decision Levels

Basis	Decision Considerations
• Data	Basic observations; measurements, transactions, etc.
• Information	Processed data; derivations, groupings, patterns, etc.
• Knowledge	Processed information plus experiences, beliefs, values, culture; explicit, tacit/conscious, unconscious.
• Wisdom	Processed knowledge plus insight and assessment over time and space; theories, etc.

(b) Decision Bases

Table 2-8 also identifies knowledge as processed information (together with experiences, beliefs, values, cultures, etc.), and wisdom as processed knowledge (together with insights, theories, etc.). In our vernacular, strategic decisions can only be made with knowledge, while systemic decisions can only be made with wisdom. Although the literature sometimes does not distinguish between data and information, it is critical to do so, especially if we wish to avoid the data-rich, information-poor (DRIP) conundrum that is identified in Section 1. In fact, if we were to strictly adhere to such a distinction, we would conclude that given the current state of information technology, it should be referred to as "data technology" and, as indicated in Section 1, we are not in a knowledge – but only a data – economy.

A decision informatics approach is needed not only to develop new innovations in services (especially e-services and/or experiences) but also, if appropriate, to be packaged within a software algorithm that can serve to automate – and thereby enhance the productivity of – the developed innovation. As depicted in Table 2-9(a), the nature of the required real-time decision (regarding the production and/or delivery of a service) determines, where appropriate and from a systems engineering perspective, the data to be collected (possibly, from multiple, non-homogeneous sources) and the real-time fusion/analysis to be undertaken to obtain the needed information for input to the modeling effort which, in turn, provides the knowledge to identify and support the required decision in a timely manner. The feedback loops in Table 2-9(a) are within the context of systems engineering; they serve to refine the analysis and modeling steps. As depicted in Table 2-9(b), the driving force behind decision informatics is the decision foci. In regard to services innovation, the decisions concern how best to a) collaborate (especially in regard to self-serving, contributing, communicating, standardizing and globalizing issues), b) customize (especially in regard to profiling and personalizing issues), c) integrate (especially in regard to supply chaining, demand chaining, data warehousing and systematizing issues), and d) adapt (especially in regard to real-timing, automating, organizing and motivating issues). Actually, collaboration, customization, integration, and adaptation may be considered to be the four major drivers for services innovation; that is, services are promulgated in order to further collaboration, customization, integration and adaptation. Not surprisingly, the four services innovation drivers somewhat overlap the nine innovation enablers that are described in Sections 1 and 2; in fact, collaboration and customization are at once both drivers and enablers for services innovation.

More specifically, decision informatics is supported by two sets of technologies (i.e., information and decision technologies) and underpinned by three disciplines: data fusion/analysis, decision modeling and systems engineering. Data fusion and analysis methods concern the mining, visualization and management of data, information and knowledge; they include statistics, mathematics, management science and cognitive science. However, from the perspective of services innovation, it should be noted that

Table 2- 9. A Decision Informatics Paradigm

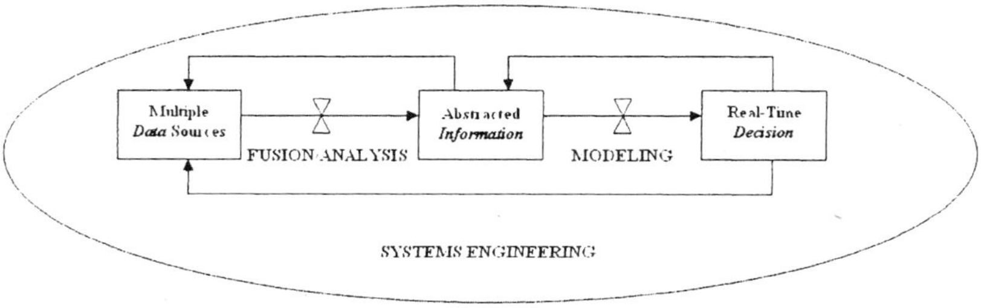

(a) Paradigm

Disciplinary Core	Related Methods
Decision Foci (For Services Innovation)	• Collaboration: self-serving, contributing, communicating, networking, standardizing, globalizing • Customization: profiling, personalizing • Integration: supply chaining, demand chaining, data warehousing, systematizing • Adaptation: real-timing, automating, organizing, motivating
Data Fusion/Analysis	• Statistics: non-homogeneous data fusion, fuzzy logic, neural networks, biometrics • Mathematics: probability, classification, clustering, association, sequencing • Management Science: expectation management, yield management • Cognitive Science: visualization, cognition
Decision Modeling	• Operations Research: optimization, simulation, prediction • Decision Science: game theory, risk analysis, dynamic pricing, Bayesian networks • Computer Science: service-oriented architecture (SoA), XML, genetic algorithms • Industrial Engineering: project management, scheduling,
Systems Engineering	• Electrical Engineering: cybernetics, networks, pattern recognition • Human Machine Systems: human factors, cognitive ergonomics, ethnography • System Performance: life-cycle, value chain • System Biology: predictive medicine, preventive medicine, personalized medicine

(b) Methods

the available data fusion and analysis methods suffer from two critical shortcomings. First, the available methods are predominantly focused on quantitative data, which is, of course, very limiting since it is estimated that over 80 percent of the available data are qualitative in nature. Second, the available methods are primarily focused, if not trained, on a fixed data set, whereas in the real-world, there is a constant stream of data that require continuous fusion and analysis. Clearly, methods must be developed that can fuse and analyze a steady stream of non-homogeneous (i.e., quantitative and qualitative) data.

It is helpful to further address data fusion, which can take place at the signal level, the feature level and/or the decision level. Signal-level fusion refers to combining the signals of a group of sensors. The signals from the sensors can be modeled as random variables, contaminated by uncorrelated noise. The fusion process is considered an estimation procedure. Only if the sensory signals are strictly homogeneous or alike can the fusion take place at the signal level. Feature-level fusion refers to combining the features that are extracted from sensory data. A set or vector of primary features is first obtained, then composite features can be created, and analysis is typically undertaken on the composite features. Thus, Ayache and Faugeras [1989] use extended Kalman filtering to efficiently integrate sequences of images at the feature-level in order to determine the surfaces of three-dimensional objects. The feature-level fusion enables the overall uncertainty concerning the location of objects to be reduced in the presence of environmental and sensory noise. Gunatilaka and Baertlein [2001] extract geographic features by nonlinear optimization techniques, and then they determine whether a certain type of mine is located in the region by applying Bayesian decision theory to the composite features.On the other hand, decision-level fusion refers to combining information extracted from sensory data at the highest level of abstraction; it is commonly employed in applications where multiple sensors are of a different nature or are located in different regions of the environment. Fusion is accomplished by judicious processing of the individual sensory information, or through symbolic reasoning that may make use of prior knowledge from a world model or sources external to the system. The prevailing techniques for decision- or symbol-level fusion include Bayesian (i.e., maximum a posteriori) estimation [Gunatilaka and Baertlein, 2001] and Dempster-Shafer evidential reasoning [Garvey et al., 1981]. Evidential reasoning is actually an extension of the Bayesian approach; it makes explicit any lack of information concerning a proposition's uncertainty by separating firm belief for the proposition from just its plausibility. In the Bayesian approach, all propositions (e.g., objects in the environment) for which there are no information are assigned an equal a priori probability. When additional information from a sensor becomes available and the number of unknown propositions is large relative to the number of known propositions, an intuitively unsatisfying result of the Bayesian approach is that the probabilities of known propositions become unstable. In the Dempster-Shafer approach, this is avoided by not assuming an a priori probability. Instead, the unknown propositions are assigned to "ignorance", which is reduced only when supporting information becomes available. Evidential reasoning is introduced to allow each sensor to contribute information at its own level of detail. For example, one sensor may be able to provide information that can be used to distinguish individual objects, whereas the information from another sensor may only be able to distinguish classes of objects.

Decision modeling methods concern the information-based modeling and analysis of alternative decision scenarios; they include operations research, decision science, computer science and industrial engineering. Likewise, decision modeling methods suffer from two shortcomings. First, most of the available – especially optimization – methods are only applicable in a steady state environment, whereas in the real-world, all systems are in transition. (Note that steady state, like average, is an analytical concept that allows for a tractable, if not manageable, analysis.) Second, most of the available methods are unable to cope with changing circumstances; instead, we need methods that are adaptive so that decisions can be made in real-time. Thus, non steady-state and adaptive decision methods are required. More importantly, real-time decision modeling is not just about speeding up the models and solution algorithms; it, like real-time data fusion and analysis, also requires additional research and development.

Systems engineering methods concern the integration of people, processes, products and operations from a systems perspective; they include electrical engineering, human-machine systems, systems performance and systems biology. Again, the real-time nature of co-producing services – especially human-centered services that are computationally-intensive and intelligence-oriented – requires a real-time, systems engineering approach. Ethnography, a branch of anthropology that can help identify a consumer's unmet needs, is being used to spot breakthrough product and service innovations; as examples, it is being credited with developing a Motorola cell phone that allows text messaging using Chinese characters, a portable Sirius satellite-radio player, and a PayPass tag that provides Citigroup customers with a debit service. Another critical aspect of systems engineering is system performance; it provides an essential framework for assessing the decisions made – in terms of such issues as satisfaction, convenience, privacy, security, equity, quality, productivity, safety and reliability. Similarly, undertaking systems engineering within a real-time environment will require additional thought and research.

The decision informatics paradigm can be very appropriately employed to develop new approaches or innovations. Two such example innovations are summarized in Table 2-10. The first was an NSF-funded effort, entitled, "Automated Discovery of Novel Pharmaceuticals," in which Embrechts et al. [2000] focus on identifying novel candidate pharmaceuticals. Molecular

Table 2-10. Innovation Examples Using Decision Informatics

FOCUS	DRUG DISCOVERY EXAMPLE	AGILE MANUFACTURING EXAMPLE
Effort	"Automated Discovery of Novel Pharmaceuticals" (NSF, $1.2M, 9/99-8/02); a bioinformatics application.	"Electronic Agile Manufacturing Research Institute" (NSF/Industry, $11.2M, 4/94-8/00); a distributed manufacturing approach to circuit board design and assembly, resulting in a patent and a new incubator company called "ve-design.com".
Decision	Molecules that could be novel drug candidates.	Design, fabrication and assembly of a printed circuit board.
Data Fusion/Analysis	Molecular data are analyzed and information is derived concerning some 1000 descriptors for each molecule.	Based on possible design configurations, software or intelligent "agents" obtain relevant cost and cycle time information from the vast data sets resident in computers of possible suppliers (Cisco, Pitney Bowes, Lucent, Rockwell Automation).
Decision Modeling	Obtained information is input into various neural network and genetic algorithm models to determine those qualitative structural activity relationships that might be of interest or yield improved bio-activities.	Obtained information is input into a genetic algorithm model that assists in deciding the best design (in terms of components, supplies, geometries, technologies).
Systems Engineering	Entire process is to be automated, employing a systems framework that includes returning the non-selected molecules to the information base for further processing.	Entire virtual design environment is developed to operate in a network of distributed databases/alternative designs resident with members of supply chain.

data are analyzed and information is obtained concerning some 1000 descriptors for each molecule; based on various neural network and genetic algorithm models, the quantitative structural activity relationships (QSARs) are determined to help screen and decide on those molecules which could be candidate drugs due to their interesting or improved bioactivities. The entire process is automated, employing a systems engineering framework that includes returning the non-selected molecules to the information base for further QSAR analysis, screening and selection.

In the second example, Graves et al. [1999] completed another NSF-funded effort, entitled, "Electronic Agile Manufacturing," with a focus on the design of a printed circuit-board assembly (PCBA). Cost and cycle time data in design, fabrication, and assembly are statistically analyzed to yield a networked information environment of relationships between PCBA characteristics and their effect on cost and cycle time; these relationships are, in turn, input into a genetic algorithm model that helps the designer to decide on the best PCBA design (in terms of components, suppliers, geometries and technologies) from literally thousands of possible alternatives. The entire virtual design environment is systems engineered to operate in a network of distributed databases and alternative designs, resident at and maintained by members of a supply chain. An automated, real-time information prototype has been developed and tested, employing real design files and data from collaborating companies, including Cisco Systems, Pitney Bowes, Rockwell Automation and Lucent Technologies.

Yet a third example of applying the decision informatics paradigm is in the context of major urban disruptions [Tien, 2005]. Urban infrastructures are the focus of terrorist acts because, quite simply, they produce the most visible impact, if not casualties. While terrorist acts are the most insidious and onerous of all disruptions, it is obvious that there are many similarities in the way one should deal with these willful acts and those caused by natural and accidental incidents that have also resulted in adverse and severe consequences. However, there is one major and critical difference between terrorist acts and the other types of disruptions: the terrorist acts are willful – and therefore also adaptive. One must counter these acts with the same, if not more sophisticated, willful, adaptive and informed approach. Real-time, information-based decision making (i.e., decision informatics) is the approach that can be employed to make the right decisions at the right time in the various stages of a disruption. As discussed above, it is focused on decisions and based on multiple data sources, data fusion and analysis methods, timely information, stochastic decision models and a systems engineering outlook. The approach provides a consistent way to address real-time emergency issues, including those concerned with the preparation for a major disruption, the prediction of such a disruption, the prevention or mitigation of the disruption, the detection of the disruption, the response to the disruption, and the recovery steps that are necessary to adequately, if not fully, recuperate from the disruption. As a consequence, we must trade off between productivity and security; between just-in-time interdependencies and just-in-case inventories; and between high-probability, low-risk life-as-usual situations and low-probability, high-risk catastrophes.

Finally, it should be noted that decision informatics is, as a framework, generic and applicable to most, if not all, decision problems. Actually, it is likewise applicable to any design problem, inasmuch as the essence of design is about making decisions concerning alternative scenarios or designs. (Not surprisingly, innovation is sometimes characterized as "design thinking".) Additionally, since any data analysis, modeling or design effort should only be undertaken for some purpose or decision, all analyses, modeling and design activities should be able to be viewed within the decision informatics framework, including the development of new decision-theoretic tools that can integrate sensed data in support of real-time decision making. In short, decision informatics represents a decision-driven, information-based, real-time, continuously-adaptive, customer-centric and computationally-intensive approach to intelligent decision making by humans and/or software agents. Consequently, it can be very appropriately employed to address decisions regarding the design and delivery of innovative services; it is a necessary tool for or enabler of services innovation.

5. SERVICES INNOVATION

Sections 1 through 4 have, in essence, defined a process for undertaking services innovation. Table 2-11 provides a summary of the process. It identifies the relationships between goods, services and experiences (which are typically integrated products and services); shows how the nine enablers and four drivers interact to yield new innovations in goods, services and experiences; and highlights why decision informatics is a necessary enabler. As noted earlier, decision informatics constitutes a pivotal step in developing or deciding on a new services innovation; additionally, it is, if appropriate, central to (i.e., the brain in) any software algorithm that can serve to automate – and thereby enhance the productivity of – the developed innovation. As we focus on services innovation, it is helpful to reexamine the four innovation drivers: collaboration, customization, integration and adaptation. All four are directed at empowering the individual – that is, at recognizing that the individual can a) contribute in a collaborative situation,

b) receive customized or personalized attention, c) access an integrated system or process, and d) obtain adaptive real-time or just-in-time input.

Table 2-11. Services Innovation: Drivers, Enablers and Decision Attributes

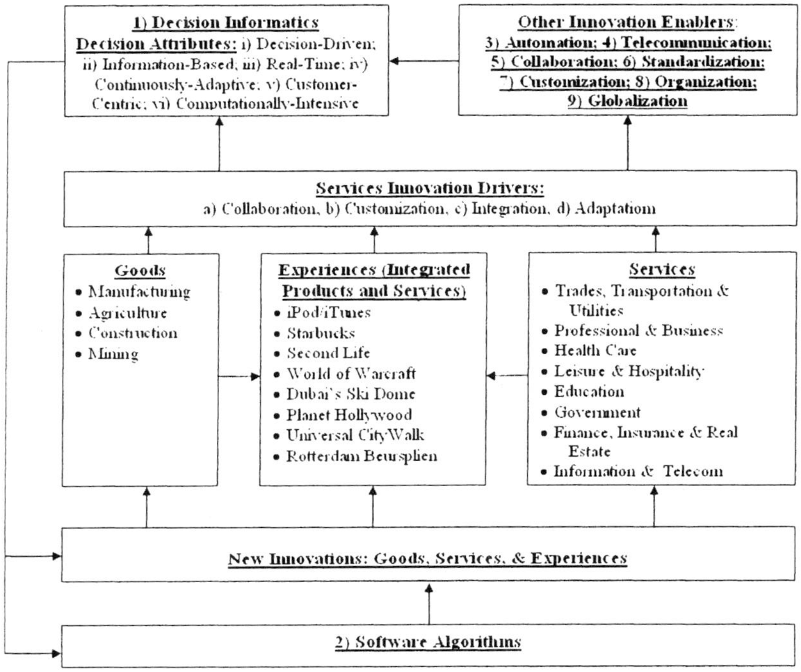

Nevertheless, the question remains: where are the areas or white spaces for possible new innovations in services (and/or experiences)? The answer can be found by considering the nine innovation enablers (described in Section 1 and 2), the six services-related decision attributes (identified in Section 3), and the four services innovation drivers (discussed in Section 4); their coverage serve to identify the potential white spaces. As examples, Table 2-12 identifies the primary drivers, enablers and decision attributes associated with 45 services innovation areas, assuming 5 in each of the 9 service categories or domains. Although both the domain areas and the identification process are quite subjective, it is interesting to note that the drivers, in order of impact, are: integration (16 out of 45), adaptation (13), customization (12), and collaboration (4). Similarly, the enablers are:

automation (19), organization (7), globalization (5), customization (5), standardization (5), telecommunication (2), and collaboration (2). (Inasmuch as decision informatics and software algorithms are somewhat pervasive and pertinent to all areas, only 7 of the 9 enablers are considered.)

Although Table 2-12 lists the existent innovations in the 45 areas, there is considerable room for many more innovations in these same areas. As examples, with sophisticated wireless and global positioning technologies, highway commuters should be able to put their cars on autopilot; with multimedia and wideband technologies, entire degree programs with just-in-time learning capabilities should be able to be accessed online [Tien, 2000]; and with real-time customized management of both the supply and demand chains, a jacket, for example, should be able to be personalized (in size, color and style) and produced in a matter of hours [Tien et al., 2004; Gershenfeld, 2005].

Indeed, the services landscape is full of white spaces. Paradoxically, one set of white spaces concern innovations that can mitigate the unforeseen consequences or abuses of earlier innovations. Antivirus companies like Symantec and Trend Micro are barely able to cope with the avalanche of new viruses and virus delivery schemes. Ad spamming is taking over the email system, much like junk mail took over the traditional postal system. Spyware, a form of adware that tracks an individual's every click and sends the data to advertisers, has now infected some 80 percent of all personal computers in the U. S. Indeed, fraudulent clicks by robotic viruses have cost advertisers millions of dollars. In "phishing" or creating a replica of an existing Web page to fool users into submitting personal, financial or password data, hackers are stealing individual identities and committing fraud. Sadly, the same innovations that have enhanced global interconnectedness have engendered new vulnerabilities, including cyber attacks. Thus, electronic viruses, biological agents and other toxic materials can turn a nation's "lifelines" into "deathlines", in that they can be used to facilitate the spread of these materials – whether by accident or by willful act. In this vein, the Internet – with over a billion users – has become a terrorist tool; jihad websites are recruiting members, soliciting funds, and promoting violence (e.g., by showing the beheading of hostages). Also, as evidenced by the 9/11 attack, components of an infrastructure (e.g., airplanes) can be used as weapons of destruction. In sum, new and more powerful innovations are required to secure and safeguard those innovations – including mobile devices, electronic systems, and, more recently, even RFID tags – that define and underpin our advanced economies.

A related set of white spaces concern innovations that can safeguard our rights to privacy. In fact, in 2003 the U. S. Congress stopped the Terrorism Information Awareness program sponsored by the Department of Advanced

Table 2-12. Services Innovation and Decision Informatics

Example Innovations			**Decision Attributes***					
Service Categories **Trade, Transportation & Utilities**	**Primary Driver**	**Primary Enabler**	**D D**	**I B**	**R T**	**C A**	**C C**	**C I**
Trading (eBay, Green Energy Tags, E-Waste Recycling)	Collaboration	Standardization	✔	✔	✔	✔	✔	✔
RFID (Supply Chain, Automated Checkout, P&G, Wal-Mart)	Customization	Automation	✔	✔	✔	✔	✔	✔
Travel Sites (Expedia, Orbitz, Travelocity, Travelzoo, Priceline)	Integration	Globalization	✔	✔	✔	✔	✔	✔
Intelligent Transportation Systems (Interoperability, Standards)	Integration	Standardization	✔	✔	✔	✔	✔	✔
Payment Systems (PayPal/eBay, Peppercoin, Paystone, BitPass)	Adaptation	Automation	✔	✔	✔	✔	✔	✔
Professional & Business								
Web Commerce (Amazon, Wal-Mart, ToysRUs)	Integration	Globalization	✔	✔	✔	✔	✔	✔
Real-Time Routing (JetBlue, UPS, FedEx, BostonCoach)	Adaptation	Customization	✔	✔	✔	✔	✔	✔
GPS-Based Services (Traffic, Emergencies, Local Info)	Adaptation	Customization	✔	✔	✔	✔	✔	✔
Targeted Marketing (Amazon, Harrah's, BMW, Wells Fargo)	Adaptation	Customization	✔	✔	✔	✔	✔	✔
Business Processes (Textron's Streamlining, Nucor's Incentives)	Adaptation	Organization	✔	✔	✔	✔	✔	✔
Health Care								
E-Health (Imaging, Diagnostic AmpliChips)	Customization	Automation	✔	✔	✔	✔	✔	✔
Bionic Parts (Limbs, Heart, Lungs, Liver, Eyes, Ears)	Customization	Automation	✔	✔	✔	✔	✔	✔
Health Reform (Mandatory Insurance, Digital Records)	Customization	Standardization	✔	✔	✔	✔	✔	✔
One-Stop Wellness Facility (Medical, Dental, Spa, Therapy)	Customization	Organization	✔	✔	✔	✔	✔	✔
Bioinformatics (Drugs, Genomics, Proteomics, Glycomics)	Adaptation	Automation	✔	✔	✔	✔	✔	✔

Leisure & Hospitality								
Social Networking (MySpace, Craigslist, Visible Path)	Customization	Collaboration	✔	✔	✔	✔	✔	✔
Retail Tourism (Mall of America)	Customization	Organization	✔	✔	✔	✔	✔	✔
Experiential Venues (Starbucks, ESPN Zones, IMAX Theatres)	Customization	Organization	✔	✔	✔	✔	✔	✔
Virtual Environments (Second Life, World of Warcraft)	Customization	Collaboration	✔	✔	✔	✔	✔	✔
Simulated Environments (Dubai's Ski Dome)	Customization	Organization	✔	✔	✔	✔	✔	✔
Education								
Smart Games (Sudoku, Brain Age, Big Brain Academy, IQ)	Adaptation	Automation	✔	✔	✔	✔	✔	✔
New Foci (Services Science, Innovation Engineering)	Integration	Organization	✔	✔	✔	✔	✔	✔
Online Degrees (U. of Phoenix, EArmyU, Florida Virtual School)	Adaptation	Globalization	✔	✔	✔	✔	✔	✔
E-Training (Certifications, Microsoft, Cisco, Kinko)	Adaptation	Globalization	✔	✔	✔	✔	✔	✔
E-Reference (WebMD, FindLaw, Wikipedia)	Integration	Automation	✔	✔	✔	✔	✔	✔
Government								
Imaging (Airport Screening, Target Tracking, Predator Drone)	Integration	Automation	✔	✔	✔	✔	✔	✔
Security (CAPPS II, Biometrics, Coplink, Relationships Ident)	Integration	Automation	✔	✔	✔	✔	✔	✔
Research (GPS Profiling, WMD Sensing)	Integration	Automation	✔	✔	✔	✔	✔	✔
Civil Service (Motivation, Morale, Retention, Recruitment)	Adaptation	Organization	✔	✔	✔	✔	✔	✔
National Counterterrorism Center (Email, Voice, Databases)	Integration	Automation	✔	✔	✔	✔	✔	✔
Finance, Insurance & Real Estate								
Credit Ratings (TransUnion, Equifax, Experian)	Integration	Automation	✔	✔	✔	✔	✔	✔
Web Trading (Schwab,	Integration	Automation	✔	✔	✔	✔	✔	✔

Fidelity, TD Ameritrade, ETFs)								
Web Realty (zipRealty, HomeGain, LendingTree, Zillow)	Integration	Automation	✔	✔	✔	✔	✔	✔
Web Insurance (Insweb, Progressive's Auto, Aon's TechShield)	Integration	Automation	✔	✔	✔	✔	✔	✔
Wealth Care Investments (Portfolios Reflecting Life and Living)	Integration	Automation	✔	✔	✔	✔	✔	✔
Information & Telecom								
Web Search (Google, Yahoo, AOL, MSN, Windows Live)	Integration	Customization	✔	✔	✔	✔	✔	✔
Voice Over Internet (Vonage, Skype, Comcast, Time Warner)	Collaboration	Telecomm.	✔	✔	✔	✔	✔	✔
Content Collaboration (Wikipedia, YouTube, Flickr)	Integration	Globalization	✔	✔	✔	✔	✔	✔
Software Collaboration (Red Hat, JBoss, MySQL)	Collaboration	Automation	✔	✔	✔	✔	✔	✔
Advanced Mobile Devices (PDAs, Satellite Radio, OnStar Autos)	Collaboration	Telecomm.	✔	✔	✔	✔	✔	✔
Other								
Assemble-to-Order (BMW, Dell, Whirlpool, FreshDirect)	Adaptation	Standardization	✔	✔	✔	✔	✔	✔
Made-to-Order (Siemen's Hearing Aids, Fab Labs)	Adaptation	Automation	✔	✔	✔	✔	✔	✔
On-Demand (IBM, Microsoft Dynamics, Accenture)	Adaptation	Customization	✔	✔	✔	✔	✔	✔
E-Advertising (Display Banners, Search Ads/Clicks, Productions)	Customization	Automation	✔	✔	✔	✔	✔	✔
Brand Marketing (Tide, Always, Pampers, iPod, Intel Inside)	Customization	Standardization	✔	✔	✔	✔	✔	✔
*DD (Decision-Driven), IB (Information-Based), RT (Real-Time), CA (Continuously-Adaptive), CC (Customer-Centric), CI (Computationally-Intensive)								

Research Projects Agency (DARPA) because it was going to mine massive amounts of data, including personal transactions of U. S. citizens, in order to connect the dots leading to terrorists and terrorism. Moreover, the continuing anti-terrorist surveillance program by the U. S. government and the widely acclaimed and increasingly profitable search, marketing and even social networking innovations on the Internet could easily be considered to be an invasion of privacy. As an example, constitutional scholars feel that current wiretapping by the National Security Agency (NSA) on communications between individuals outside the U. S. and citizens inside the country is both unconstitutional and against the 1978 Foreign Intelligence Surveillance Act (FISA). Additionally, identifying one's buying habits, broadcasting one's location and submitting data to social network sites about one's friends (without their explicit permission) are also questionable from a privacy perspective. Clearly, sophisticated innovations are required to prevent incursions into our private lives.

Another set of white spaces concern innovations that can protect us from the always-on, interconnected world. With a 24/7 electronic world and wireless mobile devices, we are unfortunately always reachable – for mostly business purposes – from anywhere in the world. Increasingly, our business life extends into and takes over or displaces our home life. Thus, although our work output has increased (mostly due to our increased working hours), we are not necessarily more productive. Furthermore, as Surowiecki [2005] suggests, more electronic devices and gadgets do not necessarily increase our well-being; instead, over time, we tend to take these innovations for granted and to raise our expectations for what future innovations can bring, thus mitigating our overall satisfaction – which, as Tien and Cahn [1981] confirmed, is a function of our expectation. Hallowell [2006] argues that the 24/7 frenzy has drained us of creativity, humanity, mental well-being, and the ability to focus on what truly matters – we suffer from a culturally induced attention deficit disorder. He suggests that we can teach ourselves to move from the F-state (i.e., frenzied, flailing, fearful, forgetful, and furious) to the C-state (i.e., cool, calm, clear, consistent, curious, and courteous). Nevertheless, new innovations are required to protect ourselves from the F-state.

Yet another white space for services innovation is the development of an authoritative search engine. At present, for example, Google provides a weighted or prioritized set of output pages when a word or phrase search is initiated; unfortunately, several hundreds of pages are presented and sometimes with conflicting, if not confusing, information – a classic case of the aforementioned data rich, information poor (DRIP) conundrum. Likewise, Wikipedia – with an anyone-can-contribute ethos and a 200 gigabyte database, containing 3 million articles in 200 languages – suffers from the same problem, even though some contributions can be deleted by a Wikipedia elite of some 800 longtime contributors. Interestingly, in a recent comparison between Wikipedia and its major peer, Encyclopedia Britannica,

Nature [2005] asked experts from several disciplines to review 50 articles – with identical subject matter and of similar length – from each encyclopedia and assess them for their accuracy, resulting in 2.9 errors per article for Encyclopaedia Britannica versus 3.9 errors per article for Wikipedia. Nevertheless, it is obvious that an authoritative Google (Agoogle) is needed, one which provides fewer pages of output and a higher degree of accuracy for each search. Such an Agoogle would not only replace the various search engines but may well become the largest capitalized company in the world.

A final white space concerns the economic measurement of services itself. Corrado et al. [2005] are concerned that while the government's decades-old system of data collection and statistical analysis are appropriate for capturing tangible investments in equipment, buildings and even software, they are inadequate in reflecting the growing knowledge economy, one driven by intangible ideas and services innovation. In other words, the Bureau of Economic Analysis in Washington, D. C., is not tracking the billions of dollars that companies spend each year on innovation and product design, brand-building, employee training, or any of the other investments – not consumption costs – that are required to compete in today's global economy. As a result, services-oriented economies – like those of the U. S. and Japan – are probably much stronger than the official statistics indicate. Such a measurement innovation may result in a "knowledge-adjusted" GDP metric.

6. CONCLUDING REMARKS

In conclusion, several remarks should be made. First, it should be stated that although so called, "business intelligence" (BI) software (offered by MicroStrategy, Hyperion Solutions, SAS, Cognos, etc.) could have been developed by employing the decision informatics paradigm that is advanced herein, we are not aware that any of the proprietary software actually followed such a purposeful, systematic and decision-driven approach. Moreover, to our knowledge, most of the BI software attempts to make sense of the transactions data and to present it in a way that anyone, from a sales representative to a chief executive, can understand and use; indeed, for the most part, the software represents a query window into data warehouses. Thus, it is unclear whether the BI software contains any sophisticated, real-time data fusion, data analysis, decision modeling, or systems engineering methods.

Second, as emphasized throughout this paper, significant research is required to fully and fruitfully apply the proposed real-time, information-based approach to services innovation. Indeed, the decision informatics paradigm must continuously undergo upgrades and refinements, especially as computing becomes faster and cheaper and as powerful new tools are developed. For example, research into cognition (i.e., understanding how people process input) could result in findings that may have a significant impact on not only services innovation, but also the decision making process itself.

Third, as real-time decisions must be made in an accelerated manner, the human decision maker or service provider will increasingly become a bottleneck; he/she must make way for a smart robot or software agent. For example, everyone could use a smart alter ego or agent which could analyze, and perhaps fuse, all the existing and incoming e-mails, phone calls, Web pages, news clips, and stock quotes, and assigns every item a priority based on the individual's preferences and observed behavior. It should be able to perform a semantic analysis of a message text, judge the sender-recipient relationships by examining an organizational chart and recall the urgency of the recipient's responses to previous messages from the same sender. To this, it might add information gathered by watching the user via a video camera or by scrutinizing his/her calendar. Most probably, such an agent would be based on a Bayesian statistical model – capable of evaluating hundreds of user-related factors linked by probabilities, causes and effects in a vast web of contingent outcomes – that infers the likelihood that a given decision on the software's part would lead to the user's desired outcome. The ultimate goal is to judge when the user can safely be interrupted, with what kind of message, and via which device. Perhaps the same agent could serve as a travel agent by searching the Internet and gathering all the relevant information about airline schedules and hotel prices, and, with the user's consent, returning with the electronic tickets. Clearly, such innovative agents can be developed by employing the decision informatics paradigm.

Finally, the decision attributes, innovation enablers and innovation drivers advanced in this paper provide an effective calculus for identifying, developing and promulgating services innovation. Thus, the paper serves as a critical step towards understanding the science, management and engineering of services.

REFERENCES

Ayache, N., and Faugeras, O., 1989, "Maintaining Representations of the Environment of Mobile Robot," *IEEE Transactions on Robotics and Automation,* Vol. 5, No. 6, pp. 804-819.

Baumol, W. J., Batey-Blackman, S. A., and Wolff, E. N., 1989, *Productivity and American Leadership: The Long View*, Cambridge, MA: John Wiley & Sons.

Berg, D. and Einspruch, N. G., 2006, "Analyzing Corporate Innovation Using The Data Surface Mining Technique," *Proceedings of the 3rd IEEE Conference on Management of Innovation and Technology,* Singapore, June 21-23.

Berg, D., Tien, J. M., and Wallace, W. A., 2001, "Guest Editorial: Technology Management in the Service Industry," *IEEE Transactions on Engineering Management: Special Cluster,* Vol. 148, No. 3, pp. 330-332.

Cairncross, F., 1997, *The Death of Distance: How the Communications Revolution is Changing Our Lives,* Boston, MA: Harvard Business School Press.

Friedman, T. L., 2005, *The World Is Flat: A Brief History of the Twenty-First Century,* New York, NY: Farrar, Strauss & Giroux.

Chesbrough, H. W., 2003, *Open Innovation: The New Imperative for Creating and Profiting from Technology,* Boston, MA: Harvard Business School Press.

Corrado, C., Hulten, C., and Sichel, D., 2005, *Intangible Capital and Economic Growth*, Baltimore, MD: Federal Reserve Board.

Dychtwald, K., Erickson, T. J., and Morison, R., 2006, *Workforce Crisis: How to Beat the Coming Shortage of Skills And Talent*, Boston, MA: Harvard Business School Press.

Embrechts, M., Lee, I. N., and Liao, S.C., 2000, "Data Mining Techniques Applied to Medical Information," *Medical Information*, Vol. 25, No. 2, pp. 81-102.

Garvey, T. D., Lowrance, J. D., and Fischler, M. A., 1981, "An Inference Technique for Integrating Knowledge from Disparate Sources," *Proceedings of the Seventh International Joint Conference on Artificial Intelligence*, pp. 319-325.

Gershenfeld, N. A, 2005, *FAB: The Coming Revolution on Your Desktop – From Personal Computers to Personal Fabrication,* Boston, MA: Basic Books.

Govindarajan, V. and Trimble, C., 2005, *Ten Rules for Strategic Innovators: From Idea to Execution,* Boston, MA: Harvard Business School Press.

Graves, R. J., Subbu, R., Sanderson, A. C. and Hocaoghu, C., 1999, "Evolutionary Decision Support for Distributed Virtual Design in Modular Product Manufacturing," Vol. 10, No. 7, *Production Planning and Control*, pp. 627-642.

Gunatilaka, A.H., and Baertlein, B. A., 2001, "Feature-Level and Decision-Level Fusion of Noncoincidently Sampled Sensors for Land Mine Detection," *IEEE Transactions on Pattern Analysis and Machine Intelligence,* Vol. 23, No. 6, pp. 577-589.

Hallowell, E. M., M.D., 2006, *CrazyBusy : Overstretched, Overbooked, and About to Snap! Strategies for Coping in a World Gone ADD,* New York, NY: Ballantine Books.

Hammond, J. S., Keeney, R. L. and Raiffa, H., 1999, *Smart Choices: A Practical Guide to Making Better Decisions*, Boston, MA: Harvard Business School Press.

Moore, G. E., 1965, "Cramming More Components Onto Integrated Circuits", *Electronics*, Vol. 38, No. 8, April, pp. 38-41.

National Academy of Engineering, 2000, *The Great Achievements Project*, Washington, DC: National Academies Press, February.

Nature, 2005, "Internet Encyclopedias Go Head to Head", *Nature,* vol. 438, 15 December, pp. 900-901.

National Science Foundation (NSF), 2006, *Partnerships for Innovation,* Washington, DC: NSF 06-550.

Norwegian Ministry of Industry and Trade (NMIT), 2006, *Innovation in Services: Typology, Case Studies and Policy Implications,* Oslo, Norway: ECON Report 2006-025, February.

Organisation for Economic Cooperation and Development (OECD), 2005, *Enhancing the Performance of the Service Sector: Promoting Innovation in Services,* Paris, France: OECD Publications.

Palmisano, S. J., 2004, *Global Innovation Outlook,* Armonk, NY: IBM.

Parasuraman, A., Zeithaml, V.A., and Berry, L. L., 1998, "Servqual: A Multiple Item Scale for Measuring Consumer Perceptions of Service Quality", *Journal of Retailing,* Vol.64, No. 1, pp.12-40.

Pine II, B. J., and Gilmore, J.H., 1999, *The Experience Economy,* Boston, MA: Harvard Business School Press.

Quinn, J. B., Baruch, J. J., and Paquette, P. C., 1987, "Technology in Services," *Scientific American,* Vol. 257, No. 6, pp. 50-58.

Sanford, L. S. and Taylor, D., 2005, *Let Go To Grow: Escaping the Commodity Trap,* Upper Saddle River, NJ: Pearson Education.

Surowiecki, J., 2005, "Technology and Happiness", *Technology Review,* January, pp.72-76.

Tien, J. M., 1986, "On Automated Correctional Data Systems," *Computers, Environment and Urban Systems,* Vol. 10, No. 3/4, April, pp. 157-163.

Tien, J. M., 2000, "Individual-Centered Education: An Any One, Any Time, Any Where Approach to Engineering Education," *IEEE Transactions on Systems, Man, and Cybernetics Part C: Special Issue on Systems Engineering Education,* Vol. 30, No. 2, pp. 213-218.

Tien, J. M., 2003, "Towards A Decision Informatics Paradigm: A Real-Time, Information-Based Approach to Decision Making," *IEEE Transactions on Systems, Man, and Cybernetics, Special Issue,* Part C, Vol. 33, No. 1, pp. 102-113.

Tien, J. M., 2005, "Viewing Urban Disruptions from a Decision Informatics Perspective", *Journal of Systems Science and Systems Engineering,* Vol. 14, No. 3, September, pp. 257-288.

Tien, J. M., and Berg, D., 1995, "Systems Engineering in the Growing Service Economy," *IEEE Transactions on Systems, Man, and Cybernetics,* Vol. 25, No. 5, pp. 321-326.

Tien, J. M. and Berg, D., 2003, "A Case for Service Systems Engineering", *Journal of Systems Science and Systems Engineering,* Vol. 12, No. 1, pp. 13-38.

Tien, J. M., and Cahn, M. F., 1981, *An Evaluation of the Wilmington Management of Demand Program,* Washington, DC: National Institute of Justice.

Tien, J. M., Krishnamurthy, A. and Yasar, A., 2004, "Towards Real-Time Customized Management of Supply and Demand Chains", *Journal of Systems Science and Systems Engineering,* Vol. 13, No. 3, September, pp. 257-278.

U. S. Congress, 2005, *National Innovation Act,* Washington, DC: U. S. Congress S2109/HR4654.

von Hippel, E., 2005, *Democratizing Innovation,* Cambridge, MA: The MIT Press.

Chapter 3

REENGINEERING THE ORGANIZATION WITH A SERVICE ORIENTATION

François B. Vernadat
European Commission, DG DIGIT, Unit for e-Commission, Interoperability, Architecture and Methododology, L-2920 Luxemburg

Abstract: The need to build agile interoperable enterprise systems requires tools and methods to be able to reengineer the organization or a networked organization with a service orientation coupled with the more traditional business process orientation. This Chapter presents a mixed approach combining business process and business service principles for enterprise engineering with focus on enterprise modeling aspects and IT implementation aspects.

Key words: Enterprise Engineering, Enterprise Modeling, Business Processes, Business Services, Service-Oriented Architectures (SOA)

1. INTRODUCTION

Many organizations, be they large or small industrial corporations, service companies, administrative organizations, or government agencies, face the need to more frequently reengineer their operations, review alignment of their IT systems with their business goals, and improve their efficiency to cope with changing business conditions.

Recent computing technologies, and especially Internet computing, have drastically impacted operations of organizations by removing distance, time reactivity, or interoperability barriers[1]. From transactional processing, then distributed processing followed by tight enterprise application integration, we are moving toward more interoperable, loosely coupled, and asynchronous processing to support more reactive environments, *i.e.*, business environments that can be quickly and timely adapted to new business conditions. This requires revisiting concepts, methods, and tools for enterprise engineering.

Enterprise Engineering (EE)[2,3] is concerned with intra and inter enterprise operations and with improving their efficiency and effectiveness. EE can be defined as the art of analyzing, restructuring, designing – or redesigning – and, as much as possible, optimizing whole or part of a business entity with respect to its mission and objectives, where a business entity is any socio-economic system built to produce goods or services. In this Chapter, a business entity can be, for instance, a department of an organization, the organization itself, a network of business partners (networked enterprise), or a complete supply chain.

Traditionally, enterprises were modeled and analyzed in terms of their business functions (sales, R&D, finance, production...) and essential flows (material and information/document flows). This hierarchical or vertical approach has prevailed until the late 80's but was far too disjunctive in the sense that it either created organizational boundaries or islands of information, which have resulted in the many information silos that exist today as legacy systems in which functionality and data are locked.

Since the early 90's, the state of the art has been to apply a horizontal or transverse approach to describing and specifying business entities in terms of business processes, irrespectively of divisional or organizational barriers. First, this is a more logical and natural way of representing the structure, functionality, and behavior of a business entity. Second, this was an answer to the need of building more flexible business entity structures, *i.e.*, structures that can cope with several types of situations. However, enterprise operations are not always strictly governed in the form of business processes.

The current challenge is to build agile interoperable enterprise systems, *i.e.*, business entities that can work together, even if they belong to different legal entities, and that can be easily tailored to fast changing conditions (*e.g.*, markets, economic conditions, political regulations, energy crisis, etc.). An answer to this challenge is to build systems made of a combination of business processes (for partially ordered and synchronized sequences of activities) and/or business services (for on-line and asynchronous activities).

This chapter explains how to design or redesign business entity structures using a mixed process/service approach on the basis of a business scenario. It then shows how this can be implemented at the IT level in the form of a Service-Oriented Architecture (SOA).

2. A BUSINESS SCENARIO

Because the material presented in this Chapter equally applies to profit and non-profit organizations, we have selected a business scenario that deals with human resources management (HR domain) to remain at a sufficient generic level to be understood by the widest audience.

Let us consider a medium-sized company ABC producing manufactured goods. To manage personnel matters, five IT legacy systems are used:

- Pay System (PS) producing monthly pay statements for every employee
- Time Management System (TMS) recording time spent at work (number of hours) or on leave (number of days) per month by each employee
- HR Database Management (HRDB), which is the human resources database recording personal data, positions, job descriptions, personnel qualifications, career history, and promotion data
- Mission Management System (Mission), used to encode travel requests and follow up mission execution (approval, travel expense claims)
- Training Management System (Training), used to encode training requests and follow up their execution

Currently, each system is stand-alone, has been developed at different points in time with different technologies (TMS and HRDB are in PL/SQL, Mission and Training are in ColdFusion, and PS is in Java/ WebLogic), and relies on a 3-tier architecture, *i.e.*, has its own user interface at the presentation layer, application logic at the business layer, and database access at the data layer. Communication among systems is direct (point to point) and synchronous and is made either via shared database tables or file exchange.

Some problems with this situation come from the facts that redundancy may exist across databases and that users may have to access several systems to perform one task because basic functional operations have been implemented per specialized system (functional specialization principle). For instance, problems with the following personnel event life cycles are:

- Change personal address: Any time someone notifies a change in his personal address, both HRDB and Mission databases have to be updated.
- Declare birth of a child: The birth of a child implies a change in the social security rights of the employee with possible impact on his salary. This information must therefore be recorded in PS and HRDB systems.
- Go on training mission: Any time an employee must go on training outside the company, he must first fill in a training request and get approval and then fill in a mission request. He must therefore log in to two successive systems: Training and Mission (using two separate user interfaces and login/passwords), which may create inconsistencies (errors on dates, cancellation of one request without canceling the other, etc.).

3. TRADITIONAL ENTERPRISE MODELING

Instead of jumping straight away to the service orientation, it is essential to make sure that the basic principles of the business process orientation as well as those of enterprise modeling are properly understood.

3.1 Enterprise Modeling

Enterprise Modeling (EM)[4] is concerned with the representation and specification of various aspects of the enterprise operations – *functional* (what is being done, in which order), *informational* (which and how many objects are used, required, or processed), *resource* (what or who carries out tasks and what policy applies), and *organizational* (the responsibility and authority framework within which things are done). Enterprise Modeling is therefore essential for Enterprise Engineering; it is also a prerequisite for Enterprise Integration, *i.e.*, removing organizational boundaries and increasing synergy across the organization[4,5,6,7].

EM has been defined as the art of expressing facts and knowledge about various aspects of an enterprise, especially the structure, the behavior, and the organization of the enterprise. The goal is to represent, analyze, design, evaluate, and even control the business entity subject to the study.

Enterprise Modeling methods and tools enable decision makers to represent, visualize, understand, communicate, redesign, and improve operations of an enterprise with a focus on timeliness, cost, and quality[8].

Various enterprise modeling tools are commercially available on the market place. These include: ARIS ToolSet, Metis, MEGA suite, KBSI's IDEF suite, FirstSTEP, CaseWise, or Enterprise Modeler, to name the most famous ones.

3.2 Enterprise Modeling Constructs

State of the art enterprise modeling languages and notations all place the concepts of activity and process at the heart of their modeling paradigm. Indeed, the core modeling constructs, or basic modeling language building blocks, of the functional view are *event*, *process*, and *activity*. Using those, an event-driven process-based architecture of a business entity can be devised. These constructs can be complemented by concepts of *enterprise object* and their state manifestations called *object views* in the information view as well as concepts of *resource* and *capability set* (or *role*) in the resource view.

This terminology is part of the forthcoming standard IS 19440 on enterprise modeling constructs jointly prepared by CEN and ISO[9]. The standard consists of an exhaustive set of modeling constructs, each one being specified in the form of a template made of three parts: a standard header with the name and identifier of the construct, a body grouping descriptive properties, and a footer defining relationships with other constructs of the model. Construct definition of IS 19440 has its roots in the modeling language proposed as part of the CIMOSA architecture issued from a EU funded project, AMICE[5].

For the detailed definition of the constructs, the reader is referred to the CEN/ISO standard document[9]. In this Chapter, we only use the concepts of business event, business process, and enterprise activity as previously defined in CIMOSA and the IS 19440 and analyzed by Berio and Vernadat[10].

Business Event: A business event is a fact or happening that occurs in the enterprise operations and that will trigger the execution of some action, *i.e.*, start one or more business processes. An event corresponds to a change in the state of the enterprise that must be acted upon. Business events can be solicited events (*e.g.*, requests or management orders), unsolicited events (*e.g.*, machine breakdowns or exception handling requests), scheduled events (*e.g.*, a timer or a specific clock time, a list of scheduled orders), or synchronization events (*e.g.*, start or end of an activity).

Business Process: A business process is a partially ordered sequence of steps executed to perform some enterprise goals. It represents a full chain of processing, from its starting point to its finish characterized by the delivery of its end-result(s) as expected by the process owner.

Business process execution is triggered by the occurrence of one or more events (if several events are involved in the process triggering condition, this condition will be a logical expression combining event occurrences with AND, NOT, or OR operators). A process step is either a sub-process or an enterprise activity (*e.g.*, human facing, application, machine, or human-based activities). For instance, *Update_Personal_Address* can be one of the business processes of the HR domain of the ABC Company, triggered by the need of a company's employee to communicate his new personal address.

Business processes define the control flow, or logical order in which activities of an enterprise are executed. They represent the enterprise behavior. To do so, the following control flow operators are used:

- Pure sequential flow: upon completion of step *A*, do step *B*
- Branching flow (or parallel execution): upon completion of step *A*, do step *B* AND step *C* AND ... Two cases must be differentiated: synchronous branching (all downstream steps start at the same time) and asynchronous branching (downstream steps can start at different times)

- Rendez-vous (or synchronization): once all upstream steps have been done, do next step. Rendez-vous is usually asynchronous but synchronous rendez-vous can be defined as well
- Spawning flow (or forking): upon completion of step *A*, if ending status is case 1 do step *B*, if ending status is case 2 do step *C*, etc. The semantic of this operator is an exclusive OR (XOR)
- Loops: no specific operator exists. Loop structures are constructed with the spawning flow and a looping condition which must be true or false

Enterprise Activity: An enterprise activity is an elementary step in a business process (*i.e.*, a leaf in the functional decomposition tree of a business process). It is the locus of action and, therefore, transforms inputs into outputs over time using resources to produce expected results. Inputs and outputs are object views of enterprise objects. Resources are enterprise objects (humans, agents, or IT applications) defined as resources in the resource view. For instance, *Fill_In_Address_Form* could be one of the activities of the *Update_Personal_Address* process. In this case, the resource would be the employee who declares his new personal address, the input would be the empty form, and the output would be the filled in form.

A standard representation of any activity has been proposed as early as 1977 by D.T. Ross in his SADT/IDEF0 formalism. The activity is depicted by a rectangular box, also called ICOM box, the name of which must be a verb and having four types of input and output defined as follows (see Figure 3-1):

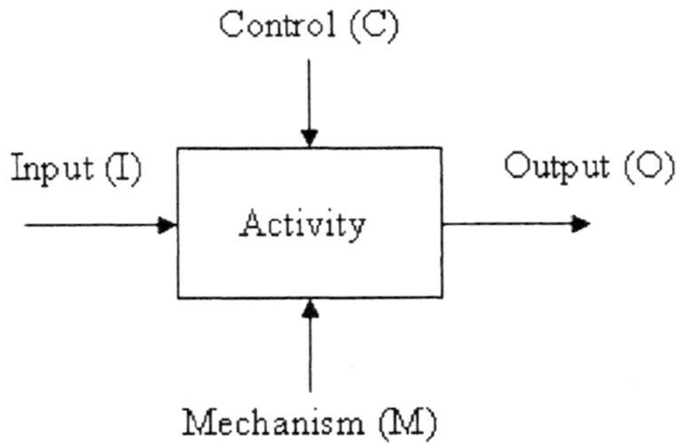

Figure 3-1. SADT/IDEF0 ICOM box for activity representation.

- Input (I): is the set of all objects to be used or processed by the activity
- Control (C): is the set of all objects constraining the execution of the activity but not modified by the activity
- Output (O): is the set of all objects produced or modified by the activity
- Mechanism (M): is the set of all objects used as resources by the activity

CIMOSA uses the same notation but adds the concept of ending status to depict all possible termination statuses of the activity (*e.g.*, correctly done, incomplete completion, error status, etc.). It also adds the concept of control output (to issue the ending status value but possibly events raised by the activity as well) and resource output (*i.e.*, consumption of the resources).

To specify the transfer function δ associated to activity *A* (O(*A*) = δ (I(*A*), C(*A*), M(*A*)), CIMOSA and IS 19440 add the concept of *functional operation* to describe the elementary actions performed by each resource involved in the execution of the activity *A*. A functional operation is canonically defined as a message sent to an executing agent in the form:

Resource_Name.Operation_Name (list of arguments)

For instance, *Employee.Provide_New_address (New_Address_data, Address_Change_Form)* could be one of the functional operations of the activity *Fill_In_Address_Form.*

3.3 Examples

Using concepts and notations introduced in the previous section as well as the graphical symbols shown in Figure 3-2, two of the three scenarios of the ABC Company mentioned in section 2 could be modeled as indicated hereafter. These models represent the AS-IS situation, *i.e.*, the current operations of the company before reengineering.

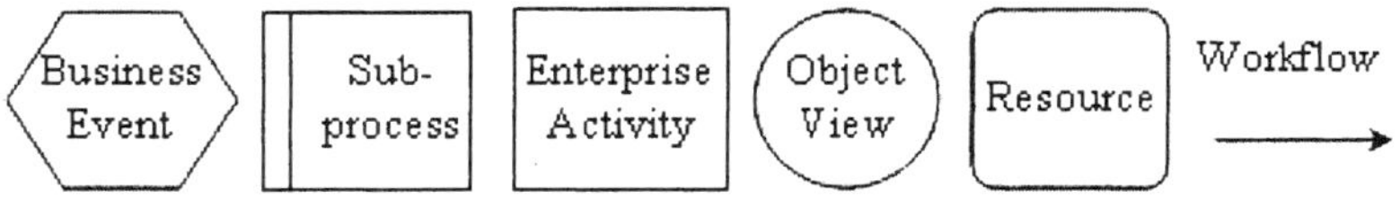

Figure 3-2. Graphical notation for business process representation.

Scenario 1: Update personal address. Figure 3-3 describes the control flow of this business process. First, the employee gets the form for address change from his unit secretariat. This is a paper form that he fills in with his personal data and that he returns to the secretariat. The secretary checks the form and sends a copy to the human resources department (HR Dept) and to the Mission department (Mission Dept). A clerk in each of these departments will update the respective database. Figure 3-4 gives a more complete view of the process by indicating the flow of object views (*e.g.*, different states of the form) and the use of resources in addition to the flow of control.

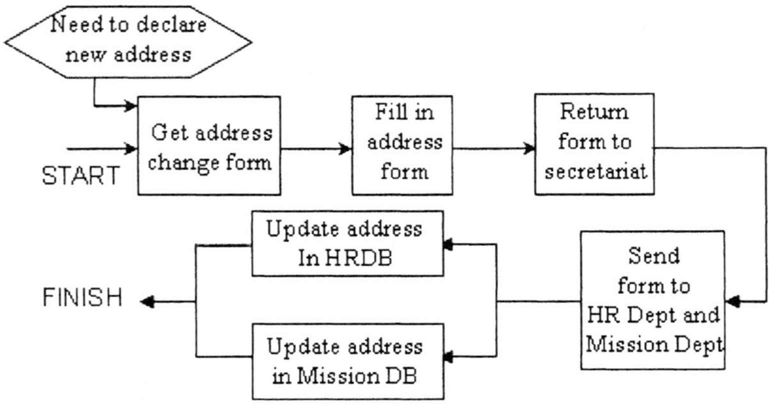

Figure 3-3. Example of a business process (control flow only).

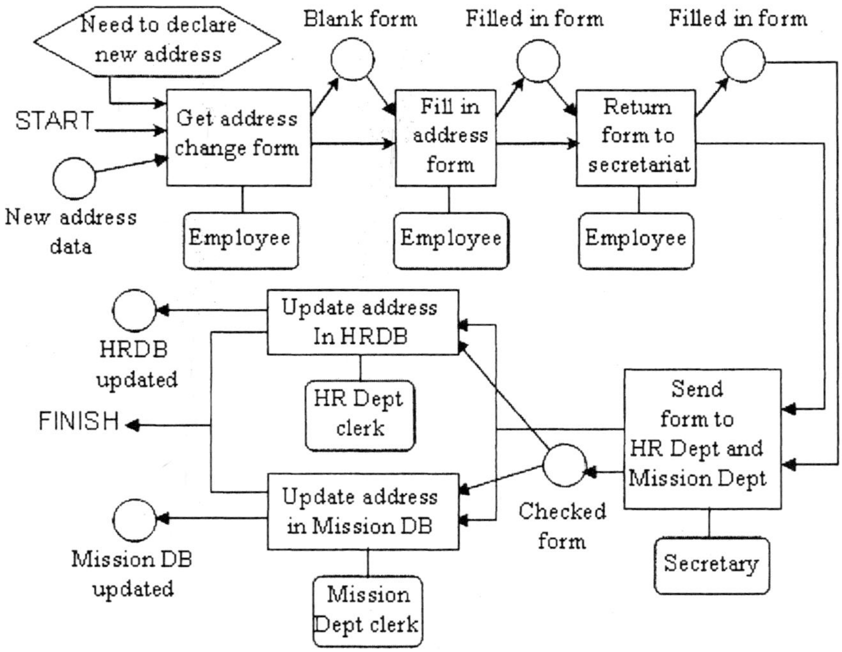

Figure 3-4. Example of a business process (full description).

In this case, the manual procedure implies at least four different actors (employee, unit secretary, HR Dept clerk, and Mission Dept clerk).

Furthermore, the employee gets no feedback on the completion of his request. There is therefore a need to simplify and reengineer this process.

Scenario 2: Request a training mission. This process is made of two subsequent sub-processes: Request external training and, once the training is approved, Request mission authorization (Figure 3-5). Notice that in this case ending statuses have been used in the flow of control to model a spawning flow (*Approved*, *Rejected*).

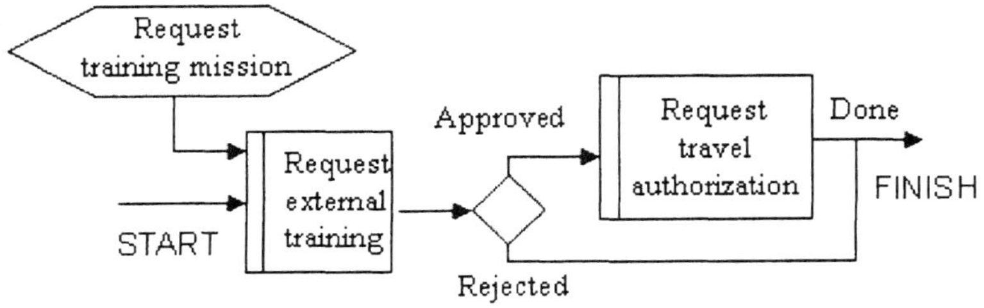

Figure 3-5. AS-IS model of the Request training mission process.

The problem with this process is that, in addition to the risk of inconsistencies mentioned in section 2, the head of unit of the employee does not have all the information at hand to make his approval decision in the first step to control his budget: he will know the cost of the training required from the request but he has to make a guess about the travel and accommodation cost. Furthermore, if he approves the training request, it is only a few days later that he will have to approve the travel request, as long as he remembers to make the association between the two. A better design of this process would be to ask the employee to enter both requests at the same time (which currently requires access to two different IT systems – Training and Mission) and to submit the requests for approval to the head of unit (HoU). If the training is refused, this would imply canceling the travel request.

Figure 3-6 gives an outline of the TO-BE model of this process once reengineered. In this case, it is drastic reengineering. The first step consists in entering the training and the travel requests using the associated IT systems (Training and Mission). Using them as they are, this would require entering the requests separately, *i.e.*, sequentially. A better solution would be to provide the user with a single interface to enter all data and create requests in the relevant systems. Once done, the two requests are passed to the head of unit who will be notified that he has to approve a training mission. He now has full knowledge of the training and travel costs and he can decide to accept or reject the employee's request. If he rejects the training request, the travel request is automatically canceled. Whatever his decision is, a notification message is sent to the employee via the internal e-mail system.

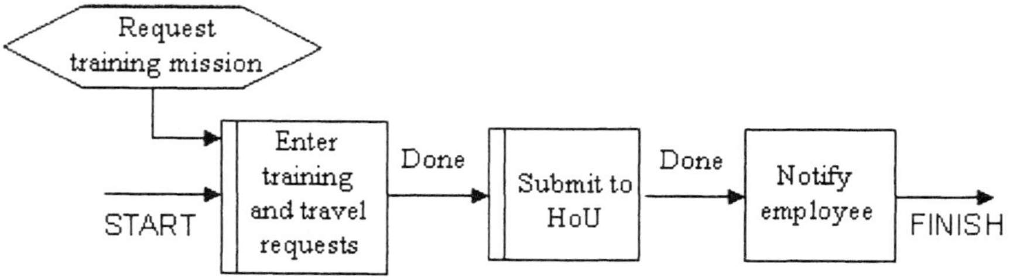

Figure 3-6. TO-BE model of the Request training mission process.

3.4 Automating Business Processes as Workflow

Once business processes have been modeled, reengineered, analyzed, and possibly evaluated at the engineering level from the point of view of alternatives ("what-if" scenarios) or for system performance (for instance, using analytical or simulation tools), some of them will be automated or computerized at the implementation level to improve enterprise efficiency.

From the IT perspective, a business process to be computerized will be specified and implemented in the form of a workflow, either using a commercial workflow management system or in a programmatic and ad hoc way.

In IT terms, a *workflow* is a formal representation of a business process to be interpreted by computers to monitor execution of the business process.

The process specification expressed in a workflow language is called a *workflow schema*. Each execution of a workflow schema is called a *workflow instance*. The *workflow management system* (WfMS) is the engine that interprets the workflow schema and controls and monitors the execution of each instance of the workflow schema.

There are many commercial tools available on the market from small or large vendors. Examples include Ultimus Workflow Suite, SAP Workflow, Oracle Workflow, HP Process Manager, or IBM WebSphere workflow, but many others could be cited. The reader more interested in this technology is referred to a book by Leymann and Roller[11].

Automating business processes as workflow offers many advantages and can generate significant improvements in terms of cost and quality. First, execution of each individual step of a process can be made faster and more accurate, *i.e.*, no time is wasted between two steps because someone has forgot to do something and no step is skipped. Second, each step and action can be logged and traced, which allows *process tracking*, *i.e.*, one can know what happened after the fact or one can know at which step the process is currently at (check process progress). Finally, if something goes wrong (*e.g.*, time-out or delay too long, missing data, resource not responding, etc.), this can be detected and an *exception handling* procedure (or exception process) can be started.

An enterprise system automated as a workflow system typically adopts an event-driven process-based architecture in the sense that its behavior is governed by occurrences of events that trigger process chains implemented as workflows. Some mechanisms must be implemented to capture real-world events (*e.g.*, arrivals of customer orders, sending requests, start actions, etc.) and convert them into process triggering conditions.

4. SERVICE ORIENTATION – SOA PRINCIPLES

The business process approach as practiced throughout the 90's has introduced a more natural and horizontal way in organizing business systems as opposed to application centric approaches. However, rapidly changing market conditions and business requirements tend to increase the gap between what the business requires and what IT can deliver. To build more flexible, extensible, and evolvable environments in which IT can be more quickly and easily aligned with the business, many organizations are turning to Service-Oriented Architecture (SOA) principles to close the gap.

4.1 Enterprise Agility

Agility is the ability to quickly react to changing conditions. Nevertheless, depending on choices either made at the organization level or at the IT level, enterprise agility can be inhibited or enhanced!

At the organizational level, agility means to be able to quickly reshape enterprise behavior, *i.e.*, the flow of control of business processes. However, defining the entire enterprise operations as business processes and implementing them as heavily programmatic workflows would "rigidify" the organization, making modification difficult and costly.

At the IT level, agility means to be able to reconfigure and extend applications systems quickly with minimal rewriting of code or database modifications. However, if systems are tightly interfaced, work in synchronous mode, and their data and functionality are locked inside, this will prevent agility.

It is therefore necessary to consider more loosely coupled and asynchronous solutions that can be easily reshaped, *i.e.*, in which components can be added, modified, or removed with minimal impact. This is one of the essential promises of service orientation. It nevertheless does not quick out or supersede the process orientation – it complements it.

4.2 Service-Oriented Architectures (SOA)

Service-Oriented Architectures are emerging as a new wave for building agile and interoperable enterprise systems. It is an IT strategy consisting in exposing as encapsulated services the business functions of an application. Broadly speaking, an SOA is essentially a collection of services[12, 13].

In technical terms, SOA is about designing and building IT systems using heterogeneous network addressable software components (preferably communicating over Internet). These interoperable standards-based components or *services* (*i.e.*, callable and reusable functions accessible by their interface) can be directly invoked by business users or executed as steps of business processes. They can be combined, modified, or reused quickly to meet business needs. They can be implemented as Web Services or functions of Web applications and, therefore, be located anywhere on the Web[12, 14].

In this sense, SOA could not happen without HTTP (Internet) and XML technologies, which are fundamental building blocks for achieving loose integration and system ubiquity.

Using such an architectural approach, the capabilities of applications or the access mechanisms to information sources (*e.g.*, file systems, databases, or websites) will be exposed as services. This will hide their underlying implementation intricacies from the application developer who has just to call these services and orchestrate their flow of execution. Furthermore, it is interesting to mention that the use of services provided by external providers can also easily be incorporated as part of the enterprise application.

4.3 Services and Messages

Services are functional or informational business components designed to be accessed as such by service clients or consumers. They represent business functions of the real world as a whole (*e.g.*, Declare birth of a child, Update personal address, or Get daily company news).

From a business user perspective, a service is an invokable piece of functionality that will return a result (*i.e.*, provide a service) under the conditions defined in its service level agreement (SLA).

From an IT perspective, a service is a piece of business or infrastructure functionality that can be invoked by its locator and its interface(s) as publicly published in a standard format (see Figure 3-7). Details of its implementation are hidden. The service can be implemented using any IT technology (C program, PL/SQL, Java/J2EE, EJB...).

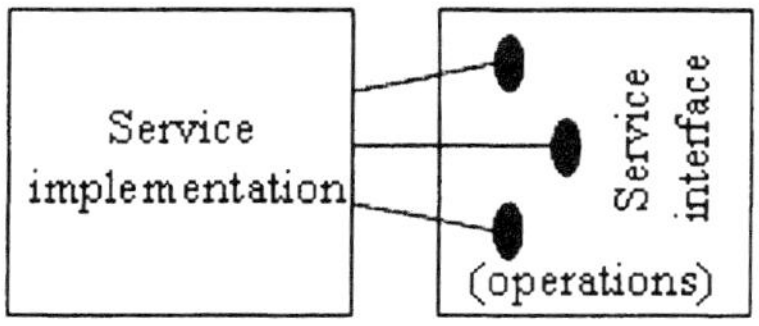

Figure 3-7. Service definition.

The standard format usually used for describing operations accessible in the service interface is known as WSDL (*Web Service Description Language*). This is a language proposed by W3C[15]. WSDL enables dynamic interaction and interoperation between Web services. It not only describes service interfaces, but also the corresponding bindings involved. For instance, in WSDL a service is described through a number of endpoints. An endpoint is composed of a set of operations. An operation, or unit of task supported by the service, is described in terms of messages received or sent out by the service.

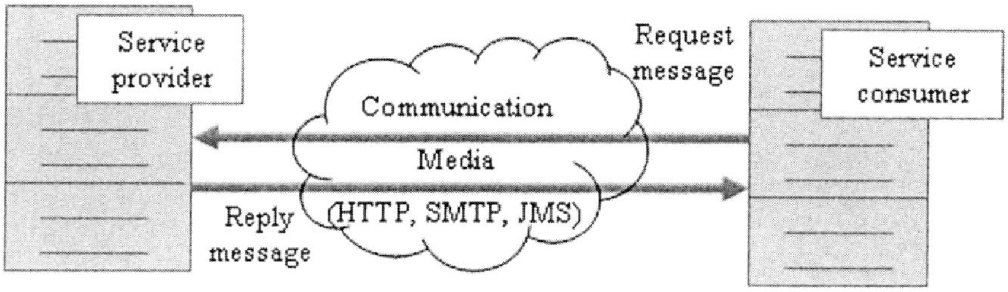

Figure 3-8. Communicating services.

A *message* is any unit of information to be exchanged from the sender's perspective. It has therefore a sender and a consumer (see Figure 3-8). A message is an abstract definition of data being communicated, consisting of message parts (header, properties, and body or payload). In SOA technology, messages are usually expressed in XML format[16], but HTTP messages can also be used. Messages can be transported using different simple transport protocols such as the e-mail transfer protocol SMTP, the hypertext transfer protocol HTTP, or message queuing protocols (for instance, JMS).

Finally, services can call each other, which may have a cascading effect, or they can be grouped together to form composite applications (see Figure 3-9). To coordinate their flow of execution or their collaboration, concepts of orchestration and choreography will be introduced in a subsequent section.

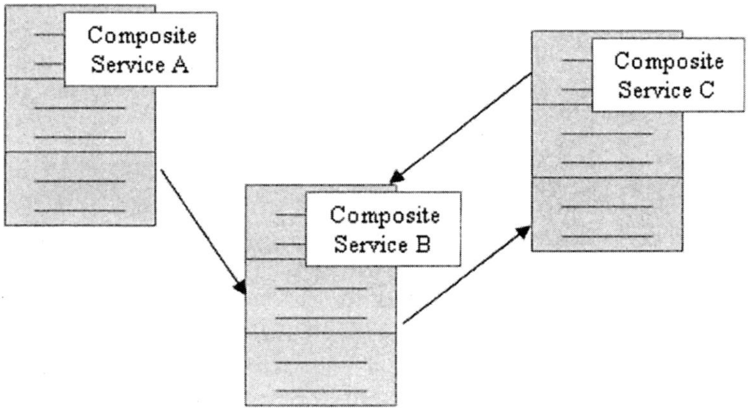

Figure 3-9. Composite application made of communicating services.

5. ENTERPRISE MODELING FOR SOA

As shown in Section 3, Enterprise Engineering strongly relies on Enterprise Modeling. Therefore, modeling is a crucial step for a successful journey on the road to SOA. However, the traditional enterprise modeling paradigm discussed in the previous sections needs to be adapted for service-oriented enterprise engineering.

In this Chapter, we show that in order to architect and make operational whole or part of an enterprise from an SOA perspective, there are three key concepts to consider for modeling the organization capabilities and behavior. Namely these are: *event*, *service*, and *process*. Each of these must be contextualized and materialized at the business level and at the application level of the organization.

At the business or organizational level, these three concepts will naturally be called business event, business service, and business process. Concepts of business event and business process defined earlier still hold. The concept of business service is added.

5.1 Business Service Definition

Business Service: A business service is a discrete piece of functionality that appears to be platform-independent, logically addressable, and self-contained from the point of view of the service caller. It must be uniquely identified within the enterprise and has a service owner. Logically addressable means that it can be dynamically invoked simply by calling its logical address or universal resource identifier (URI), thus without having to know where it is physically located. Self-contained means that the service exists as a whole and that it maintains its own state. In practice, it is recommended to develop only stateless services (*i.e.*, each service call is independent of previous calls), especially if they are implemented as Web services. However, stateful services may also exist (they require that both the consumer and the provider share the same consumer-specific context – passed in the message).

Physically, a business service can either be performed by a human agent or a technical agent. In this paper, we consider IT-based services.

Figure 3-10. Business service representation.

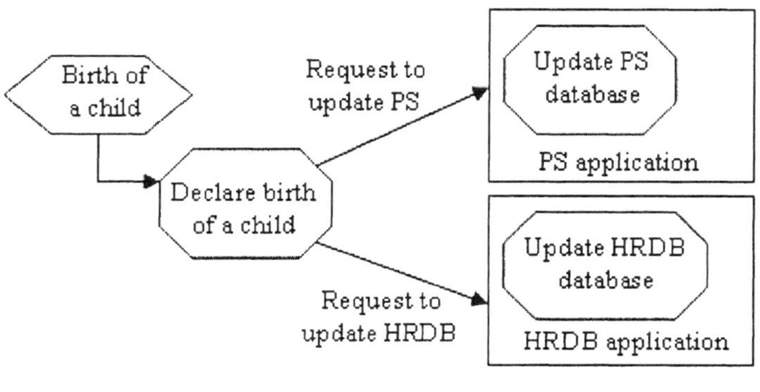

Figure 3-11. Declare birth of child service with call to back-office services.

For instance, *Declare_Birth_of_Child* could be a stateless business service offered by the HR domain as a function accessible on the intranet portal of the ABC Company. The service gets on-line data from the employee via an electronic form and sends an update message both to the PS and HRDB systems asking to update their database.

Assuming that we use the notation shown in Figure 3-10 to graphically represent a business service, Figure 3-11 gives a graphical illustration of the *Declare_Birth_of_Child* service. The service is triggered by an event (*Birth_of_a_Child*) and sends two message requests respectively to the PS and HRDB applications that will trigger their database update service.

5.2 Business Services, Business Processes and Activities

When modeling business processes and business services, different types of situations can be encountered. Among these, we can have:

- Case 1: A business service can be used independently of anything else (asynchronous execution). In this case, it is equivalent to a business process comprising only one step, the service. Thanks to Internet and Web services, this is typically the case for many services made available on company's intranets that can be accessed via a Web browser at any time from any PC connected to the internal company network.
  For instance, this could be the case of two of the previous examples encapsulated as self-contained functions: *Update_Personal_Address* and *Declare_Birth_of_Child*. Other examples include looking at the value of stock exchanges on Yahoo or checking the weather forecast in a specific city on Internet.
- Case 2: A business service can be invoked to perform a given step within a business process (synchronized action flow). In this case, the service would be equivalent to an activity of a process.
  For instance, the *Update_Personal_Address* service, which can be used as a stand-alone service, can also be used as one step in an administrative process dealing with asking a special leave for personal moving reason.
- Case 3: A business service can be used by several processes.
  For instance, the *Update_Personal_Address* service could be reused in different administrative processes.
- Case 4: A business service can be made of other services (composite service).
  For instance, the *Declare_Birth_of_Child* service of Figure 3-11 could be split into the following elementary steps: *Get person data*, *Get child data*, *Send request to update PS*, and *Send request to update HRDB*. *Get person data* could itself be a service that retrieves usual data about the

employee from HRDB (*e.g.*, employee name, employee id, grade, position...) based on the authentication user id of the employee and automatically pre-fills relevant fields of the form on the screen. The same service can be used as one of the first steps of the Mission and Training applications exactly for the same purpose.

From what precedes, it appears that a business service can be an elementary step of a business process or a business process reduced to one step. So, what is the difference between a business service and an enterprise activity?

The only difference relies in the fact that an activity only exists in the context of a business process (it is never directly triggered by an event) while the business service has existence on its own and can be triggered by an event, but can also be used in a control flow.

5.3 Service Orchestration vs. Choreography

In pure SOA terminology, two concepts are defined to deal with service coordination: namely, service orchestration and service choreography.

Service orchestration refers to some business behavior or control flow in which all steps are business services. It is the SOA term for workflow in the formal specification of a business process.

It describes a process flow and includes execution order of service interactions. It can refer to both internal and external services of the enterprise, but the control flow must always be controlled by one party (centralized control).

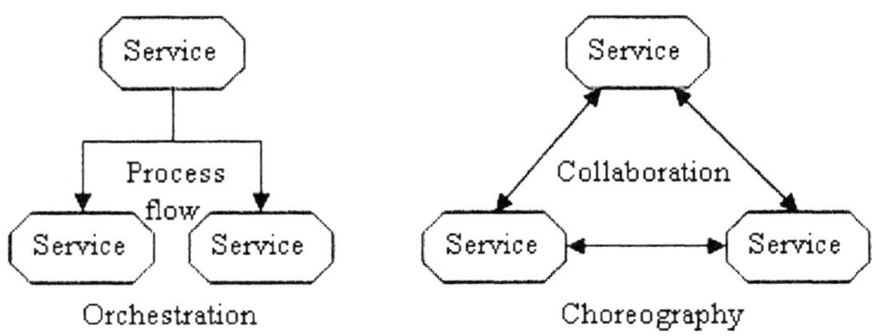

Figure 3-12. Service orchestration versus choreography.

Service choreography deals with service collaboration (or interaction). It tracks the sequence of messages sent by multiple parties and sources involved in a communication exchange. It is associated with public message exchanges, not service execution order, although that, in a conversational mode, the concept of a token can be used to control the order or sequence of message sending (only the service which has the token is allowed to send a message at a given time – the token is then passed to another service).

Figure 3-12 illustrates the difference between the two modes.

5.4 Example

Let us consider the reengineering of the example shown in Figure 3-4. The ABC Company has decided to automate this business process that was previously manual, paper-based, and involved three persons in addition to the employee who had to declare his new private address.

This process must become a workflow starting with a new service accessible on the company's intranet (*Update_Personal_Address*) that will get data about the new personal address of the employee, send the electronic form to the secretary for validation, and then send messages in XML format with relevant data for updating HRDB and Mission databases.

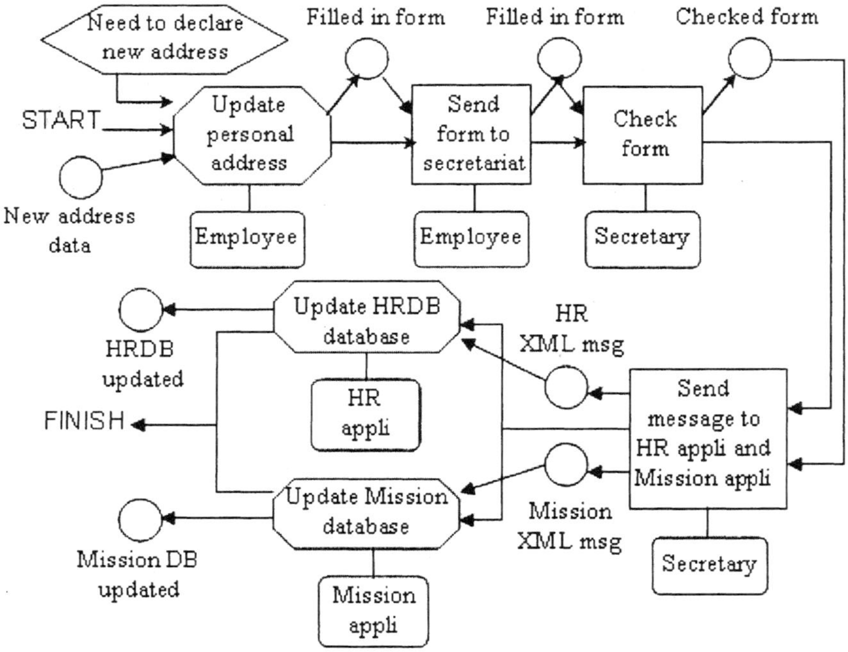

Figure 3-13. TO-BE model of the Update personal address process.

The TO-BE model of the new process combining business services and enterprise activities is given by Figure 3-13. The process starts with the

Update personal address service that could be common to other administrative processes. Once filled in, the form is sent to the secretary of the employee's unit who checks data in the form and validates it. Upon validation, the workflow sends a message to the HR application (HR XML msg) and a message to the Mission application (Mission XML msg). Upon reception of the message, an update service is activated in the HRDB application to update the HR database. The same happens in the Mission application. The database update step is defined as a generic service in both applications because it can be used by similar requests from other processes, only the input data in the XML message will change. This simplifies the application design.

6. TECHNOLOGICAL ASPECTS OF SOA

In terms of implementation, a business service can either be performed by a human agent or a technical agent. In the case of IT-based services, they can be implemented as Web services (in this case, they are made accessible via a URI), Web pages on a website or an enterprise portal (accessible via a URL), programmatic entities (procedure calls for a client/server application, functions of an API, or servlets and EJBs in a Java J2EE environment), or existing applications encapsulated within a Web service interface.

6.1 Web Services

The aim of Web Services is to connect computers and devices with each other using Internet protocols to exchange data and to process data dynamically, *i.e.,* on-the-fly.

Web services can be defined as interoperable software objects that can be assembled over the Internet using standard protocols and exchange formats to perform functions or execute business processes[12, 14].

In a sense, Web Services can be assimilated to autonomous software agents hosted on some servers connected to the Web. These services can be invoked by means of their URI by any calling entity via Internet and using XML and SOAP to send requests and receive replies. Their internal behavior can be implemented in whatever computer language (*e.g.*, C, Java, PL/SQL...) or provided by software packages (*e.g.*, SAP, Business Objects, portlets in a portal...). Their granularity can be of any size. The great idea behind Web services is that a functionality can be made available (or published) on the Web and accessed (or subscribed) by whoever needs it without having to know neither its location nor its implementation details, *i.e.*, in a very transparent way. Direct data exchanges are made possible among Web services and applications and take the form of XML flows.

Web service technology relies on the following essential standards:

- WSDL (Web Service Description Language): as already mentioned, it is a contract language used to declare Web service interface and access methods using specific description templates[15].
- XML: is the language used to structure and formulate messages between services (requests or replies)[16].
- SOAP: is used as the messaging protocol for sending request and response messages among Web services[17].
- UDDI (Universal Description, Discovery and integration): is an XML-based registry, or catalog, of businesses and the Web services they provide (described in WSDL). It is provided as a central facility on the Web to publish, find, and subscribe Web services[18].

As indicated earlier, for the transport layer of messages between services the following transport protocols are the usual ones used in practice: SMTP, HTTP, or JMS (Java Messaging Systems)[19].

6.2 Service-Oriented Application Architecture

A typical architecture of a pure service-oriented application or IT environment will look like the structure depicted by Figure 3-14. In this case, the architecture includes a Web user interface using a Web server that gives access to the application clients via the URI of the application.

The whole application is developed on an application server. It is made of a number of software modules that can be services (Service1, Service2...) providing the application functionality or access to databases or other information sources (DB1, DB2...) as well as file system managers to get access to specific file directories. Two additional central modules are usually present (that could be combined in one management module): the central management system, which acts as the main program, and the orchestrator or scheduler, which controls the execution sequence of the services in the case of event-driven or process-based operations (orchestration).

Business Process Execution Language for Web Services (BPEL4WS or simply BEPL)[20] is a standard business process language used for service orchestration by several application server vendors including BEA Systems, IBM, or Microsoft. A BPEL process links several Web services in a flow of control. Service entry points are defined in the BPEL specification of a process. These entry points either consume WSDL operations' incoming messages from input-only or input-output (request-response) operations as declared in the service interface.

A BPEL specification of a business process is composed of activities. BPEL provides the following primitive activities:

- Invoking an operation of a Web service (<invoke>)
- Waiting to receive a message for an operation of the service (<receive>)
- Creating a response to an input-output operation (<reply>)
- Waiting for some time without doing anything (<wait>)
- Indicating an error (<throw>)
- Copying data from one place to another (<assign>)
- Closing the entire service instance down (<terminate>)
- Doing nothing through (<empty>)

These basic primitives may be combined in a workflow using the following operators: combining through (sequence), branching through (switch), defining loops (while), executing one of the chosen control paths (pick), or executing activities in parallel (flow).

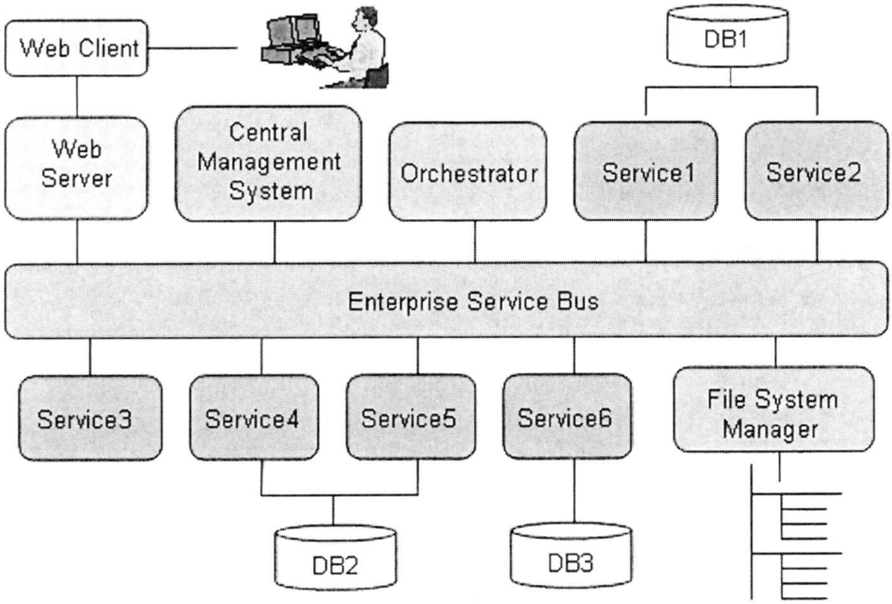

Figure 3-14. Typical architecture of a service-oriented IT application.

As shown on Figure 3-14, all components of the service-oriented application communicate with one another via a common middleware message exchange platform, called Enterprise Service Bus.

6.3 Enterprise Service Bus

An *Enterprise Service Bus*[13] is a standards-based integration platform that combines capabilities of a message-oriented middleware (MOM), Web services, data transformation, database access services, intelligent routing of messages, and even business process execution to reliably connect and coordinate the interaction of significant numbers of diverse applications across an extended organization with transactional integrity. It is capable of being adopted for any general-purpose integration project and it can scale beyond the limits of more traditional Enterprise Application Integration (EAI) platforms.

A *Message-Oriented Middleware* (MOM) is a messaging system that provides the ability to connect applications in an asynchronous message exchange fashion using message queues. It provides the ability to create and manage message queues, to manage the routing of messages, and to fix priorities of messages. Messages can be delivered according to three essential messaging models:

- Point-to-Point model: in which only one consumer may receive a message that is sent to a queue.
- Publish-and-Subscribe: in which multiple consumers may register, or subscribe to, receive messages from the same queue (messages are in this case called topics).
- Request/Reply: in which a sending queue and a reply queue are used.

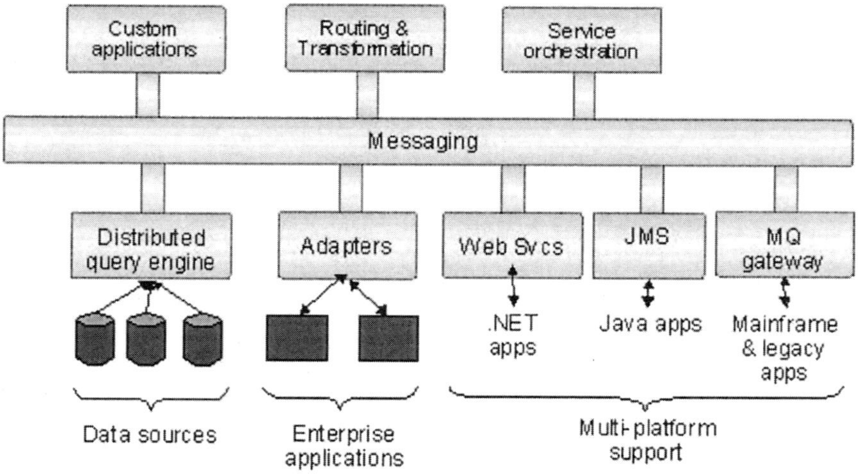

Figure 3-15. Enterprise Service Bus (ESB) structure.

Data transformation capability of an ESB is the ability to apply XSLT transformations to XML messages to reformat messages during transport depending on the type of receivers that will consume the messages (for instance, a person address may be formatted with postal code and city name in one field by one message consumer while they appear as two separate fields for another message consumer). Intelligent or rule-based routing is the ability to use message properties to route message delivery to different queues (*i.e.*, services) according to message content. Database services simplify accesses to database systems using standard access methods such as SQL and JDBC (Java Database Connectivity).

Figure 3-15 gives an illustration of a typical ESB infrastructure. A necessary companion component to the ESB in a SOA is a service registry to keep track of all service descriptions and logical addresses.

7. CONCLUSION

SOA can be understood as a form of event-driven architecture (EDA) in which business capabilities are delivered as services. There is therefore no point in opposing SOA, EDA, or more traditional process-based architectures, but instead, from a systemic and holistic point of view, there are many arguments for using these paradigms in synergy because real-world systems are made of event-driven, process-based, and service-oriented situations. The world is neither only made of processes, nor only of services.

The process orientation brings a horizontal view of activity chains that flow across the organizational boundaries. The event-driven architectures apply to reactive systems made of modules sending messages to one another to react to events. The service orientation unlocks data and functions from monolithic applications and favors reuse of functionality (you don't access a full-blown application anymore, you call a location-independent service).

Other frequently cited advantages of the service orientation are:

- Agile reconfiguration of technical infrastructure and organizational structure as business requirements change because it becomes easier to add, remove, or modify services.
- Better protection of IT investments on the long term due to service encapsulation (the interface of the service may change while protecting the internal code, or vice versa, the internal code can be upgraded without affecting the rest of the architecture).
- Alignment of IT capabilities with business goals is made easier because of the modular and dynamic structure of SOA-based environments.

One difficulty at the implementation level that has not been addressed in this text is identity management and authentication when accessing services from a Web browser, especially in the case of using services that call other services. While security standards exist, such as WS-Security or WS-Trust, to provide means to obtain security credentials that represent the identity of the requestor, there are still hard security problems when services should be open to external users. This mostly applies for those who have to deal with services accessible from Internet. The problem is less crucial if services are used inside the protected company's network where their use is recommended.

REFERENCE

1. M.P. Singh (Ed.), *The Practical Handbook of Internet Computing* (Chapman & Hall/CRC, Boca Raton, 2005).
2. K. Kosanke K. and J.G. Nell J.G. (Eds.), *Enterprise Engineering and Integration: Building International Consensus* (Springer-Verlag, Berlin, 1997).
3. K. Kosanke, F. Vernadat, and M. Zelm, CIMOSA: Enterprise Engineering and Integration, *Computers in Industry*, 40 83-97(1999).
4. F.B. Vernadat, *Enterprise Modeling and Integration: Principles and Applications* (Chapman & Hall, London, 1996).
5. AMICE, *CIMOSA: Open System Architecture for CIM*, 2nd edition (Springer-Verlag, Berlin, 1993).
6. C.J. Petrie C.J. (Ed.), *Enterprise Integration Modeling* (The MIT Press, Cambridge, MA, 1992).
7. B. Gold-Bernstein and W. Ruh, *Enterprise Integration: The Essential Guide to Integration Solutions* (Addison-Wesley, Boston, MA, 2005).
8. D. Delen, N.P. Dalal, and P.C. Benjamin, Integrated Modeling: The key to holistic understanding of the enterprise, *Communications of the ACM*, 48(4) 107-112 (2005).
9. CEN/ISO, Enterprise Integration – Constructs for enterprise modelling, prEN 19440, CEN/TC 310 and ISO/TC 184, BSI secretariat, London, UK, 2006.
10. G. Berio and F. Vernadat, F., Enterprise modeling with CIMOSA: functional and organizational aspects, *Production Planning & Control*, 12(2) 128-136 (2001).
11. F. Leymann and D. Roller, *Production Workflow: Concepts and Techniques* (Prentice-Hall, New York, 1999).
12. P. Herzum, Web Services and Service-Oriented Architecture, Cutter Consortium, Executive Report 4, No. 10, 2001.
13. D. Chappell, *Enterprise Service Bus* (O'Reilly Media, Sebastopol, CA, 2004).
14. R. Khalaf, F. Curbera, W.A. Nagy, N. Mukhi, S. Tai, M. Duftler, Understanding Web Services, in: *Practical Handbook of Internet Computing*, edited by M. Singh (Chapman & Hall/CRC Press, Boca Raton, FL, 2004), Chap. 27.
15. W3C, World Wide Web Consortium, WSDL: Web Service Description Language, http://www.w3.org/TR/wsdl, 2001.
16. W3C, World Wide Web Consortium, XML: eXtensible Mark-up Language, http://www.w3.org/xml, 2000.

17. W3C, World Wide Web Consortium, SOAP: Simple Object Access Protocol, http://www.w3.org/TR/SOAP, 2002.
18. OASIS. UDDI: Universal Description, Discovery, and Integration, http://www.uddi.org, 2002.
19. Sun, Java Messaging System (JMS), http://java.sun.com/products/jms.
20. IBM, Business Process Execution Language for Web Services, Version 1.0, BEA, IBM, Microsoft, www.ibm.com/developerworks/webservices/library/ws-bpel1/, 2002.

Chapter 4

CUSTOMER INCENTIVES IN TIME-BASED ENVIRONMENT

Jian Chen and Nan Zhang
Tsinghua University, China

Abstract: In this chapter, we explore customer incentive issues. Time-based competition was first highlighted explicitly in the literature in the late 1980s by Stalk who argued that time has become a significant source of competitive advantage. Since Stalk's introduction of this paradigm, it has attracted a lot of attentions, and its importance apparently has been recognized. In time-based environment, customers have become more and more sensitive to the range of choices and the degree of responsiveness provided by firms. However, production and consumption happen simultaneously in service production, which makes waiting in queue inevitable. Demand management is an effective way to solve this problem. Since customers' private information such as delay cost is critical for demand management, a key question is how a firm can provide incentives to its customers so that it is in their interest to truthfully disclose their information.

This chapter seeks to provide a comprehensive review of the literature and explore further research of customer incentive issues. We begin our review of the literature by introduction of some pre-requisite knowledge, including the objective of the firm and the customer's utility function. Then we discuss the literature of mechanism design and categorize the existing literature into two broad classes: price auction and direct mechanism. In direct mechanism, a customer is required to report his delay cost when he arrives at the firm. Based on his announcement, the firm assigns a priority to him and imposes a corresponding priority toll. Through designing the assignment and pricing rules properly, customers will disclose the truth. There are also some articles referring to price auction. In their settings, customers should bid for priorities when they arrive. The key of price auction is to find the equilibrium bid function.

Most of the literature discusses the problem of priority assignment, i.e., managing demand in the same period. For service enterprises, it is more meaningful to assign demand to different periods. In the third section of this chapter, we present a model with several periods each providing different value. Actually, heterogeneous service is a main reason that results in imbalance between demand and supply. We first obtain the optimal assignment and pricing rules when the firm is omniscient and acts on a centralized administrative basis. Then we prove that this optimal mechanism is also incentive compatible, i.e., the mechanism enables the decentralization of decisions while maintaining optimality. According to the optimal mechanism, high-value periods will serve more customers who are more patient.

We then conclude the chapter with an overall summary and the further research to be carried out in this realm, including models with general delay cost structure and perishable value, integrated capacity decision and real-time decision models.

Key words: Time-based competition; customer incentive; queuing; mechanism design.

1. TIME-BASED PARADIGM IN SERVICE SECTOR

1.1 Time-based competition

To outperform competitors, service firms must develop a service strategy that addresses the important competitive features of their respective industries. Porter (1980) had argued that three generic competitive advantages exist: overall cost leadership, differentiation and market focus. An overall cost leadership strategy requires firms to develop policies aimed at becoming and keeping a low-cost position in the market. The differentiation strategy involves the offering of a product or service that is perceived as being unique to create customer loyalty. The focus strategy is built around the idea of serving a particular target market very well by addressing the customers' specific needs. He regarded time (speed) as one of the important aspects of the differentiation strategy.

Then in the article of Stalk (1988), time-based paradigm was first highlighted explicitly. Stalk argued that time had become a significant source of competitive advantage. In Stalk's opinion, firms especially Japanese firms illustrated four evolutionary stages of competitive advantage (seen in Table 4-1). In the period following World War II, by employing low-cost labor, Japanese firms achieved low production cost. Then with the development of technologies, they shifted to scale-based strategies. To achieve even higher levels of productivity, they adopted focused factory strategy, i.e., focused on specific products and key elements of production competence. However, this strategy restricted the variety of products. The flexible factory emerged and balanced scale and variety. Finally, fierce competition resulted in the need for introducing new products at rapid rates, leading to the emergence of today's newest competitive paradigm: time-based competition.

Table 4-1. Evolution of competitive advantage

Stage	Competitive Strategy	Source of Competitive Advantage
1945~1960	Low cost	Low-cost labor
1960~mid-1970s	High productivity, low cost	Scale economy Focused factory
mid-1970s~1990	Low cost, variety	Flexible factory
1990~	Quick response	Time-based paradigm

Source: Adapted from Stalk, G.Jr., 1988, Time-the next source of competitive advantage, Harvard Business Review. 66(4): 41-51.

By Stalk and Hout (1990), time-based competition mandates a strategy of customer responsiveness and rapid new product introduction, together with competitive quality and cost. The essence of time-based competition involves compressing time in every phase of the product creation and delivery cycle.

Since Stalk (1988) introduced the paradigm of time-based competition, it has been attracted a lot of attentions and its importance apparently has been recognized. Some literature describes the nature of time-based competition, its strategies and characteristics, its benefits and limitations, and its application and implementation. Some literature makes a contribution by highlighting the potential of time-based competition and its implications for firms. This concern has contributed to the adoption of new management techniques such as just-in-time (JIT) and quick response (QR), as well as the adoption of new technologies such as electronic data interchange (EDI).

1.2 The role of time in service sector

Significant improvement has been made in manufacturing sector through adopting time-based strategies. However, in service sector, things are not so bright. Service sector consists of all economic activities whose output is not a physical product or construction, is generally consumed at the time it is produced and provides added value in forms that are essentially intangible (Quinn et al., 1987). In many countries, service sector accounts for a large and increasing proportion of GDP and employs a large and growing proportion of employees. In the U.S., service employment is at 80%[1]. In China, service accounts for about 40% of GDP in 2005[2].

[1] Source: Bureau of labor statistics, 1998.

[2] Source: China Statistics Yearbook, 2005.

Tien and Berg (2003) provided an additional comparison between the goods and service sectors. In their opinion, the goods sector requires material as input, is physical in nature, involves the customer at the design stage, and uses mostly quantitative measures to assess its quality. On the other hand, the service sector requires information as input, is virtual in nature, involves the customer at the production/delivery stage, and employs mostly qualitative measures to assess its quality.

These characteristics lead to multi-dimensionality of service quality. And since production and consumption happen simultaneously which makes waiting inevitable, time plays an important role in service quality. The value of the potential waiting time may be quite significant relative to other competitive elements, such as price. Some research verified the significant role of time in service sector. Both Federal Express (Blackburn, 1991) and United Parcel Service (Daniels and Essaides, 1993), which dominate the U.S. air express industry, are guided by a time-focused strategy, such as JIT concepts and time-based delivery. Domino Pizza (Tucker, 1991), with its competitive niche built on speed of delivery rather than on the quality of pizza itself, rises to the second largest pizza chain in the U.S. by virtue of high-speed management. Besides these cases, statistic data in gasoline stations showed that retail demand was sensitive to service time. Customers were willing to pay about 1% more for a 6% reduction in congestion (Png, 1994).

1.3 Customers in time-based environment

In time-based environment, some customers are sensitive to the degree of responsiveness and the time-based firms focus on this type of customers (Stalk and Hout, 1990). As emphasized by Becker (1965), when they buy the service, these customers pay two prices: an explicit price to the firm and, in addition, an implicit price in the time spent waiting. To represent the customer's sensitivity to time, Kleinrock (1967) defined an *impatience factor* that measured how many dollars it cost a customer for each second that he spent in the system. Balachandran (1972) and Lui (1985) used *time cost* or *the value of the waiting time* to represent it. Since the cost related to service delays, Mendelson (1985) called it *delay cost.* Delay cost mainly includes opportunity cost and anxiety cost caused by waiting. This term is continued to use.

It should be noted that customers are always different in their delay cost or other factors (e.g., required service time, service valuation, etc.). Such circumstances provide competing business with an opportunity of differentiating itself on price and thereby service time. Firms can segment the market and provide different delivery time and corresponding price for each segmented market, to manage demand and accordingly increase their profit.

Unlike price given by the firms, delay cost is implicit and is always private information of customers. Firms may get some statistic data from market research, but they may not know the exact delay cost of every customer when he sets foot in the store. Since customers' private information such as delay cost is critical for demand management, a key issue that arises in this context is customer incentives, that is, how a firm can provide incentives to its customers so that it is their interest to truthfully disclose their information. The incentive mechanisms would assist a firm to improve its profit, and at the same time, the welfare of the customers. In the next section, we will review related literature. In the third section, we will present a multi-period model for assigning demand to different periods. Section 4 concludes the chapter.

2. LITERATURE REVIEW

This section seeks to provide a comprehensive review of the literature and explore further research of customer incentive issues. We will firstly discuss the objective of the service firm and the customer's utility function in the time-based environment. Then we review the literature of mechanism design by two lines: price auction and direct mechanism.

2.1 Objective of the firms

Hiller and Gerald (1990) classified the service systems into four types, i.e., commercial service, social service, internal service and transportation service. In commercial service systems, including commercial banks, barber shops and department stores, customers arrive and buy the service. Delay will reduce the demand and lead to profit loss. Social services, such as justice systems and health care, do not generate directly measurable profits. In these sectors, delay cost often appears as a kind of social cost (the capital needed to solve the social problems caused by delay). Internal services mainly include internal departments and they serve several user departments. Internal services and social services are similar in some ways, such as the objective of the service systems and the appearance of delay cost. Unlike the above three types of services, in transportation services, the "customers" are often vehicles, for example, the automobiles waiting for the traffic light or the sails waiting for loading.

We do not consider transportation services in our study for their customers are vehicles. And from the firm's point of view, we reclassify the service systems as Table 4-2 shows. In a commercial service, customers come from outside and the firm aims to maximize its profit, while the objective of a social service or an internal service is to optimize the whole system's (including the firm/department and the customers) benefit.

Table 4-2. Two types of service systems

Characteristic	Commercial service	Social service and internal service
Instance	Bank, restaurant	Health care Department of administration
The source of customers	Outside	Outside, Inside
Objective of the firm	Profit maximization	Net-value maximization

As we have mentioned, customers are heterogeneous (e.g., they have different delay cost per unit time). Impatient customers prefer short waiting time, and in order to get speedy service, they would like to pay higher price. On the contrary, some patient customers like low price and they do not care how long they will wait. So a firm that targets several specific markets will promote its services more effectively than a firm aiming at the "average" customer. A firm can differentiate on price and waiting time. The manager should firstly partition the market to n segmented markets based on certain criteria, and then optimize the price for each segmented market.

Most of the literature models a firm as a queueing server in the time-based environment. In a commercial system, the manager first partitions the market to n segmented markets, and then he maximizes the firm's expected stationary profit,

$$\max_{P} \sum_{i=1}^{n} \lambda_i(P) \cdot (p_i - q_i) - FC \qquad (1)$$

where i is the index of the segmented market. P is the vector of price p_i. $\lambda_i(\cdot)$ denotes the arrival rate (demand) per unit time of segment i, which is a function of the price vector P. q_i is the variable cost of server i. FC denotes the fixed cost.

In a social service or an internal department, the firm/department and the customers are regarded as a whole system. Similarly, the manager should first partition the market to n segmented markets, and then optimize the whole system's expected benefit through determining P,

$$\max_{P} \sum_{k=1}^{N} (v^k - E[C^k(W^k)]) - \sum_{i=1}^{n} \lambda_i(P) \cdot q_i - FC \qquad (2)$$

where N is the total number of the customers per unit time, v^k is the value customer k gets from the service (or called customer valuation). C^k is his delay cost function of his waiting time W^k which is a random variable, so we employ its expected value. Similarly, λ_i's are relative to p_i's. Actually, the above net value is the sum of the firm's profit and all the customers' utilities.

To optimize the objective, the manager must obtain the relationship between the arrival rates (demand) λ_i's and the pricing policy P. Hence he has to consider the reaction of the customers to P, which we will discuss in the following sub-section.

2.2 Customer's utility

Generally, a customer's utility u can be formulized as,

$$u(v, W, p) = U(v - C(W) - p) \tag{3}$$

where v is the value of the service, or the customer's valuation. W is the customer's waiting time which is a random variable. p is the price of the service he buys. $C(\cdot)$ is the delay cost function of the waiting time W. $U(\cdot)$ is the utility function, which transfers monetary value to utility and represents a customer's risk attitude.

Table 4-3. Assumptions of the parameters

Parameter	Literature	Assumption
$U(\cdot)$	Most of the literature	Linear, $U(x) = x$
	Chen and Frank (2004)	Piecewise linear
v	Edelson and Hildebrand (1975)	Service value
	Mendelson and Wang (1990)	Customer valuation
	Afeche and Mendelson (2004)	Perishable value, $v \cdot D(w)$
$C(\cdot)$	Most of the literature	Linear, $C(W) = c \cdot W$
	Kittsteiner and Moldovanu (2005)	Convex (concave) with respect to W

The existing literature makes different assumptions of these parameters. We summarize them in Table 4-3. In regard to $U(\cdot)$, most of the researchers assumed it a linear function (i.e., assumed that the customer is risk neutral). Chen and Frank (2004) considered the case of piecewise linear function, but some properties could not be reserved in this case. There are two opinions about v. One is that v is the service value, which is the attribute of the service. The other is that v is customer valuation. Afeche and Mendelson (2004) further considered the perishable service, such as a financial trade, and added a delay discount function $D(w)$ to v, where w is the customer's expected waiting time, $D(w) \leq 1$ is decreasing in w and deflates the value

v. Referring to $C(\cdot)$, most of the literature assumed that $C(W) = c \cdot W$, where c is the delay cost per unit time (unit delay cost for short).

Assumed that the whole market is partitioned to n segmented markets, i.e., the firm will provide n types of services. In that case, a customer can maximize his expected utility by choosing a type of services,

$$\max_i \quad E[U(v - C(c, W_i) - p_i)] \tag{4}$$

where i is the index of the segmented market, W_i and p_i are corresponding waiting time and price. The customer valuation is v and his unit delay cost is c. Generally, there exists a lower expected utility threshold u_0. $u_0 = -\infty$ means that the customer will not leave the firm, thus describing the case of monopoly. There are also some researchers who set that $u_0 = 0$. In this case, if the prices given by the firm are so high that no matter what kind of services a customer chooses, his utility will be lower than u_0, then the customer will leave the firm to other firms, which models the competitive case.

We can integrate all the customers' choices to obtain the relationship between each arrival rate λ_i and the pricing policy P. Then, Eqs. (1) and (2) can be optimized.

2.3 Centralized system

In a centralized system, information is symmetry and all the players in the system aim to optimize a common objective, that is, all the players are selfless. In fact, a centralized system does not exist in the real world, for all the customers have private information (e.g., the delay cost function, the valuation, etc.) and they make decisions to maximize their own utilities. We call this situation a decentralized system, which is common in reality. We will firstly study the centralized system, and derive the first best solutions as benchmarks. Then a mechanism is employed to optimize the decentralized system, and we will analyze the effectiveness of this mechanism by comparing the results of the two systems.

In the centralized system, we only consider the objective of net value maximization. There often exists a leader (maybe the manager of the firm), and all the players will act according to the leader's decision. In this case, the most important thing we need to do is to find the optimal assignment rule. An *assignment rule* assigns different delivery time to different segmented markets. Cox and Smith (1961) brought forward the well-known c/rt rule, where c is the unit delay cost and rt is the expected required service time. In an $M/M/1$ queueing system, if the delay cost function is linear, to minimize the expected average delay cost per unit of time, the optimal assignment rule is to serve customers in decreasing order of their "priority index" c/rt. We can see that, in a single server queueing system, the delivery time arrangement is simplified to priority assignment.

When there is no leader in the system, pricing or bidding is necessary. Price auction allows a customer himself to affect his own queue length, rather than the above approach of pre-assignment. Kleinrock (1967) considered this problem in the case of $M/G/1$. In his settings, the customers are not self-interested and their common objective is to minimize the total cost of all the customers. The customers are heterogeneous in their unit delay cost c. When he arrives, a customer bids b based on c, and his relative position in the queue is determined according to all the customers' bids. The author derived the average waiting time w for a customer as a function of the customer's bid b. He also proved that, if and only if $b(c)$ is a strictly increasing function of c, the function $b(c)$ will be an optimum bid function. This result is consistent with the c/rt rule. So in a centralized system, as long as the customers are selfless, no matter a leader exists or not is not important.

But in the real world, as we have mentioned in section 2.2, a customer always wants to maximize his own utility. Clearly, every customer prefers short waiting time. Hence externality exists. By Johnson (2006), *externality* is a situation in which the private costs or benefits to the producers or purchasers differs from the total social costs or benefits entailed in the production and consumption. An *external cost* or *negative externality* results when part of the cost of producing or consuming a good or service is borne by others other than the producer or purchaser. An *external benefit* or *positive externality* results when part of the benefit of producing or consuming a good or service accrues to others other than that who produces or purchases it. Externalities generate a problem for the effective functioning of the market to maximize the total utility of the society because rational profit-maximizing buyers and sellers do not take into account costs and benefits they do not have to bear. Naor (1969) found that, when a customer joined the queue, other customers' expected waiting time would increase. That is, negative externality exists in a decentralized queueing system.

Mechanisms are needed to bridge the gap between the customer's private cost and the social cost. A mechanism that can make a customer's benefit be consistent with the firm's is *incentive compatible*. Our target is to find an incentive compatible mechanism that can also optimize the firm's objective. Two mechanisms are explored by the researchers, which will be our next topic.

2.4 Mechanism design

We categorize the existing literature according to the mechanisms they undertake, i.e., price auction and direct mechanism. By using price auction, a customer should bid when he arrives, and his waiting time is determined by all customers' bids. In a direct mechanism, a customer is required to report his private information (e.g., unit delay cost) when he arrives at the firm. Based on his announcement, the firm assigns a priority to him and imposes a corresponding priority toll.

2.4.1 Price auction

As mentioned in section 2.3, Kleinrock (1967) studied a centralized system, where customers' behavior is omitted. Based on his model, Lui (1985) considered a decentralized system, that is, the customers are self-interested. When he arrives, a customer bids based on his unit delay cost c. Since c is the customer's private information, others (other customers and the manager) can only know the probability distribution function $F(c)$.

A Nash equilibrium bid strategy $b(c)$ is derived as,

$$b(c) = \int_{c_0}^{c} x \cdot (-w'(x)) dF(x) + P_0 \tag{5}$$

where c_0 is the minimal unit delay cost of the customers. Kleinrock (1967) derived the expected waiting time function $w(b(\cdot))$ that was related to the distribution function of $b(\cdot)$, and since $b(\cdot)$ should be a strictly increasing function of c, the function $w(c)$ could be easily derived. $w'(c)$ is the differential function of $w(c)$. Because $w(c)$ is a decreasing function of c, $w'(c) < 0$. We can see that, the customer with unit delay cost c will not impact the customers whose unit delay cost is greater than c, because these customers will get higher priority than him. But the customers whose unit delay cost x is below c will be impacted by this customer. When he joins the queue, it equals that the unit delay cost of all the customers with unit delay cost $x < c$ decreases one unit. Hence the expected waiting time of the customer with unit delay cost x increases $-w'(x)$, which results in an increase of $x \cdot (-w'(x))$ in delay cost. So the first term of the right hand side of Eq. (5) represents the expected cost inflicted on all other customers in the flow by this customer. We call it priority price. P_0 is the admission or reserve price. The customer who bids P_0 will get the lowest priority. So the bid consists of two parts, priority price and reserve price. Actually, the manager can optimize his objective function by setting an appropriate P_0. But this article did not discuss this problem further. The utility of the customer with unit delay cost c is $v-b(c)-c\cdot w(c)$, where v is the service value that is fixed. It can be easily proved that a customer's utility is a decreasing function of c. Therefore, given the lower utility threshold u_0, there exists a higher threshold $\bar{c}$, and when a customer's unit delay cost $c>\bar{c}$, he will not join the queue, i.e., not buy the service.

Afeche and Mendelson (2004) considered a general delay cost function $C(w)+v\cdot(1-D(w))$, where $D(w)\le 1$ is decreasing in the expected waiting time w. In this way, the value deflates with delay, so this function models the case of perishable service. Based on Eq. (5), they gave an equilibrium bid function. Through determining P_0, they optimized the firm's objective. They proved that, only when the priority is preemptive, and the objective is to maximize the net value of the system, $P_0=0$. Otherwise, $P_0>0$. Because when the priority is preemptive, the customer with lowest priority will not impact other customers' waiting time, that is, the external cost caused by this customer is zero, so $P_0=0$. They also discussed some properties in the perishable environment that is different from the traditional ones. Readers can refer to this article for your interest.

In the above models, unit delay cost c is the customer's private information. Kittsteiner and Moldovanu (2005) assumed that the stochastically arriving customers are privately informed about their own service time. Since the required service time is private information, Kleinrock's (1967) equation cannot be applied. So the authors focused on the properties of assignment rules in the bidding equilibrium. The main results showed that, the convexity/concavity of the delay cost function determined the assignment rule (shortest-processing-time-first (SPT) or longest-processing-time-first (LPT)) arising in a bidding equilibrium.

The above literature assumed that the customers could not see the queue length, while in Balachandran's (1972) model, when arriving, a customer could see the queue length l, and based on this information, he bid $b(l)$. The author aimed to find a Nash equilibrium bid function. He derived the formula of $b(l)$ and proved that $b(l)$ could not be a decreasing function of l. If the unit delay cost satisfied some conditions, then an increasing function $b(l)$ could be stable.

2.4.2 Direct mechanism

A static Bayesian game in which each player's only action is to submit a claim about his type (private information) is called *direct mechanism* (Gibbons, 1992). Direct mechanism is a special type of auction. Unlike price auction, a player should claim his type instead of bidding a price. A direct mechanism in which truth-telling is a Bayesian Nash equilibrium is called

Bayesian incentive compatible (In the following paragraphs, we use incentive compatibility directly to denote Bayesian incentive compatibility).

By using direct mechanism, a complex mechanism design problem can be converted to an optimization problem which is relatively simple. The *revelation principle*, by Myerson (1979), says that, any Bayesian Nash equilibrium of any Bayesian game can be represented by an incentive compatible direct mechanism.

In a direct mechanism, a customer is required to report his private information (such as unit delay cost) when he arrives at the firm. Based on his announcement, the manager assigns a priority to him and imposes a corresponding price. Through designing the assignment and pricing rules properly, the customers would tell the truth. The question, then, is how to construct an incentive compatible mechanism which can maximize the firm's objective.

Mendelson and Wang (1990) considered an $M/M/1$ queueing system with n user classes. Each class was characterized by its unit delay cost c_i. When he arrived, a customer reported his unit delay cost, and then the manager assigned a priority to him based on the c/rt rule. The authors derived a pricing mechanism that was optimal and incentive compatible in the sense that the arrival rates and execution priorities jointly maximized the expected net value of the system. A closed-form expression of the price structure was presented and studied,

$$p_i = \sum_{k=1}^{n} \lambda_k \cdot c_k \cdot \partial w_k(\Lambda)/\partial \lambda_i \tag{6}$$

where λ_k, c_k and w_k are the arrival rate, unit delay cost and expected waiting time of class k customers, respectively. The authors firstly considered the centralized system. They optimized λ_i's and then derived the price function. Therefore the expected waiting time was a function of $\Lambda = \{\lambda_1, \lambda_2, \cdots, \lambda_n\}$. When the customer with unit delay cost c_i joins the queue, the arrival rate of class i increases one unit; so the right hand side of Eq. (6) represents the expected cost inflicted on all other customers in the flow by this customer - that is, the external cost. The difference between Eqs. (5) and (6) is that Lui (1985) considered a continuous distribution function of the unit delay cost c, but Mendelson and Wang (1990) considered n user classes with each characterized by its unit delay cost c_i. The optimal price for a customer is equal to the associated external cost, so this mechanism is also incentive compatible. Even under the circumstance of asymmetric information, we can reach the optimal case of the centralized system. Since in the social or internal service, the objective of the firm is to maximize the expected net value of the system, this pricing policy is particularly useful.

Bradford (1996) considered multi-server. In an $M/G/m$ queueing system, customers are heterogeneous in their unit delay cost. A customer with unit delay cost c_i is called class i customer. Unlike single server, by current research, it is hard to find the optimal assignment rule. So he gave an assignment rule directly. In his rule, each arriving class i customer was sent to server k with probability π_{ik}. The manager must make two decisions, π_{ik} and the prices p_i's to maximize his objective. The author did not discuss the properties of π_{ik}, but focused on the incentive compatible pricing policy. He proved that, based on his assignment rule, the optimal pricing policy was also incentive compatible. This assignment rule is very clear and somewhat reasonable, but is it optimal? It is a question needed further analysis.

2.4.3 Summary

We summarize the existing literature in Table 4-4. The solving processes and the key issues of the two mechanisms are listed in the table. If we decide to use price auction, we should firstly find an equilibrium bid function, and then optimize this function to maximize the objective. In price auction, if the unit delay cost is private information, we can find a Nash equilibrium bid function based on Eq. (5) and then optimize the function. But if the auction is based on other information, such as the required service time or the queue length, then the bidding equilibrium is hard to find. When we decide to use direct mechanism, the first thing that should be done is to find the optimal assignment rule. But the c/rt rule can only be applied in the circumstance of the single server queue and the linear delay cost function. Much research remains to be done in this field.

Table 4-4. Literature summary

Mechanism	Literature	Solving processes	Key issues
Price auction	• Kleinrock (1967) • Lui (1985) • Afeche and Mendelson (2004)	• Find an equilibrium bid function; • Optimize the bid function.	Find a bidding equilibrium
Direct mechanism	• Mendelson and Wang (1990) • Bradford (1996)	• Find the optimal assignment rule; • Derive the incentive compatible constrains; • Based on the optimal assignment rule, and considering the constraints, optimize the pricing policy.	Get the optimal assignment rule

Generally speaking, these researchers focused on single server queueing system, so they only needed to study the priority assignment problem, i.e., they only considered one business period and arranged demand in this period. But in reality, the business hours (may be one day, one week or one year, etc.) can be classified into several periods. For example, in a restaurant, lunch and dinner times are peak periods. Customers should wait much longer time for service in peak periods. In addition, there are not enough facilities. These all lead to lost sales. But in other periods, there are so few customers that facilities remain idle. In other service industries, such as bank, department store, barber shop, etc., similar problems exist. So it is more practical to arrange demand in multi-period in service sector. In the following section, we will try to discuss the period assignment problem.

3. A MULTI-PERIOD MODEL

Based on the above overview, a multi-period model is developed. Consider a service firm that faces seasonal demand. The business time can be classified to n periods, with period i providing value v_i. The difference of the value causes congestion in peak periods and idle facilities in non-peak ones, which results in waste of capacity and lost sales. This problem is practical in service sector. In contrast with manufacture, services are produced and consumed almost simultaneously, so they cannot be stored for future sale. Besides, the high degree of producer-consumer interaction also leads to congestion or lost sales in peak periods. So keeping the balance between demand and supply creates a challenge for service managers.

Sasser (1976) proposed two strategies to match demand and supply, that is, chase demand which is also called supply management, and level capacity which is also called demand management. We try to use the demand management policy to match demand with supply. Different from the existing literature, we consider heterogeneous service, which is practical in the real world, and build two models (the net value maximization model and the revenue maximization model). Then the two models will be compared by a simple numerical example.

3.1 Assumptions and model

Consider a service firm that faces seasonal demand. The business time can be divided to n periods, with period i providing value v_i. We assume that $v_1 < v_2 < \cdots < v_n$. The service time of each period is assumed to follow an exponential distribution with mean service time $1/\mu$.

Each customer is characterized by his delay cost per unit time c, which is uniformly distributed in $[c_{\min}, c_{\max}]$. We assume that customers make individual decision on whether or not to join the service system based on self-optimizing and regardless of the impact on other customers. Generally, a customer's decision includes n steps. When period i is coming, he makes a decision on whether purchasing the service or going to the next period (balking when $i = n$). We can also consider a static decision structure, in which a customer chooses a period to enter (choosing 0 means balking) before the first period, and in each period, he behaves according to the initial decision. Actually, if the travel cost (the cost spent in going to the firm) is high enough, the static decision structure makes sense. Therefore, the multi-period models can be transformed into the multi-server models from the mathematic point of view.

Assume that the total arrival process follows a stationary Poisson process with fixed mean arrival rate λ which can be regarded as the market capacity, i.e., the upper bound of the mean arrival rate. The queues are first-come-first-served. For the sake of tractability, we also assume that the assignment rule involves randomly splitting the total arrival process, so that the arrival process of each period also follows a Poisson process and has a price-dependent arrival rate $\lambda_i, i = 0,1,\cdots,n$. We assume that $\mu > \lambda$ to prevent the queue of each period from growing indefinitely. Taking into account the customers' decisions, the manager makes an assignment rule and pricing policy to maximize his objective.

In the following two sub-sections, we will discuss two models, the net value maximization model and the revenue maximization model, which corresponds to the social/internal firm and the commercial firm respectively.

3.2 Net value maximization

Since the direct mechanism is employed, we first consider a centralized system. In a centralized system, the arrival rate λ_i (i=1,2,..., n) is determined by the service manager. In our model, we do not use priority assignment, but consider a period segmentation policy, i.e., segment the customers to $n+1$ classes (note that there is a virtual period 0 which means that customers balk), and then assign a kind of customers to a specific period (server), and the customers who enter the same period will obtain the same priority. Period assignment policy is common in reality. In many service industries, e.g., travel sector and bank, all the customers who arrive in the same period will get the same priority.

The system expected net value nv is $\Sigma_{i=1}^{n} \lambda_i \cdot (v_i - \bar{c}_i(\Lambda) \cdot w(\lambda_i))$, where λ_i is the arrival rate of server i. v_i is the service value provided by server i. $\Lambda = \{\lambda_1, \lambda_2, \cdots, \lambda_n\}$ is the vector of the arrival rates. $\bar{c}_i(\cdot)$ denotes the expected unit delay cost of the customers assigned to server i. $w(\lambda_i)=1/(\mu-\lambda_i)$ denotes the average waiting time of the customers assigned to server i in the system. We then use the notation w_i to denote $w(\lambda_i)$. Capacity cost is ignored for it is fixed per unit time, and we also omit service cost since it is fixed and can be considered in service toll if necessary.

3.2.1 The optimal assignment rule

An assignment rule AR is a mapping from the interval $[c_{\min},c_{\max}]$ to the set $\{0,1,\cdots,n\}$. We can formulize it as, $AR:[c_{\min},c_{\max}]\rightarrow\{0,1,\cdots,n\}$. An assignment rule must solve two problems. The first one is how it divides the interval, and the second one is how it assigns each subinterval to the servers.

For the first problem, a natural approach is that, divide the interval to $n+1$ subintervals and make each subinterval correspond to a certain server. This approach is equal to, $\forall x,y,z\in[c_{\min},c_{\max}]$ and $x<y<z$, if $AR(x)=i$ and $AR(z)=i$, then $AR(y)=i$. Besides, we obtain another property in the proof procedure, which is also listed in Property 1.

PROPERTY 1. The optimal assignment rule AR^{nv} divides the interval $[c_{\min},c_{\max}]$ to $n+1$ subintervals, and

1) each subinterval corresponds to a certain server, i.e., $\forall x,y,z\in[c_{\min},c_{\max}]$ and $x<y<z$, if $AR^{nv}(x)=i$ and $AR^{nv}(z)=i$, then $AR^{nv}(y)=i$.
2) the more impatient customers will be assigned to the less congested servers.

The proof of this property is given in the appendix. AR^{nv} denotes the optimal assignment rule of the net value maximization model. In the following paragraphs, we use the superscript nv to denote the optimal solutions to the net value maximization model. The second part of Property 1 says that, the manager should guarantee less waiting time for more impatient customers. Consider two customers whose unit delay is x and y respectively and $x>y$. Then the customer with unit delay cost x will be assigned either to the same server as the other one or to the sever which is less congested. To describe Property 1 more clearly, here we introduce a notation (i). For any given λ_i, i=1,2,...,n, if they can be arranged as $\lambda_{k1}\leq\lambda_{k2}\leq\cdots\leq\lambda_{kn}$, we denote ki as (i), i.e., $\lambda_{(1)}\leq\lambda_{(2)}\leq\cdots\leq\lambda_{(n)}$. This notation seems like the subscript of *order statistics* in statistics. Given Property 1 and the definition of (i), the optimal assignment rule can be illustrated in Figure 4-1.

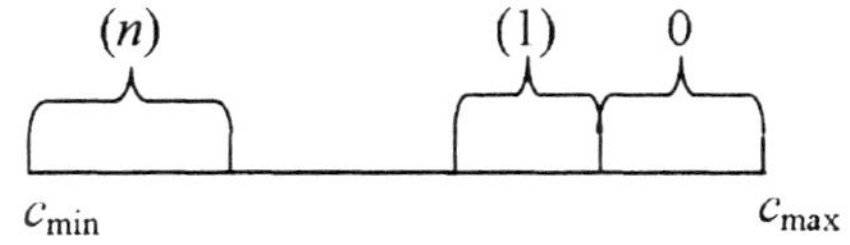

Figure 4-1. Interval divided by the optimal assignment rule AR^{nv}

From Property 1, we know the optimal assignment rule divides the customers to $n+1$ classes, $0,(1),\cdots,(n)$. Then we should answer the second question, i.e., how to assign each class (i) customers to the server, i.e., what is the relationship between (i) and i. Property 2 gives the answer.

PROPERTY 2. The optimal assignment rule AR^{nv} assigns class (i) customers to server i.

The proof of property 2 is given in the appendix. Note that $\lambda_{(1)} \le \lambda_{(2)} \le \cdots \le \lambda_{(n)}$, and $v_1 < v_2 < \cdots < v_n$, so Property 2 says that, the more value a server can provide, the more customers it should serve, to maximize the total value. From the viewpoint of the customers, AR^{nv} assigns more impatient customers to the less valuable servers, because in these servers, waiting time is shorter. From the two properties, we derive the optimal assignment rule AR^{nv} and illustrate it in Figure 4-2.

AR^{nv}: There exist n points $c^{nv}_{i,i+1}, i = 0,1,\cdots,n-1$, s.t., $\forall i$, $c^{nv}_{i,i+1} \in [c_{\min}, c_{\max}]$ and $c^{nv}_{i,i+1} \le c^{nv}_{i-1,i}$. These n points divide customers to $n+1$ classes. The customer with unit delay cost c will be assigned according to the following rules.

a) If $c \in [c^{nv}_{i,i+1}, c^{nv}_{i-1,i}], i = 1,2,\cdots,n-1$, assign the customer to server i;
b) If $c \in [c_{\min}, c^{nv}_{n-1,n}]$, assign the customer to server n;
c) If $c \in [c^{nv}_{0,1}, c_{\max}]$, assign the customer to server 0, i.e., the customer will balk.

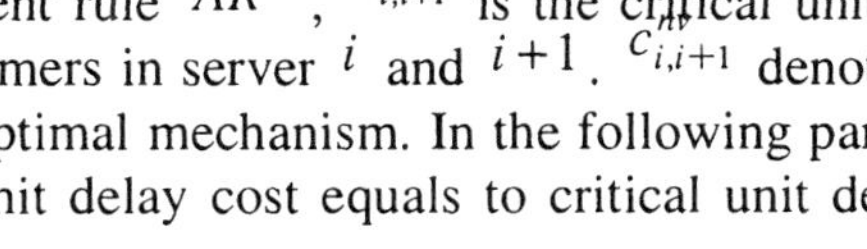

Figure 4-2. The sketch map of the optimal assignment rule AR^{nv}.

In the assignment rule AR^{nv}, $c^{nv}_{i,i+1}$ is the critical unit delay cost which separates the customers in server i and $i+1$. $c_{i,i+1}$ denotes the critical unit delay cost in the optimal mechanism. In the following paragraphs, we call a customer whose unit delay cost equals to critical unit delay cost a critical customer.

3.2.2 The optimization problem

In our model, c is uniformly distributed in $[c_{\min}, c_{\max}]$, with AR^{nv}, we have,

$$c_{i,i+1} = c_{\min} + (c_{\max} - c_{\min}) \cdot \sum_{j=i+1}^{n} \lambda_j / \lambda, \quad i = 0,1,\cdots,n-1 \tag{7}$$

We also have $\bar{c}_i = (c_{i-1,i} + c_{i,i+1})/2$ for c is uniformly distributed, and then we can solve the following optimization problem to maximize the system net value,

$$\begin{aligned} \max_{\Lambda} \quad & nv = \sum_{i=1}^{n} \lambda_i \cdot (v_i - \frac{c_{i-1,i} + c_{i,i+1}}{2} \cdot w_i) \\ s.t. \quad & \sum_{i=0}^{n} \lambda_i = \lambda \\ & \lambda_i \geq 0 \qquad\qquad i = 0,1,\cdots,n \\ & c_{i,i+1} = c_{\min} + (c_{\max} - c_{\min}) \cdot \sum_{j=i+1}^{n} \lambda_i / \lambda, \quad i = 0,1,\cdots,n-1 \\ & c_{n,n+1} = c_{\min} \end{aligned} \tag{8}$$

where $w_i := w(\lambda_i) = 1/(\mu - \lambda_i)$ denotes the expected waiting time of the customers assigned to server i. Note that we need to decide the vector of arrival rates $\Lambda = \{\lambda_1, \lambda_2, \cdots, \lambda_n\}$ instead of P in a centralized system. Besides the relationship between $c_{i,i+1}$ and Λ, we should also guarantee that the sum of the arrival rate λ_i is λ.

3.2.3 Incentive compatibility

Now we consider the decentralized system, in which customers are self-interested. Here a pricing policy is necessary to incent customers. In the decentralized model, based on the price vector P given by the firm, a customer with unit delay cost c would select a server (period) to minimize his expected total cost,

$$\min_i \{p_i + c \cdot w_i - v_i\} \tag{9}$$

Each customer minimizes his expected total costs, i.e., the service fee plus the expected delay cost minus the value he obtains from the service. He will choose the period that brings minimal cost to him. If the optimal $i = 0$, then the customer will balk, and in this way, his total cost is zero.

Now we would like to find an incentive compatible price vector. In the stationary state of the decentralized system, the incentive compatible pricing policy must guarantee that no matter which period, i.e., i or $i+1$, he chooses, the customer whose unit delay cost equals the critical unit delay cost $c_{i,i+1}$ will get the same total cost, that is,

$$p_i + c_{i,i+1} \cdot w_i - v_i = p_{i+1} + c_{i,i+1} \cdot w_{i+1} - v_{i+1} \tag{10}$$

From the above equation, we obtain the following price function,

$$p_i = v_i - \sum_{j=0}^{i-1} c_{j,j+1} \cdot (w_{j+1} - w_j) \tag{11}$$

This pricing policy only guarantees that the critical customers will not choose the adjacent period from the period assigned by the firm. This is a necessary condition of incentive compatibility. Furthermore, we can prove that, this pricing policy can also make all customers accept the manager's assignment, that is, the pricing policy is incentive compatible.

THEOREM 1. The optimal price vector P^{nv} given by

$$p_i^{nv} = v_i - \sum_{j=0}^{i-1} c_{j,j+1}^{nv} \cdot (w_{j+1}^{nv} - w_j^{nv}) \qquad i = 1, 2, \cdots, n \tag{12}$$

is incentive compatible in the decentralized net value maximization model, where $c_{i,i+1}^{nv}$ $(i = 0, 1, \cdots, n-1)$ is the optimal critical unit delay cost and w_i^{nv} $(i = 1, 2, \cdots, n)$ denotes the optimal expected waiting time of server i in the centralized net value optimization problem Eq. (8).

To get Theorem 1, we only need to prove that if he is assigned to server i in the centralized model, a customer cannot reduce his total cost by not accepting the original assignment. The proof is given in the appendix. From Theorem 1, we can see that, if the manager derives optimal λ_i's from the centralized system and assigns the customers with high unit delay cost to the less congested servers, then under the pricing policy derived from Theorem 1, the self-interested customers will take the assignment rule, and then it achieves the system-wide optimization. This pricing policy is particularly useful for an internal service department because an internal department should be evaluated by the total net value it creates. We prove that a policy to incent customer can be found and at the same time achieve the optimal net value of the centralized case. This result is inspiring.

In the proof procedure of Theorem 1, Property 1 and Eq. (11) are the sufficient and necessary conditions of incentive compatibility. Theorem 2 can be derived directly.

THEOREM 2. If and only if an assignment rule satisfies the following properties, it is incentive compatible.

1) The customers should be assigned as Figure 4-1 shows.
2) No matter which period, i.e., (i) or $(i+1)$, he chooses, the customer with unit delay cost $c_{(i),(i+1)}$ will get the same total cost.

The necessary and sufficient conditions of incentive compatibility will be used in the next revenue maximization model as well.

3.3 Revenue maximization

In this sub-section, we consider a commercial service firm. The manager wants to maximize the expected revenue per unit time. We do not discuss the centralized decision, because from the viewpoint of the manager, it is optimal to make infinite prices and let all customers purchase the service. This is unrealistic in a decentralized decision system. So we consider the decentralized problem directly. Assumptions are the same as the first model's except the objective of the organization.

The expected revenue per unit time of the firm is,

$$r = \sum_{i=1}^{n} \lambda_i \cdot p_i(\Lambda) \tag{13}$$

where $p_i(\cdot)$ is the price of server i, which is a function of the arrival rate vector Λ. The function $p_i(\cdot)$ is determined by the optimal incentive compatible assignment rule AR^r. Similarly, we use the superscript r to mark the optimal and incentive compatible solutions to the revenue maximization model. We first establish AR^r.

From Theorem 2, i.e., the constrains of incentive compatibility, we have,

$$p_{(i)} = v_{(i)} - \sum_{j=0}^{i-1} c_{(j),(j+1)} \cdot (w_{(j+1)} - w_{(j)}) \tag{14}$$

Substitute Eq. (14) into Eq. (13), the expected revenue of the firm is,

$$r(\Lambda) = \sum_{i=1}^{n} (\lambda_{(i)} \cdot v_{(i)} - \lambda_{(i)} \cdot \sum_{j=0}^{i-1} c_{(j),(j+1)} \cdot (w_{(j+1)} - w_{(j)})) \tag{15}$$

For any given λ_i's, the second item of the right hand side of Eq. (15) is not related to the servers. By the Hardy-Littlewood-Polya (HLP) inequality, we know that, the inner product of the increasing arrangement of two vectors is maximal. To maximize the revenue, the manager should let (i) be i, because $v_1 < v_2 < \cdots < v_n$ and we always have $\lambda_{(1)} \le \lambda_{(2)} \le \cdots \le \lambda_{(n)}$. Then the optimal incentive compatible assignment rule AR^r is obtained.

AR^r: There exist n points $c^r_{i,i+1}, i = 0,1,\cdots,n-1$, s.t., $\forall i$, $c^r_{i,i+1} \in [c_{\min}, c_{\max}]$ and $c^r_{i,i+1} \le c^r_{i-1,i}$. These n points divide customers to $n+1$ classes. The customer with unit delay cost c will be assigned according to the following rules.

a) If $c \in [c^r_{i,i+1}, c^r_{i-1,i}], i = 1,2,\cdots,n-1$, assign the customer to server i;

b) If $c \in [c_{\min}, c^r_{n-1,n}]$, assign the customer to server n;

c) If $c \in [c^r_{0,1}, c_{\max}]$, assign the customer to server 0, i.e., the customer will balk.

Note that $c^r_{i,i+1}$ may be different from $c^{nv}_{i,i+1}$. But the forms of AR^r and of AR^{nv} are similar. They both make impatient customers wait less time, and since the manager wants to maximize the net value or the revenue, he keeps more customers in the servers with high value or high price, so the impatient customers have to receive less valuable service. Given AR^r, we can optimize the firm's expected revenue,

$$
\begin{aligned}
\max_{P} \quad & r = \sum_{i=1}^{n} \lambda_i \cdot (v_i - \sum_{j=0}^{i-1} c_{j,j+1} \cdot (w_{j+1} - w_j)) \\
s.t. \quad & \sum_{i=0}^{n} \lambda_i = \lambda \\
& \lambda_i \ge 0 \qquad i = 0,1,\cdots,n \qquad\qquad (16) \\
& c_{i,i+1} = c_{\min} + (c_{\max} - c_{\min}) \cdot \sum_{j=i+1}^{n} \lambda_i / \lambda, \quad i = 0,1,\cdots,n-1 \\
& c_{n,n+1} = c_{\min}
\end{aligned}
$$

3.4 Numerical example and analysis

In the above two sub-sections, we proved that, optimal and incentive compatible assignment rule and pricing policy exist in net value maximization and revenue maximization models. Now we focus on the comparison of these two models by using a simple numerical example. Consider the case of $n = 2$. Joint-concavity of the objective function can be easily proved from Eqs. (8) and (16). This guarantees the existence of the optimal solutions to the two models. Set the parameters as, $c_{\min} = 0$, $c_{\max} = 1$, $V = [1,2]$, $\mu = 3$, and λ takes discrete value from 1 to 7, with equal jump of 0.5.

We focus on the optimal price vectors of the two models. Firstly, we can see that, in these two models, price of the more valuable period is always higher than the less one's, i.e., $p^r_2 > p^r_1$ and $p^{nv}_2 > p^{nv}_1$. In the first model, this pricing policy guarantees more total value. In the second model, the manager uses this policy to charge more service fee from the customers. Then we compare the price vector of these two models. As Figure 4-3 shows, $p_2^r > p_2^{nv}$, but in the less valuable server 1, there exists an intersection point λ^*. When $\lambda < \lambda^*$, $p_1^r < p_1^{nv}$ and when $\lambda > \lambda^*$, $p_1^r > p_1^{nv}$.

This result is different from the conclusions of Bradford (1996), who also considered multi-server. He proved that in multi-server queues, the optimal price of a particular customer class in the revenue maximization problem was always higher than the corresponding optimal price in the net value maximization problem. Bradford assumed that the potential demand of each class was infinite. In this way, if the prices were low enough, customers would enter any server continuously. Different from Bradford, we assume that there exists a market capacity λ, which is the upper bound of the arrival rate. The sum of the arrival rates of the servers will be impacted by the pricing policy but it cannot exceed λ. This assumption is realistic because there exists a market capacity in many markets.

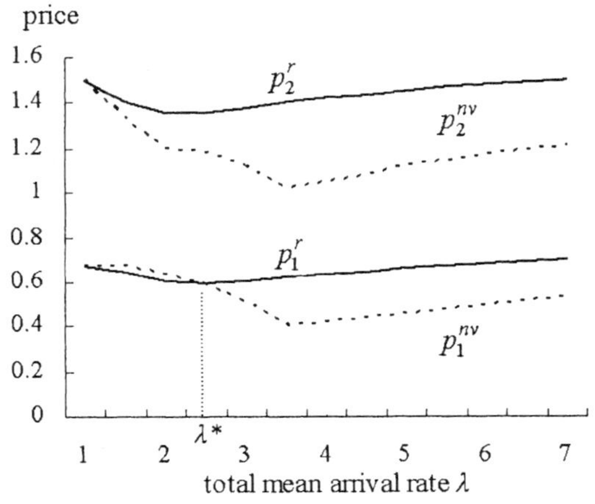

Figure 4-3. The comparison of the optimal prices in the two models

Besides, Bradford considered homogeneous servers but we consider heterogeneous servers which play different roles. This difference is especially salient when the total arrival rate is relatively small. When $\lambda < \lambda^*$, reducing prices cannot attract more customers, and hence the manager who wants to maximize the net value should charge a higher price in the less valuable period (period 1) to attract the customers to the more valuable one (period 2). While in the revenue maximization model, the manager makes a high price in the peak period, and uses the non-peak one as a supplement to attract residual demand. Therefore the manager makes a relatively low price in non-peak period. So $p_1^r < p_1^{nv}$.

When the total arrival rate is high (in this example, $\lambda > \lambda^*$ and note that λ^* is close to μ), the manager in the first model does not need to use the difference of the two prices of the servers to attract customers, so the result is consistent with Bradford, i.e., the optimal price of any period in the revenue maximization problem is higher than the corresponding optimal price in the net value maximization problem.

4. SUMMARY AND FUTURE RESEARCH

In this chapter, we firstly highlight the importance of customer incentive issues in the time-based environment. Then we review the existing literature and categorize them according to the mechanisms they undertake, i.e., price auction and direct mechanism. We describe the solving processes and key issues of the two mechanisms. Based on the overview, we develop a multi-period model and give the optimal incentive compatible assignment rule and pricing policy.

Further research should be carried out in the realm of time-based customer incentive issues. The research in this field is enslaved by the research of queueing theory. The existing literature assumes that the customer's utility and the delay cost function are linear, which are somewhat unreasonable in the real world. When the delay cost function and the utility function are nonlinear, and it is in the multi-server case, what is the optimal assignment rule? Further research is called for.

It should also be noted that several issues in this field have not been considered yet. First, although more and more services become perishable, only a few studies (e.g., Afeche and Mendelson, 2004) have focused on perishable service. Second, it is necessary to manage demand and supply simultaneously. Dewan and Mendelson (1985), Stidham (1992), Chen and Frank (2004) jointly optimized service rate and pricing policy. However it is desired to consider optimization of service rate in multi-period, employee scheduling and outsourcing, etc. Thirdly, real-time decision models are needed to support the service manager when the steady state models are ineffective.

Since time has become a critical factor in service firms' strategy in today's competitive environment, customer incentive issues become an area of recent focus, but significant work should be done as we have mentioned. We expect to see more fruitful empirical studies and theoretic research in this field.

ACKNOWLEDGEMENT

This work was supported partly by the National Natural Science Foundation of China under Grants 70321001, 70329001 and 70518002.

APPENDIXES

PROOF OF PROPERTY 1. The second part of Property 1 is a sufficient condition of the first part, so we only need to prove the second part. Denote AR^{nv} and Λ^{nv} as the optimal assignment rule and arrival rate vector in the centralized net value maximization model respectively. We can claim that, $\forall AR^{o}$ and the optimal arrival rate vector Λ^{o} based on AR^{o}, we have $nv_{AR^{nv}}(\Lambda^{nv}) \geq nv_{AR^{o}}(\Lambda^{o}) \geq nv_{AR^{o}}(\Lambda^{nv})$. In Λ^{nv}, if $\lambda_{k1}^{nv} \leq \lambda_{k2}^{nv} \leq \cdots \leq \lambda_{kn}^{nv}$, we denote ki as (i), then we always have $\lambda_{(1)}^{nv} \leq \lambda_{(2)}^{nv} \leq \cdots \leq \lambda_{(n)}^{nv}$. Assume that in the optimal assignment rule AR^{nv}, there exist (i) and (j), such that $\lambda_{(i)}^{nv} \geq \lambda_{(j)}^{nv}$, and there are some customers who are assigned as Figure 4-A1 shows, i.e., some more impatient customers wait longer time than the less impatient ones. In Figure 4-A1, the mean arrival rate of the customers we denote (i) is $\lambda_{(i)}^{A1} \leq \lambda_{(i)}^{nv}$ which means that these customers are only part of all the customers in server (i). Similarly, $\lambda_{(j)}^{A1}$ is the mean arrival rate of the customers we denote (j) in Figure 4-A1 and $\lambda_{(j)}^{A1} \leq \lambda_{(j)}^{nv}$. Denote $c_{(i)}^{A1}$ as the average unit delay cost of the customers we denote (i) in Figure 4-A1 and $c_{(i)}^{A2}$ is the corresponding average unit delay cost in Figure 4-A2. $c_{(j)}^{A1}$ and $c_{(j)}^{A2}$ are similarly defined.

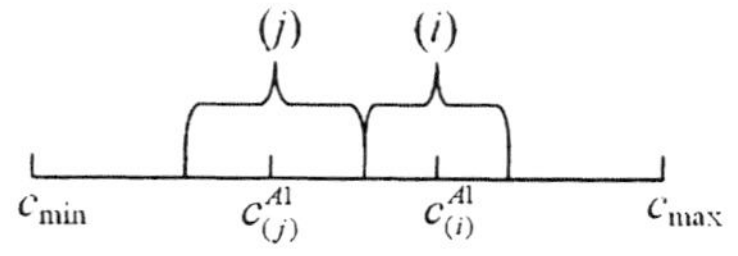

Figure 4-A1.

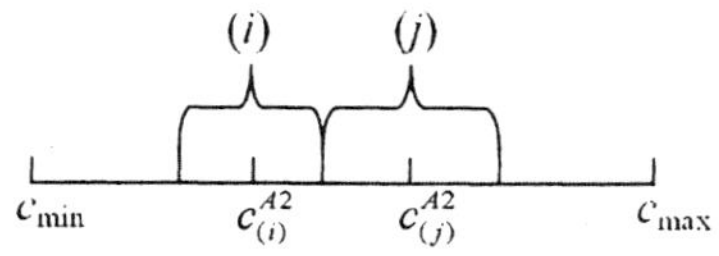

Figure 4-A2.

In Figure 4-A1, the total cost of these customers is,

$$\begin{aligned} C_{(ij)}^{A1} &= c_{(j)}^{A1} \cdot \lambda_{(j)}^{A1} \cdot w(\lambda_{(j)}) + c_{(i)}^{A1} \cdot \lambda_{(i)}^{A1} \cdot w(\lambda_{(i)}) \\ &= c_{(j)}^{A1} \cdot \lambda_{(j)}^{A1} \cdot w(\lambda_{(j)}) + (c_{(j)}^{A1} + \frac{\lambda_{(i)}^{A1} + \lambda_{(j)}^{A1}}{2\lambda} \cdot (c_{\max} - c_{\min})) \cdot \lambda_{(i)}^{A1} \cdot w(\lambda_{(i)}) \end{aligned} \tag{A1}$$

Now, if we exchange the sequence of (i) and (j) as Figure 4-A2 shows, i.e., reducing the waiting time of some impatient customers, we have, $\lambda_{(i)}^{A2} = \lambda_{(i)}^{A1}$ and $\lambda_{(j)}^{A2} = \lambda_{(j)}^{A1}$. The total cost is,

$$
\begin{aligned}
C_{(ij)}^{A2} &= c_{(i)}^{A2} \cdot \lambda_{(i)}^{A1} \cdot w(\lambda_{(i)}) + c_{(j)}^{A2} \cdot \lambda_{(j)}^{A1} \cdot w(\lambda_{(j)}) \\
&= (c_{(j)}^{A1} + \frac{\lambda_{(i)}^{A1} - \lambda_{(j)}^{A1}}{2\lambda} \cdot (c_{\max} - c_{\min})) \cdot \lambda_{(i)}^{A1} \cdot w(\lambda_{(i)}) \\
&\quad + (c_{(j)}^{A1} + \frac{\lambda_{(i)}^{A1}}{\lambda} \cdot (c_{\max} - c_{\min})) \cdot \lambda_{(j)}^{A1} \cdot w(\lambda_{(j)})
\end{aligned} \tag{A2}
$$

Note that we only exchange the servers of these two kinds of customers and leave Λ^{nv} unchanged. So if $C_{(ij)}^{A2} \le C_{(ij)}^{A1}$, we can claim that, AR^{nv} is not optimal because we can reduce the total cost of all the customers with the total value $\Sigma \lambda_i^{nv} \cdot v_i$ unchanged. The proof is quite easy as Eq. (A3) shows.

$$
\begin{aligned}
\Delta C_{(ij)} &= C_{(ij)}^{A2} - C_{(ij)}^{A1} \\
&= \frac{\lambda_{(i)}^{A1} \cdot \lambda_{(j)}^{A2}}{\lambda} \cdot (w(\lambda_{(j)}) - w(\lambda_{(i)})) \cdot (c_{\max} - c_{\min}) \le 0
\end{aligned} \tag{A3}
$$

In this way, we prove that, if $\lambda_{(i)} \ge \lambda_{(j)}$, the unit delay cost of any customer who enters server (i) is lower than all the customers' in server (j), that is, the manager should always assign the more impatient customers to the less congested servers. ■

PROOF OF PROPERTY 2. Denote Λ^{nv} as the optimal arrival rate vector based on AR^{nv}. We can claim that, $\forall AR^o$ and the corresponding optimal arrival rate vector Λ^o, we have $nv_{AR^{nv}}(\Lambda^{nv}) \ge nv_{AR^o}(\Lambda^o) \ge nv_{AR^o}(\Lambda^{nv})$. Assume that AR^o also assigns customers as Figure 4-1 shows and further it let (i) be i. Since the total delay cost is independent to the servers, the total delay cost under the mechanism (AR^{nv}, Λ^{nv}) is equal to the total delay cost under the mechanism (AR^o, Λ^{nv}). Then by the Hardy-Littlewood-Polya (HLP) inequality, we have $nv_{AR^o}(\Lambda^{nv}) \ge nv_{AR^{nv}}(\Lambda^{nv})$ immediately because $\lambda_{(1)} \le \lambda_{(2)} \le \cdots \le \lambda_{(n)}$ and $v_1 < v_2 < \cdots < v_n$. So AR^{nv} must let (i) be i. Thus we have $\lambda_1^{nv} \le \lambda_2^{nv} \le \cdots \le \lambda_n^{nv}$ which says that, the more value a server can provide, the more customers it should serve, to maximize the total value. ■

PROOF OF THEOREM 1. We only need to prove that if he is assigned to server i in the centralized model, a customer cannot reduce his cost by not accepting the original assignment. Define C_i^j as the expected total cost of a "class i customer" (a customer who should enter server i in the centralized model) when he enters server j. The proof proceeds in the following two parts,

(1) Local optimality: $C_i^j \le C_i^{j-1}$, $C_i^j \le C_i^{j+1}$;

(2) Transitivity: For $k > j > i$, if $C_i^i \le C_i^j$ and $C_j^j \le C_j^k$, then $C_i^i \le C_i^k$; For $k < j < i$, if $C_i^i \le C_i^j$ and $C_j^j \le C_j^k$, then $C_i^i \le C_i^k$.

Part (1). Choose an class i customer whose unit delay cost is c, and then we must have $c_{i,i+1}^{nv} \le c \le c_{i-1,i}^{nv}$ (recall AR^{nv}). Compute the additional cost if he chooses server $i-1$,

$$
\begin{aligned}
& C_i^{i-1} - C_i^i = (p_{i-1}^{nv} + c \cdot w_{i-1}^{nv} - v_{i-1}) - (p_i^{nv} + c \cdot w_i^{nv} - v_i) \\
& = (-\sum_{j=0}^{i-2} c_{j,j+1}^{nv} \cdot (w_{j+1}^{nv} - w_j^{nv}) + c \cdot w_{i-1}^{nv}) \\
& \qquad - (-\sum_{j=0}^{i-1} c_{j,j+1}^{nv} \cdot (w_{j+1}^{nv} - w_j^{nv}) + c \cdot w_i^{nv}) \\
& = (c_{i-1,i}^{nv} - c) \cdot (w_i^{nv} - w_{i-1}^{nv}) \geq 0
\end{aligned} \tag{A4}
$$

Similarly, we have,

$$
C_i^{i+1} - C_i^i = (c - c_{i,i+1}^{nv}) \cdot (w_{i+1}^{nv} - w_i^{nv}) \geq 0 \tag{A5}
$$

In this way, we prove the local optimality.
Part (2). If $k > j > i$, $C_i^i \leq C_i^j$ and $C_j^j \leq C_j^k$, note that,

$$
\begin{aligned}
& C_i^k - C_i^i = (C_i^k - C_i^j) + (C_i^j - C_i^i) \\
& = (p_k^{nv} + c \cdot w_k^{nv} - v_k - p_j^{nv} - c \cdot w_j^{nv} + v_j) + (C_i^j - C_i^i) \\
& w_k^{nv} > w_j^{nv}, \forall c' \in [c_{j,j+1}^{nv}, c_{j-1,j}^{nv}], c > c', then \\
& \quad C_i^k - C_i^i \\
& > (p_k^{nv} + c' \cdot w_k^{nv} - v_k - p_j^{nv} - c' \cdot w_j^{nv} + v_j) + (C_i^j - C_i^i) \\
& = (C_j^k - C_j^j) + (C_i^j - C_i^i) \geq 0
\end{aligned} \tag{A6}
$$

A similar argument proves transitivity when $k < j < i$. ■

REFERENCES

Afeche, P., and Mendelson, H., 2004, Pricing and priority auctions in queueing systems with a generalized delay cost structure, *Management science*. 50(7): 869-882.

Balachandran, K.R., 1972, Purchasing priorities in queues, *Management Science*. 18(5): 319-326.

Becker, G.S., 1965, A theory of the allocation of time, *Economic Journal*. 75(299): 493-517.

Blackburn, J.D., 1991, Time-based competition: speeding new product development, in: *Modern Production Concepts: Theory and Applications*, G. Fandel and G. Zapfel, ed., Springer-Verlag, New York.

Bradford, R.M., 1996, Pricing, routing and incentive compatibility in multiserver queues, *European Journal of Operational Research*. 89(2): 226-236.

Chen, H., and Frank, M., 2004, Monopoly pricing when customers queue, *IIE Transactions*. 36(6): 569-581.

Cox, D., and Smith, W., 1961, *Queues*, Methuen and Company, Ltd., London.

Dewan, S., and Mendelson, H., 1990, User delay costs and internal pricing for a service facility, *Management Science*. 36(12): 1502 -1517.

Daniels, N.C., and Essaides, G., 1993, *Time-based Competition*, Economic Intelligence Unit, London.

Edelson, N.M., and Hildebrand, D.K., 1975, Congestion tolls for Poisson queuing processes, *Econometrica*. 43(1): 81-92.

Gibbons, R., 1992, *A Prime in Game Theory*, Prentice Hall.

Hiller, F.S., and Gerald J.L., 1990, *Introduction to Stochastic Models in Operations Research*, 5th. ed., McGraw-Hill, Inc.

Johnson, P.M., 2006, *A Glossary of Political Economy Terms*; http://www.auburn.edu/~johnspm/gloss.

Kleinrock, L., 1967, Optimum bribing for queue position, *Operations Research*. 15(2): 304-218.

Kittsteiner T., and Moldovanu, B., 2005, Priority auctions and queue disciplines that depend on processing time, *Management Science*. 51(2): 236-248.

Lui, F., 1985, An equilibrium queuing model of bribery, *Journal of Political Economy*. 93(4): 760-781.

Myerson, R.B., 1979, Incentive compatibility and the bargaining problem, *Econometrica*. 47(1): 61-74.

Mendelson, H., 1985, Pricing computer services: queueing effects, *Communications of the ACM*. 38(3): 312-321.

Mendelson, H., and Whang, S., 1990, Optimal incentive-compatible priority pricing for the M/M/1 queue, *Operations Research*. 38(5): 870-883.

Naor, P., 1969, The regulation of queue size by levying tolls, *Econometrica*. 37(1): 15-24.

Png, I.P.L., and Reitman, D., 1994, Service time competition, *RAND Journal of Economics*. 25(4): 619-634.

Porter, M.E., 1980, Generic competitive strategies, in: *Competitive Strategy*, Free Press, New York.

Quinn, J.B., Baruch, J.J., and Paquette, P.C., 1987, *Scientific American*, 257(2): 50.

Sasser, W.E., 1976, Match supply and demand in service industries, *Harvard Business Review*. 54(6): 133–140.

Stalk, G.Jr., 1988, Time–the next source of competitive advantage, *Harvard Business Review*. 66(4): 41-51.

Stalk, G. Jr., and Hout, T.M., 1990, *Competing Against Time: How Time-based Competition is Reshaping Global Markets*, Free Press, New York.

Stidham, S., 1992, Pricing and capacity decisions for a service facility: stability and multiple local optima, *Management Science*. 38(8): 1121-1139.

Tien, J.M., and Berg, D., 2003, A case for service systems engineering, *Journal of Systems Science and Systems Engineering*. 12(1): 13-38.

Tucker, R.B., 1991, Managing the Future: Ten Driving Forces of Change for the '90s, Putnam, New York.

Chapter 5

AUCTIONS AS A DYNAMIC PRICING MECHANISM FOR E-SERVICES

Juong-Sik Lee and Boleslaw K. Szymanski

Optimaret Inc. and Department of Computer Science, Rensselaer Polytechnic Institute, 110 8th Street, Troy, NY 12180, USA

Abstract: Increasing role of services in developed economies around the world combined with ubiquitous presence of computer networks and information technologies result in rapid growth of e-services. Markets for e-services often require flexible pricing to be efficient and therefore frequently use auctions to satisfy this requirement. However, auctions in e-service markets are recurring since typically e-services are offered repeatedly, each time for a specific time interval. Additionally, all e-services offered in an auction round must be sold to avoid resource waste. Finally, enough bidders must be willing to participate in future auction rounds to prevent a collapse of market prices. Because of these requirements, previously designed auctions cannot work efficiently in e-service markets. In this chapter, we introduce and evaluate a novel auction, called *Optimal Recurring Auction (ORA),* for e-services markets. We present also simulation results that show that, unlike the traditional auctions, ORA stabilizes the market prices and maximizes the auctioneer's revenue in e-service markets.

Key words: e-commerce; e-services; dynamic pricing; recurrent auction; bidder drop.

1. INTRODUCTION

In recent years, expansion of electronic markets (abbreviated as e-markets) triggered an increase in the role and importance of efficient pricing mechanism. In many existing e-markets, fixed pricing or static time-differential pricing mechanisms are used because of their simplicity. There is, however, a natural variation in buyer's demand over time. For this reason, such pricing mechanisms are inefficient as they result in under-utilization of resources when demand is low and under-pricing when demand is high.

A static time differential pricing mechanism in which two or more tiers of on/off peak rates are used can improve efficiency by partially matching lower (higher) demand with lower (higher) price. However, this mechanism still remains inflexible, since demands of buyers do not follow a step function, but rather gradually shift from on- to off-peaks and back[15].

A continuously adjustable dynamic pricing mechanism that adapts to changing market conditions constantly is more efficient. It maintains high resource utilization and the seller's revenue in variety of market conditions. The low price invoked by the adaptive pricing increases competition during the low utilization period. High prices imposed during the high demand period increase the seller's revenues. Moreover, with such a mechanism, the price itself becomes an important signal for controlling fair allocation of resources. Hence, by ensuring that prices match the current market conditions, fully adjustable dynamic pricing mechanisms creates optimal outcomes for both buyers and sellers. At the same time, this very dynamism of pricing makes seller's pricing decisions and buyers' budget planning difficult. An auction mitigates such difficulties, since prices emerge from the buyer's willingness to pay[4]. Additionally, using auction as a dynamic pricing mechanism in e-markets, thanks to their well defined rules and procedures, eases the difficulty and cost of the implementation of the automated negotiations in electronic environments[3]. As a result, the portion of the e-commerce markets that use auction is rapidly increasing.

Thanks to auction's inherent negotiation nature, there have been several attempts to extend application domain of auctions to newly arising markets for e-service, including computational services, bandwidth and network resource allocation, Internet advertisements and so on. However, because of idiosyncrasies of e-service markets, applying traditional auctions in these markets creates several problems. In this chapter we identify such idiosyncrasies and discuss their consequences and we introduce a novel auction design that addresses these idiosyncrasies. Consequently, the chapter is organized as follows. In section 2, we survey existing types of auctions and their use in e-markets. Section 3 describes emerging e-service markets and analyzes their properties together with the requirements for designing optimal auctions for those markets. A novel auction satisfying these requirements is introduced in Section 4. The simulation based verifications of this mechanism are given in Section 5. We conclude the chapter with the summary of its content in Section 6.

2. AUCTIONS AND RELATED WORK

Auctions have been widely used from ancient times have been one of the most popular market mechanism used to match supply with demand. They achieve this goal by allowing buyer and seller to agree on a price of a resource following the well defined rules and procedures[4]. There are two types of players in an auction. One is a bidder and the other is an auctioneer.

Bidder reports bid information to the auctioneer in order to buy or obtain the rights for resources traded in auction. The bid information may consist of price alone or price combined with other attributes such as quality of goods, time of their delivery, etc. Usually, the bid information is mapped onto a single value that we will refer to as 'bid value'. Auctioneer is an agent that creates and clears an auction. Hence, auctioneer opens the auction for bidding and then collects the bids, closes the auction and then selects the winners, and finally distributes resources to the winners and collects the payments.

In General Auction, buyers become bidders and the seller is an auctioneer. In Reverse Auction this is the single buyer that becomes an auctioneer while many sellers become bidders.

2.1 Classification of auction types

Based on number of bidding sides, auctions can be classified as single or double ones[3,6,7]. In a single auction, participants can take part only in one side of an auction (e.g., as a buyer). In a double auction, participants are free to take part in both side of an auction. The single auctions can be further subdivided open-cry and sealed bid. For open-cry auctions the common types are English and Dutch auctions, while sealed bid auction are further classified into First Price (FPSB) and Second Price (SPSB) auctions based on pricing. In English, Dutch and FPSB auction, a winner pays his bidding price. On the other hand, in SPSB auction, also known as Vickrey auction, a winner pays the second highest bidding price. Auctions with multiple units of resources traded are classified based on pricing rules differently. In Discriminatory Price Sealed Bid (DPSB) auction, winners pay their bid price. In Uniform Price Sealed Bid (UPSB) auction, all winners pay the same price which is the highest bidding price of losers. Finally, in Generalized Vickrey Auction (GVA), the price of a winner k is computed by deducting the sum of payments of all other bidders in the current resource allocation from the sum of the payments that would be obtained from those other bidders in the optimum allocation where the bidder k removed from the allocation[18]. GVA is an incentive compatible, direct auction in which true valuation bidding is a dominant strategy (i.e., the strategy that, when followed, maximizes each bidder's expected utility).

English auction is widely used to sell various tangible resources such as art, collectables, electronic devices, and so on. The Dutch auction is used for selling traditional perishable resources such as fresh-cut flowers and fish. The sealed bid auction type that includes FPSB, SPSB, DPSB, and UPSB auctions is widely used in procurement that employs reverse auction.

Double auctions allow multiple buyers and sellers to be present concurrently in the market. Thus, double auction must match bid prices on both sides of the market. Double auctions can be divided into Call Market and Continuous Double Auction (CDA) based on their clearing time and bidding methods. In Call Market, bids are collected for a specific time interval from both sellers and buyers in a sealed manner. Then, bids are matched at the auction clearing time. In contrast, in CDA, auction is continuously cleared each time a new bid (which is delivered in an open-outcry manner) is delivered. The Call Market and CDA are common mechanisms for financial markets, such as stock exchange.

All the above auction types use bids that comprise only of price. In contrast, Multiple-Attribute Auction, also called Multidimensional Auction, allows bidders to bid on various attributes beyond the price. Since the auctioneer selects winners based on all bidding attributes, the overall utility of a bid must be computed and vast number of utility functions has been proposed for such computation. Generic procedures for multi-attribute auction in electronic procurement have been described in references 3 and 8.

Table 5-1. Classification of types of auctions

Criterion	**Types**
Number of items per bid	Single; Many (**Combinatorial**)
Bid Attributes	Price; Many (**Multi-attribute**)
Number of winners	One; Many
Bidding method	Open-cry (**English**, **Dutch**); Sealed; Sealed
Pricing	**First**, **Second**; **DPSB**, **UPSB**, **VCG**

Finally, so far we discussed the auctions in which each bidder bids for a single unit of the resource. In Combinatorial Auction, each bidder offers a bid price for a collection of goods (of the bidder's choosing), rather than placing a bid on each item separately. This enables the bidder to express dependencies and complementarities between goods. The auctioneer selects such a set of these combinatorial bids that result in the most revenue without assigning any object to more than one bidder. However, the computational complexity of optimal winner selection that maximizes auctioneer's revenue is very high[9]. The above analysis is summarized in Table 5-1.

2.2 General procedure of an auction

A typical auction execution can be described by the six-step processes shown in Figure 5-1.

1. Bid Collection and Validation collects the bids that could be either firm (i.e., not revisable or cancelable) or changeable under predefined rules. Any set of predefined rules can be used for eligibility of the bid and bidder to participate in relevant auction, including but not limited to, legal restrictions, credit limits on particular bidders, bidders' budget limits, bid expiry, minimum/maximum bid amounts and sizes, etc. Cancellation of bids that do not meet such requirements comprises the validation portion of the procedure.
2. Auction Close occurs once a specific set of circumstances are met, as defined by the auctioneer. These could include time elapsed, receipt of sufficient bids, availability of resource, or any other conditions relevant to the specific application. Once an auction closes, bids are not be changeable.
3. Valuation and Bid Ranking operates after the auction round closes. The bid ranking procedure computes bid value for each bid collected and eligible for participation according to any specific rules. The most basic auctions equate the bid value with the price of the bid. The final result of this procedure is the list of bidders ranked according to the values assigned to their bids.
4. Resource Ranking ranks all resources available for allocation in the given round according to their intrinsic value, which may be identical or different for each resource. A resource can be placed in any arbitrary order with respect to other items from which its intrinsic value cannot be differentiated. Although generally, the ranking reflects differences in intrinsic value of each individual unit of the resources, any relevant factors can be used to assign rank order to the resources based on the

specific application. An example is a seat in the theater, where the distance from the stage and the visibility of the stage impacts the intrinsic value of a seat.

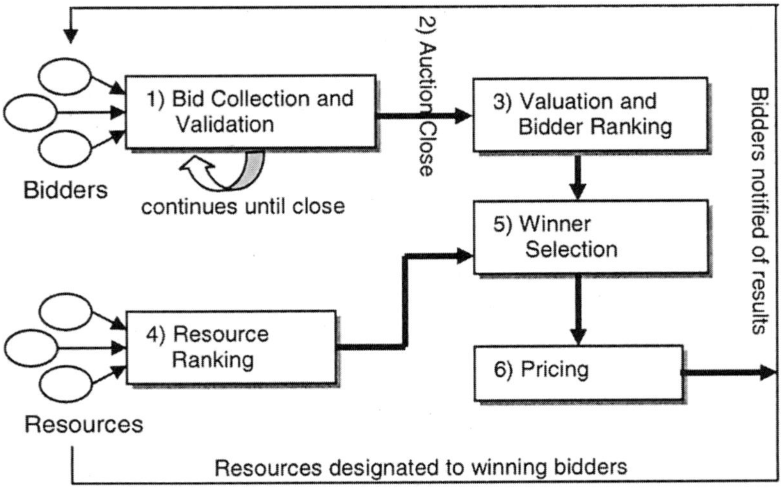

Figure 5-1. General procedures of auction

5. Winner Selection defines the way of allocating or mapping ranked resources offered in the market with specific bidders based on predefined rules. The most general winner selection method is to allocate available resources from the highest bid value bidder up to the number of available resource in decreasing order of bid values.
6. Pricing computes the payments that are charged to the winners for the allocated resources, after the winners are selected in the winner selection procedure. As discussed above, the two main variants of pricing method in the current state of the art are to pay the bid price (also known as first pricing) or the bid price of the next highest bidder (also known as second pricing).

2.3 Auction design requirements

One of the important design requirements for the basic auctions is to maximize seller's revenue. An auction that satisfies this requirement is called the '*optimal auction*'[10]. In designing auction for e-markets, the following additional requirements should be considered[3].

- Incentive compatibility: An auction is incentive compatible if bidding true valuation maximizes the expected utility for the bidder (i.e., it is the dominant strategy). This property makes implementation of agent-based automated negotiations simple.
- Efficiency: In an efficient auction, the resources are allocated to the bidders who value them the most.
- Individual rationality: The expected payoff of each bid made by a bidder is nonnegative.
- Low cost convergence to the agreement: In an electronic auction, the communication overhead of conducting negotiations and arriving at the agreement should be minimized. An auction in which a bidder can communicate with the auctioneer directly (i.e., via the sealed bids) will be called direct. Direct auctions have low communication overhead.

SPSB and UPSB auctions are incentive compatible, efficient and direct, so they are well-suited for various applications in e-markets.

2.4 Auctions in current e-markets

Recently, a vast number of auctions have been conducted over the Internet. Forester Research forecasts that auctions in e-markets will grow from $13 billion in 2002 to $54 billion in 2007[17]. Current e-markets can be classified as B2C (Business to Customer), C2C (Customer to Customer), B2G (Business to Government), and B2B (Business to Business) markets. In B2C and C2C market, English auction is the most popular auction type since it provides simple negotiation structure, and is particularly well suited for negotiation for short time period. Additionally, bidders enjoy placing bids in competition with others, and this entertainment value of the online English auction is an important feature in customer oriented markets[3]. In B2G and B2B markets, sealed bid auction types (i.e., FPSB, SPSB, DPSB, or UPSB auctions) are widely used. Those markets rely on a procurement process that requires 'Reverse Auction'.

Typically, resources traded in those e-markets are physical goods such as collectibles including antiques, stamp, coins, electronic equipments, real estate, used equipments, etc[13].

3. EMERGING E-SERVICE MARKETS

E-service is defined as a modular, nimble, Internet-based service that most often requires various computational resources such as bandwidth, computational cycles or memory to guarantee the Quality of Service (QoS)[15,19,20]. Wide-spread access to the Internet and dominance of service-oriented segment make e-services a fast growing segment of economy. Customer-centric nature of e-service[19], favors auction as a pricing mechanism for e-services markets.

3.1 Markets for application computing services

Recently, the interests in and demands for application computing services (ACS), including on-demand computing, utility computing, grid computing and so on, have been growing rapidly[12,21]. With the development of grid computing infrastructures, the fully implemented application computing services provide a transparent access to a wide variety of large scale geographically distributed computational resources (i.e., CPU, memory, storage, etc.). Hence, markets for ACS are the one of the most important e-markets.

The ACS buyers demand desired computing services, and the ACS providers temporarily allocate the necessary computer hardware and software resources to the buyer's application to produce the desired results[22]. This is radically different from the traditional approach in which the customer buys the hardware and licenses the software for lifetime ownership. Hence, application computing services bring new business model of outsourcing computer operations. For efficient contracting in such a market, the ACS providers need a tool for expressing their pricing polices and mechanisms that can maximize their profits and the computational resource utilization. Various auction based mechanisms, based either on reverse or general auctions, have been proposed for this role[11,12].

In reverse auction, a ACS buyer (i.e., auctioneer) invites sealed (or open-outcry) bids from several ACS providers by advertising his desired application computing service and the required quality of service, such as time constraints, including the deadlines for receiving the results. The buyer selects the bid that offers lowest service cost and satisfies all the constraints. The selected winner provides the computing service and then returns the computing result to the buyer at his bid price.

In general auction, an ACS provider invites bids from many ACS buyers (i.e., bidders) for application computing services. Based on the auction mechanism used and on the current conditions of distributed computational resources, the ACS provider selects the winners and clears the auction.

Auctions used in this area often require that the bid based proportional resource sharing model is followed, in which the amount of computing resources allocated to each bidder is proportional to the value of his bid[11].

3.2 Analysis of emerging e-services markets

Different market structures and properties require different dynamic pricing and negotiation mechanisms for efficient resource allocation and revenue maximization. Hence analysis and characterization of newly created markets is one of the necessary conditions for designing efficient solution.

The e-service markets can be characterized as "recurring markets using short-term contracts", because the resources such as computational and network resources are renewable and their allocations to bidders are made for specific time only[15]. Hence, short-term contract is often used in those markets. Such short-term contracts are recurring, because when the allocated renewable resources become free, the auctioneer needs to offer them to the bidders again. Short-term contracts are recurring also from the bidder's perspective, since each bidder repeatedly enters into them for a specific time interval. This solution provides financial benefits to both sides. Buyers avoid long-term contracts and outsource resources required for service[19,20]. On the other hand, sellers increase resources utilization and increase their revenue via dynamic pricing of such short-term contracts.

In addition to recurring nature, time sensitive perishable property of traded resources (i.e., the fact that unused resources perish) in e-service markets is another important factor. The resources needed for the services cannot be stored in warehouse for future sale, and leaving them unused decreases their utilization[15]. Therefore, the e-service markets need a mechanism optimizing *recurring auction trading perishable resources*.

The previous designs for auction focus on one-time auction for selling physical resources that often can be stored for future sale[2,4,5,6,7,8,10]. Hence, they do not address recurring nature and perishable property of the resources in emerging e-service markets. These two features strongly affect the bidder's bidding behavior and the revenue of the auctioneer. Hence, application of existing basic auctions to e-service markets may result in the following problems.

3.3 Bidder drop problem

Prices bid in an auction reflect willingness of each bidder to pay. This willingness in turn is limited by the bidder's (private) true valuation that is influenced by each bidder's wealth. An uneven wealth distribution can cause starvation of poor bidders in a recurring auction if their true valuations are below winning price. A frequent starvation for the traded resources decreases the bidder's interest in the future auction rounds. In such a situation, if some bidders conclude that it is impossible or unlikely that they will win at the price that they are willing to pay, they will drop from the future auction rounds and find other markets. In a recurring auction, each bidder's drop out of an auction decreases the number of active bidders in the future rounds. Reducing the number of bidders gradually decreases the price competition because the probability of winning increases for the remaining bidders. Hence, their attempts to decrease bidding prices without losing the winning position will be successful causing the overall drop of bid prices. In the long run, when the number of bidders drops close to the number of resources, the revenues of the auctioneer are likely to drop below the acceptable level.

This phenomenon is particularly acute in incentive compatible auctions, such as SPSB auction or UPSB auctions, in which bidder who lost in the previous auction round can easily conclude that his true valuation is not high enough to ever become a winner as all bidders bid their true valuations. Hence, there is no incentive for the loser of the last auction round to participate in the current and future rounds. In fact, continued participations would result in negative expected utility to losers who value their time. Consequently, the losers will immediately drop out of the auction. These dropped bidders decrease the average second highest bid or highest bid of losers. Such decrease results in collapse of auctioneer's revenue. We call this phenomenon '*paradox of incentive compatible mechanism in recurring auction*' because by having the bidders bid their true valuations, this kind of auction motivates low bidding bidders to drop immediately[24]. To the best of our knowledge, the bidder drop problem that is caused by the uneven wealth distribution has been first addressed by our work[15,16,23,24].

3.4 Resource waste problem

In addition to bidder drop problem, the asymmetric balance of negotiation power needs to be considered in auction design. The prices bid in a basic auction are dependent only on the bidder's willingness to pay. This means that intentions of only bidders, but not the auctioneer, are reflected in the auction winning prices. To restore the symmetric balance of negotiating power, the reservation price (RPA) and cancelable (CA) auctions were proposed[10,14]. In RPA, only bids higher than the auctioneer's reservation price are considered during winner selection. On the other hand, in CA, if the resulting revenue of an auction round does not meet the minimum requirement of the auctioneer, the entire auction round is cancelled. By providing reservation price or cancellation option to the auctioneer, the asymmetric negotiation power problem is resolved. However, when the perishable resources are traded, both of these auctions cause resource waste. In RPA, the reservation price restricts the number of winners. Hence, the resources unused because of this restriction are wasted. In CA, the cancellation of an auction round wastes the entire stock of resources that are allocated to this auction round.

4. OPTIMAL RECURRING AUCTION

Based on the additional requirements for designing auctions for e-services markets, we introduce a novel auction called **O**ptimal **R**ecurring **A**uction (ORA). The main idea of this mechanism is based on the demand-supply principle of microeconomics[1].

In Figure 5-2, D1 and D2 denote demand curves for the traded perishable resources while S1 and S2 represent supply levels of the resources. When the overall demand decreases (i.e., the entire demand curve changes from D1 to D2) during a recurring auction, the minimum market clearing price drops from p1 to p2 to maintain the supply at level S1. In such a case, to maintain the minimum market clearing price at p1, an auctioneer must decrease the supply of resources from q1 to q2. Inversely, when the overall demand increases, the auctioneer may increase the supply while keeping the same clearing price.

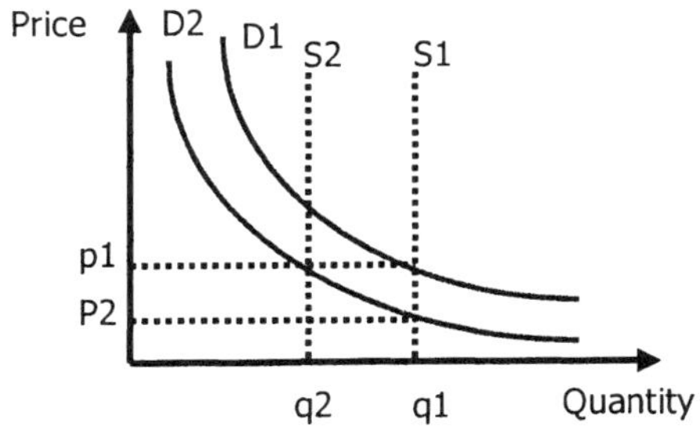

Figure 5-2. Demand and supply principle

When the auctioneer decreases the supply of perishable resources for the given time period, the unsold resources are wasted. Thus, to avoid such waste we propose to assign the "unsold" perishable resources (q1–q2 in Figure 5-2) to the bidders who have high probability of dropping out of the forthcoming auction rounds. Such an assignment prevents bidders from dropping out of auction thereby keeping enough bidders in the recurring auction to maintain the competition for resources strong. Simultaneously, using "unsold" perishable resources for bidder drop control resolves the resource waste and increases the number of winners.

To implement this idea, we introduced two types of ORA mechanisms. The first one is the Participation Incentive Optimal Recurring Auction (PI-ORA) that pursues incentive compatible mechanism, and the second one is the Discriminatory Price Optimal Recurring Auction (DP-ORA) that is based on a non-incentive compatible mechanism. From the pricing point of view, PI-ORA uses a variation of a uniform pricing scheme while DP-ORA uses a discriminatory pricing scheme. To describe the proposed auctions, we first define here the basic notions of bidders, bidding prices, and resources.

Players: There are $n+1$ players, denoted by $i=0,...,n$, including n bidders, $i=1,...,n$, and an auctioneer $i=0$. An auctioneer and each bidder enter the bidding price b_0 and $b_1, b_2, ..., b_n$, respectively, in each auction round. We also assume that each bidder is risk neutral and has private true valuation t_i for traded resources.

Resources: There are R units of perishable resources that are assigned for a specific time period in each auction round. We assume that each bidder requires one unit of a resource for the desired quality of e-service. Hence, the maximum number of possible winners in each auction round is R.

4.1 Classification of Bidders in ORA

The first step of the winner selection strategy in ORA is to define bidder's class based on each bidder's bidding price b_i, where $i=1,...,n$ and auctioneer's bid price (i.e., reservation price) b_0. The auctioneer classifies the bidders into the Definitely Winner (DW), Possible Winner (PW), and Definitely Loser (DL) classes using the following conditions:

$$\begin{array}{lll} i \in DW & \text{if } b_i \geq b_0 \ \& \ r_i > n-R, & i=1,2,...,n, \\ i \in DL & \text{if } b_i \leq 0, \ i=1,2,...,n, & \\ i \in PW & otherwise, & \end{array} \qquad (1)$$

where r_i denotes the rank of bidder i in the increasing order of bidding prices of all bidders. The numbers of bidders in the DW, PW and DL classes are denoted as N_{dw}, N_{pw} and N_{dl}, respectively. Figure 5-3 shows the bidder's classes in ORA and compares them with the classes in the traditional auctions where Traditional Losers (TL) and Traditional Winner (TW) classes are defined. WPPW represents the Winning Portion of the PW class, and the number of winners in the PW class is denoted by N_{wppw}. Hence, $N_{wppw} = R - N_{dw}$.

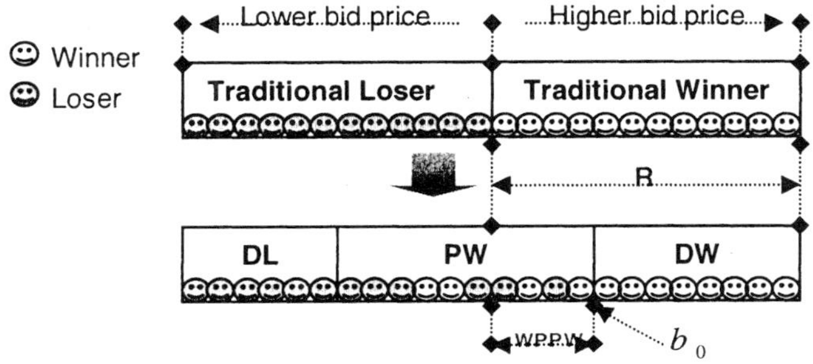

Figure 5-3. Classification of bidders in ORA

In each auction round, the DW class bidders become winners without any additional considerations, since they bid higher than the bid price of the auctioneer and there are enough resources to assign one to all of them. The DL class consists of bidders who already dropped out of the auction. Hence the DL class bidders become losers in each auction round. The bidders who are in the PW class can be winners or losers depending on the bidder drop control algorithm applied, described below (see Sections 4.2.1 and 4.3.1).

The auctioneer's bidding price b_0 in the ORA mechanisms plays the same role as the reservation price does in the Reservation Price Auction. Hence, ORA maintains symmetry of the negotiating power from lack of which the traditional auctions suffer.

4.2 Participation Incentive Optimal Recurring Auction

In PI-ORA, we introduced the following participation incentive bidder drop control algorithm to efficiently select winners in PW class.

4.2.1 Participation Incentive Bidder Drop Control

Enough bidders of PW class must participate in future auction rounds to maintain price competition in the recurring auction. To encourage such participation, the Participation Incentive Bidder Drop Control (PI-BDC) algorithm rewards bidder's participation in each auction round using the following winning score S_i^k for each bidder $i \in PW$:

$$S_i^k = \frac{b_i^k}{\alpha} \cdot B_i - W_i \quad , \tag{2}$$

where B_i and W_i denote the cumulative weighted number of times that bidder i participated in and won, respectively, in auction rounds up to and including the current one. The outcome of the current auction round is yet unknown and the credit for participation is at most 1. B_i is defined as $B_i = \frac{1}{b_i} \sum_{j=1}^{m} \min(b_{i,j}, b_{i,m})$, where m represents the current auction round and $b_{i,j}$ denotes the bid price of bidder i in auction round j (this price is zero in rounds that the bidder skips). This definition encourages the bidders to bid the same price in each auction round, as this is the only way in which a bidder can receive a full credit of 1 for participation in an auction round.

The term $(b_i^k / \alpha) \cdot B_i$ denotes expected number of wins based on the bidding price and the participation in the past rounds. Thus, the winning score S_i^k of a bidder i in class PW represents the difference between the expected and real number of wins. Hence, the PI-BDC algorithm is based on the insight that higher the winning score of a bidder is, higher the probability of him dropping out of the future rounds is because more below his expectations his winning are. For this reason, the PI-BDC algorithm ranks bidders of PW class in the decreasing order of their winning scores and up to N_{wppw} highest ranked bidders are selected as winners of the current auction round. α in equation (2) is a coefficient that controls the expected number of wins (i.e., win frequency). The optimal value of α depends on seller's strategy and true valuation distributions of the bidders. We set the value of α in such a way that the average value of winning score of all bidders is zero. Since in each auction round all bidders in PW class increase their winning scores cumulatively by $\sum_{j \in PW} b_j^k / \alpha$ (assuming that each bidder uses the same bid as in the previous round) and at the same time their winning scores decrease cumulatively by $R - N_{dw}$ wins, the balancing value is $\alpha = \sum_{j \in PW} b_j^k / (R - N_{dw})$. With this value, the win frequency of each bidder $i \in PW$ with bid price b_i is defined as follows:

$$w_i = \frac{b_i^k \cdot (R - N_{dw})}{\sum_{j \in PW} b_j^k} \tag{3}$$

To differentiate between DW and PW classes, win frequency w_i should be less than 1 for all bidders in PW class, which restricts the feasible values of k and the feasible size of PW class.

As shown in Figure 5-4, in traditional auctions, the win probability of a bidder outside the Traditional Winner class is zero. Hence, there is no incentive for bidders whose true valuations are in the range of bids of member of the Traditional Loser class to participate in the future auction round in incentive compatible auctions. However, in PI-ORA, the win probabilities of bidders in the PW class, including part of the Traditional Loser class, are higher than zero. For this reason, there is an incentive to participate for all bidders in the PW class regardless of their true valuations.

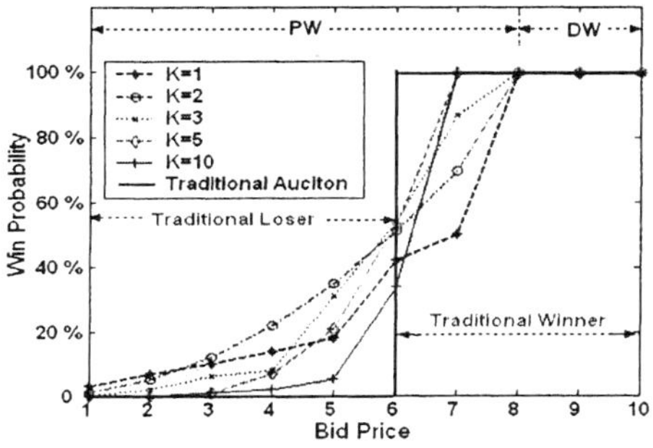

Figure 5-4. Win frequency distribution in PI-ORA

4.2.2 Pricing rules and optimal reservation price

In PI-ORA, winners in the DW and PW classes pay the price $p(b_i) = \rho \cdot \min(b_i, b_0)$, where ρ denotes payment coefficient. The value of the payment coefficient ρ that leads to incentive compatible mechanism and revenue maximization is restricted by the following condition:

$$\rho \leq \frac{k}{k + 1 + t^k_{\max PW} / s} \tag{4}$$

where *maxPW* is the index of the highest bidder in PW class, $s = \sum_{j \neq \max PW, j \in PW} b_j^k$ and, k is a constant used in Eq. (2). Hence, based on bidder's bidding price distribution, the auctioneer selects the optimal payment coefficient ρ, the auctioneer's reservation price b_0 and the constant k that satisfy the payment coefficient condition (4), as well as maximize the revenue. Since $\rho < k/(k+1)$, PI-ORA guarantees that each winner pays less than his bidding price.

4.2.3 Optimal strategies for bidders

The bidder's optimal strategy involve deciding to participate or not in the auction and in participation case, deciding the bidding price. In the reference 24, we proved that under proper selection of parameters k, b_0 and ρ, bidding each bidder's true valuation maximizes his utility in both PW and DW classes. Thus, PI-ORA is an incentive compatible auction. Likewise, participation incentive bidder drop control algorithm makes participation in as many as possible auction rounds a strategy that maximizes the expected utility. In conclusion, the bidder's optimal strategy in PI-ORA is to bid his true valuation (making the mechanism incentive compatible) and to participate in as many as possible auction rounds (see [24]).

4.3 Discriminatory Price Optimal Recurring Auction

In DP-ORA, we introduced the following Valuable Last Loser First Bidder Drop Control algorithm to select winners in PW class efficiently.

4.3.1 Valuable Last Loser First Bidder Drop Control

The purpose of selecting winners in the PW class is to encourage them to stay in the auction. Hence, those winners should include those bidders in the PW class who are considering dropping out of the auction. This insight is the basis for the Valuable Last Loser First Bidder Drop Control (VLLF-BDC) algorithm. The algorithm consists of two phases. In the first one, bidders who lost in the last auction round but bid in the current round the price higher than in the previous one are marked as potential winners. The marked bidders are ranked according to their bidding prices and up to N_{wppw} highest ranked marked bidders are selected as winners of the current auction round. If the number of the marked bidders is smaller than N_{wppw}, the remaining resources are allocated in the second phase of the algorithm in the decreasing order of their bidding prices.

The winner selection in the first phase is dictated by the bid price and winning record of the previous auction round, so there could be some loss of fairness. To compensate for it, in the second phase, the highest bidding unmarked bidders in the PW class are selected as winners of the remaining resources. By marking only those last losers who bid higher in the current round than in the previous one, the algorithm prevents bidders with low bidding patterns from becoming winners.

5. ORA VERIFICATION VIA SIMULATION

5.1 Simulation Experiments with PI-ORA

In simulations of PI-ORA, we compare the following four different auctions those are all incentive compatible mechanisms. Each one is executed 2000 times recurrently.

- *UPSB auction*: Here, we use the basic uniform price sealed bid auction that has no bidder drop control, so bidders are allowed to drop out of auction at any time.
- *UPSB-NBD auction*: This case uses the basic UPSB auction but with bidders never dropping from the auction, regardless of their results.
- *PI-ORA*: As described above, PI-ORA uses PI-BDC algorithm in winner selection of PW class.
- *PI-ORA-NBD*: Here, we use the PI-ORA mechanism with no bidder dropping out of auction during recurring auction, regardless of possible starvation.

The results of simulating UPSB-NBD and PI-ORA-NBD are used only to obtain upper bounds on the auctioneer's revenue since assuming no bidder drop is unrealistic. The wealth of each bidder limits her willingness to pay defined by the true valuation of a unit of resource. For this reason, we equate wealth distribution with a distribution of bidder true valuations. In the simulations, we consider three types of those distributions, all with the mean of 5: (1) the exponential distribution, (2) the uniform distribution over [0, 10] range, and (3) the Gaussian distribution. Once the true valuations are allocated to bidders, they do not change during recurring auction.

There are 40 bidders in our simulations and 20 units of perishable resources are available for allocation. Hence, there are 20 winners in each auction round. According to the bidder's dominant strategy and risk neutral assumption, each bidder bids his true valuation in each auction round in order to maximize his expected utility. Additionally, bidders participate in auction continuously until they drop out of the auction. Once out of the auction, the bidder never returns to it.

We define Tolerance of Consecutive Loss, abbreviated as TCL, to simulate bidders' drop out of the auction. The bidder's TCL denotes the maximum number of consecutive losses that a bidder can tolerate before dropping out of an auction. TCL of each bidder is uniformly distributed over the range of [2, 10]. If consecutive losses of a bidder exceed his TCL, then the bidder drops out of the auction and never returns to it. The TCL is set to the number larger than the number of auction round simulated for the UPSB-NBD and PI-ORA-NBD cases.

Our simulations collect data on the auctioneer's revenue and mechanism efficiency and stability in response to bidder drops. We use the average payment of winners in each auction round as a measure of auctioneer's revenue. The revenue comparison between original auction and no bidder drop assumption case is used only to measure the mechanism stability. We also measure the total number of wins of each bidder to gauge the efficiency.

As shown in Figure 5-5, the traditional UPSB auction cannot maintain the auctioneer's desired revenue in a recurring auction because the losers of each auction round have no incentive to participate in future rounds so they drop out of the auction. This is the result of phenomena that we termed the 'paradox of an incentive compatible mechanism in a recurring auction'. Since bidders reveal their true valuations in each bid, bidders learn their ability to win and those who cannot win drop out the auction. The decreased price competition for the remaining winners results in a plunge of the auction clearing price (i.e., highest price of losers), which quickly becomes zero). After 10 auction rounds (that is also the upper bound on the TCL value in our simulations), the auction clearing price collapses to 0, since every loser dropped out of the auction. Therefore, in the basic UPSB auction, the bidder drop problem is the sole cause of the seller's revenue collapse.

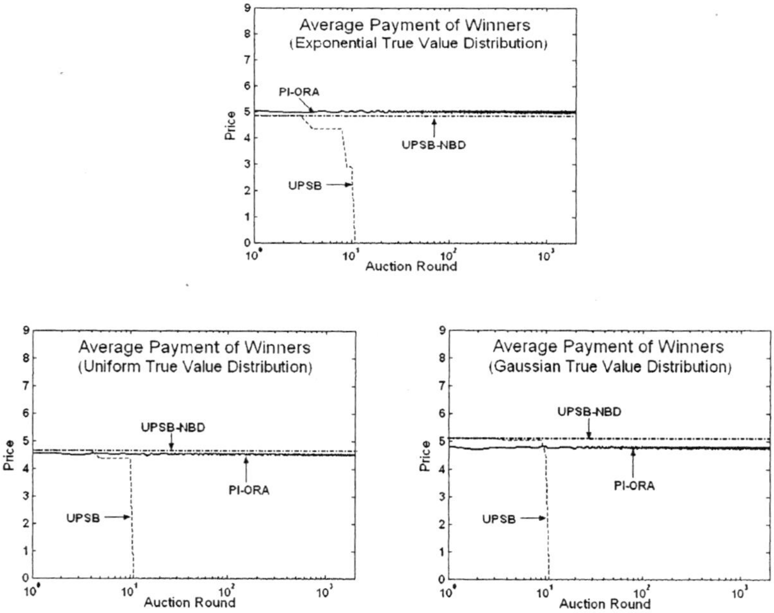

Figure 5-5. Average payment of winners in PI-ORA

An efficient bidder drop control based on PI-BDC algorithm of the PI-ORA supports auction participation of bidders in the PW class and therefore maintains the price competition between bidders in the DW and PW classes permanently. Additionally, by optimally selecting the payment coefficient ρ, the optimal auctioneer's bidding price b_0, and the constant k from Eq. (2), the auctioneer can stabilize and maximize the revenue regardless of the bidder true valuation distribution. The resource waste problem never arises, because the entire stock of available perishable resources is sold in each auction round.

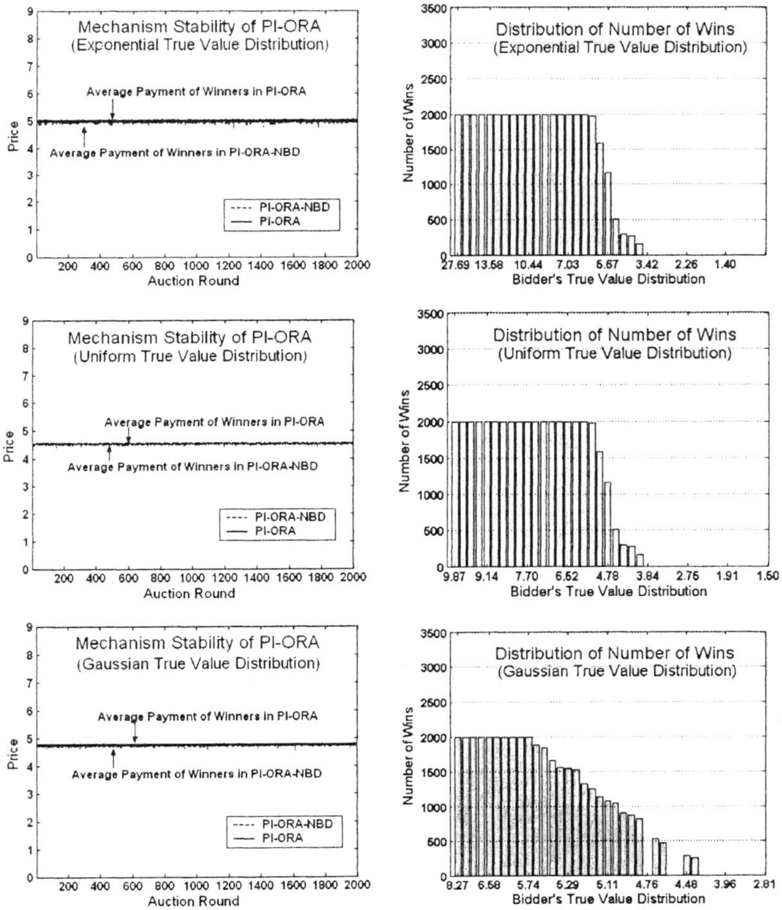

(a) Stability (b) Efficiency

Figure 5-6. Mechanism stability and efficiency

The average payment of winners in PI-ORA and PI-ORA-NBD in each auction round are almost the same, as shown in Figure 5-6 (a) for various true valuation distributions. This indicates that the efficient bidder drop control algorithm makes the PI-ORA stable.

The simulation results also show that PI-ORA is efficient. As shown in Figure 5-6 (b), it distributes the total number of available perishable resources proportionally to each bidder's true valuation. Thus, the bidder who has the higher true valuation and, thus, higher actual payment for the perishable resource, wins more often than the one with the lower true valuation and lower actual payment (under the same participation level). The win distributions of Figure 5-6 (b) also show that the bidders whose bidding prices (i.e., true valuations) are too low are eliminated from the auction automatically by exceeding the number of consecutive losses defined by their TCL. Hence, even though some resources are allocated to the bidders in PW class, the truly low bidders do not impact the revenue of PI-ORA.

5.2 Simulation Experiments with DP-ORA

In simulation of DP-ORA mechanism, we compare the following five auctions based on 2000 round recurrent executions:

- *DPSB auction*: In this case we simulate basic discriminatory price sealed bid auction that has no bidder drop control. Hence, bidders drop out of the recurring auction as a result of starvation for resource allocation.
- *DPSB-NBD*: This case represents an idealized DPSB auction in which bidders never drop during the recurring auction even if they suffer constant consecutive losses.
- *Reservation Price Auction (RPA)*: This is the case of the DPSB auction with reservation price. Hence only the bidders who bid price higher than reservation price can be winners.
- *Cancelable Auction (CA)*: This is another variant of the DPSB auction in which the auctioneer cancels an auction round when the projected revenue does not meet his expectation.
- *DP-ORA*: This case represents DP-ORA with the VLLF-BDC algorithm.

There are 100 bidders in our simulations. The sealed bidding assumption makes each bidder's bidding behavior independent of others. Hence, in a recurring auction, the bidding behavior is influenced only by the results of the previous auction rounds, i.e., the win/loss decision informed to each bidder. Based on the assumption of risk neutral bidders, each bidder will attempt to maximize its expected profit. All the above considerations motivated us to assume the following bidding behavior. If a bidder lost in the last auction round, she increases her bidding price by a factor of $\alpha > 1$ to improve her win probability in the current round. The increase of bidding price is limited by the true valuation. If a bidder won in the last auction round, she, with equal probability of 0.5, either decreases the bidding price by a factor of β or maintains it unchanged. The decrease attempts to maximize the expected profit factor in each bidder's utility. α and β are set in the simulations to 1.2 and 0.8, respectively. The minimum bidding price of each bidder is 0.1. If a bidder drops out of an auction, his bidding price is set to 0. There are 50 units of perishable resources available for allocation in each auction round. Hence, the maximum number of winners in each auction round is 50. If the resulting revenue of an auction round is lower than 250, the auction round is cancelled in CA. All other aspects of simulation scenarios, such as distributions of true valuation or TCL are same as in PI-ORA scenarios. Hence, we set the reservation price for RPA as 5.0.

The simulations of DP-ORA collect data on the auctioneer revenue and resource allocation fairness. The auctioneer's revenue is proportional to the average bidding price of winners in each auction round, so we use the latter as a measure of the former. We also measure the number of wins for each bidder in 2000 rounds of the recurring auction. The resulting distribution is a metric of fairness, because higher bidding bidders should be more frequent winners than the lower bidding ones.

Fairness of DPSB-NBD is optimal, because a bidder with the bid higher than a winner is also a winner. Additionally, by the no bidder drop assumption, DPSB-NBD never looses a bidder with high willingness to pay and low TCL. This means that DPSB-NBD prevents the loss of fairness that may result from the low TCL. Thus, we can measure the loss of fairness of DPSB, RPA, CA and DP-ORA by their degree of deviation from the fairness of DPSB-NBD.

As shown in Figure 5-7, under, various wealth distributions (i.e., true valuation distributions), DPSB cannot maintain the auctioneer's desired revenue. The inevitable bidders' drops decrease the price competition between bidders who remain in the auction. Accordingly, the remaining bidders try to decrease their bidding price in the forthcoming auction rounds to maximize their expected profit. In the long run, the revenue of each auction round plunges to a very low level (i.e., below 1.0), compared to the auctioneer's desired minimum cost (here 5.0). Therefore, in DPSB, an inevitable bidder drop problem is the dominating factor that decreases the auctioneer's revenue, because there are no wasted perishable resources.

In RPA, the revenue of auctioneer is mainly decreased by the resource waste problem. The bidder drop effect is small in this case, because the reservation price prevents the winners from decreasing their bidding price to the very low level. However, RPA does not avoid the resource waste problem. 28.6%, 28.0% and 34.2% of resources are wasted during 2000 recurrent auction rounds in exponential, uniform and Gaussian distributions of true valuation, respectively. As a result, the auctioneer cannot achieve her desired revenue in a recurring auction of this type.

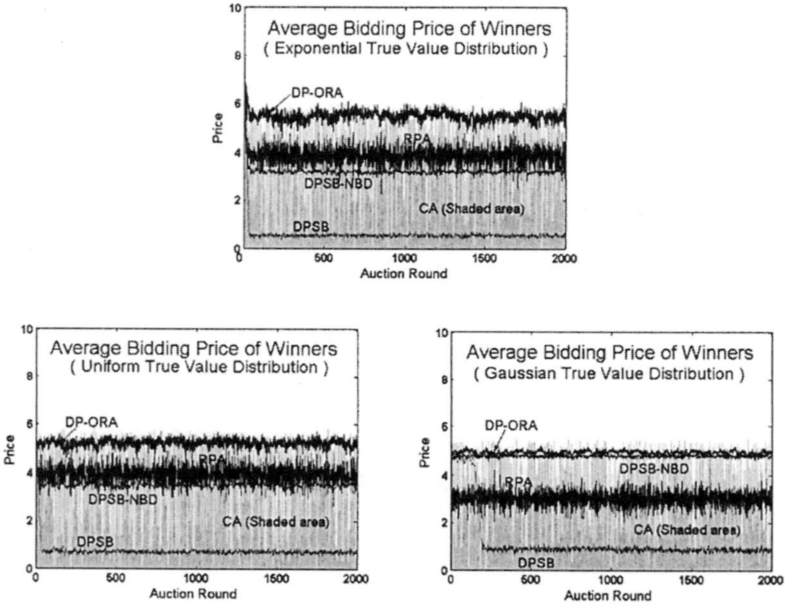

Figure 5-7. Average bidding price of winners in DP-ORA

CA suffers from the same problem as RPA. By canceling auction, CA can prevent remaining bidders from decreasing their bidding price to the very low levels. However, in cancelled auction round, the entire 50 units of perishable resources that are assigned to the auction round are wasted. 23.5%, 32.9% and 34.8% of resources are wasted during 2000 recurrent auction round in exponential, uniform and Gaussian distribution of true valuation, respectively. For this reason, the resources wasted in the cancelled auction rounds prevent the auctioneer from achieving the desired revenue. Figure 5-8 shows amount of the resource waste in exponential true valuation distribution in each auction round of RPA and CA.

DP-ORA is able to maintain price competition permanently in a recurring auction thanks to the VLLF-BDC algorithm. Moreover, in DP-ORA, the resource waste never arises, because the entire stock of perishable resources is sold in each auction round. Therefore, the auctioneer can preserve nearly optimal level of the revenue. Additionally, the bidders whose bid prices are too low are eliminated from the auction automatically based on their TCL. Hence, even though VLLF-BDC algorithm allocates resources to the PW class whose members bid lower than member of the DW class, the low true valuation bidders cannot impact auctioneer's revenue in DP-ORA.

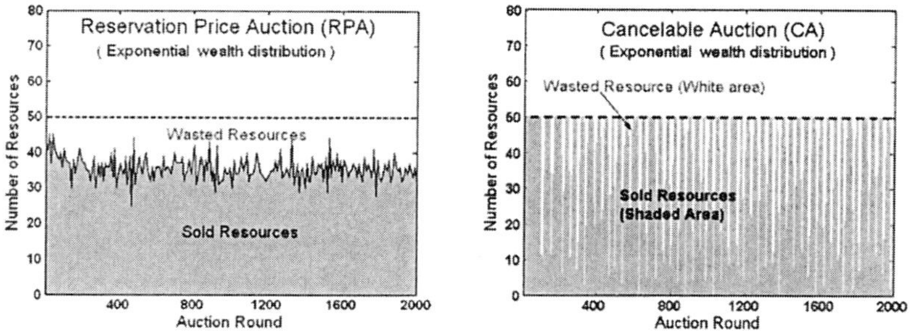

Figure 5-8. Resource waste in RPA and CA

Remarkably, the loss of fairness in DP-ORA is lower than the one observed in DPSB, RPA and CA under all simulated wealth distributions of bidders. This phenomenon results from the fact that DPSB, RPA and CA cannot prevent the loss of fairness caused by high true valuation bidders dropping out of an auction as a result of exceeding their TCLs. In other words, DPSB, RPA and CA cannot prevent a bidder who is willing to pay high prices but has low TCL from dropping out of an auction because he may exceeds his TCL at some auction round. In each auction round, DPSB, RPA and CA have highest possible fairness, because their winners are selected by the current bidding price only. Yet, remarkably, DP-ORA has lower loss of fairness over the entire recurring auction because loss of fairness that results from TCL is the dominating factor in the long run. The specific results measuring the loss of fairness under various bidder wealth distributions are provided in Table 5-2.

Table 5-2. Loss of fairness

Auctions	Exponential	Uniform	Gaussian
DPSB	34.6 %	23.9 %	29.4 %
CA	33.5 %	32.9 %	33.4 %
RPA	30.0 %	28.9 %	41.8 %
DP-ORA	9.4 %	6.0 %	11.9 %

We also simulated the more general case of an auction in which a bidder who dropped out can return when the winning price becomes sufficiently low. For this case, the simulation results show that the revenue of the auctioneer settles somewhere between the revenues of DPSB and DPSB-NBD because those are the border cases of the general one. The revenue of the DPSB case sets the lower bound for the revenues in the general case because there are no bidders returning during the recurring auction. The revenue of DPSB-NBD sets the upper bound because all bidders return immediately to the recurring auction in that case.

In summary, DP-ORA can achieve the increased revenue and the decreased loss of fairness in the recurring auction for perishable resources by resolving the bidder drop problem and the resource waste problem.

6. SUMMARY OF THE CHAPTER

As the current e-market paradigm evolves towards e-service oriented markets, auctions used in such e-services markets are recurring and trade perishable resources. During such auctions, bidders can drop out of an auction at any time. Since an auction relies on a competition based dynamic pricing mechanism, keeping bidders interested in participating in the auction stabilizes the market by preventing a collapse of the price competition. Hence, the bidder drop problem is one of the most important aspects of the designing winner selection strategies for the recurring auction. The resource waste is another problem that needs to be considered in such context.

In this chapter, we introduced two optimal recurring auctions for e-services markets: the Participation Incentive Optima Recurring Auction (PI-ORA) that is incentive compatible, and the Discriminatory Price Optimal Recurring Auction (DP-ORA) that is not. In PI-ORA, each bidder's participation is rewarded by increase in his win frequency. In DP-ORA, the auctioneer allocates a resource to a bidder before he drops out of the auction. Such bidders are identified on the basis of their bid prices and history of wins in the recurring auction. Therefore, the ORA mechanisms using bidder drop control algorithms encourage participation of bidders in the recurring auction and therefore stabilize the e-service markets using short-term contracts and increase auctioneer's revenue in such markets.

REFERENCES

1. R. H. Frank and B.S. Bernanke, "Principle of Economics: 2nd edition", McGraw Hill, New York, 2004.

2. V. Krishna, Auction Theory, Academic Press, San Diego, 2002
3. M. Bichler, "The Future of e-Markets: Multidimensional Market Mechanism", Cambridge University Press, 2001.
4. R. McAfee and P.J. McMillan, "Auction and Bidding", Journal of Economic Literature, 25:699 – 738, 1997.
5. W. Vickrey, "Counter speculation, Auction, and Competitive Sealed Tenders", Journal of Finance, 16(1), March 1961.
6. Agorics, Inc., "Going, Going, Gone! A Survey of Auction Types", available at http://www.agorics.com/Library/auctions.html
7. M.P. Wellman, W.E. Walsh and P.R.Wurman, "Auction Protocols for Decentralized Scheduling", Game and Economic Behavior, (35), 271-303, 2001.
8. M. Bichler, M. Kaukal, and A. Segev, "Multi-attribute auctions for electronic procurement", Proc. 1st IBM IAC Workshop on Internet based Negotiation Technologies, Yorktown Heights, NY 1999.
9. T. Sandholm, "Approaches to winner determination in combinatorial auctions", Decision Support System, 28 (1):165 - 176.
10. J.G. Riely and W.F. Samuelson, "Optimal Auction", The American Economic Review, 71(3):381 - 392, June 1981.
11. B. Chun and D. Cullar, "Market based proportional resource sharing for cluster", Technical Report, University of California, Berkeley, September 1999.
12. R. Buyya, D. Abramson, and J. Giddy, "A Case for Economy Grid Architecture for Service-Oriented Grid Computing", Proc. 15th International Parallel & Distributed Processing Symposium, 2001.
13. D. L. Reiley, "Auctions on the Internet: What's Being Auctioned, and How?", Journal of Industrial Economics, 48(3): 227-252.
14. A. Fiat, A.V Goldberg, J.D. Hartline , and A.R. Karlin, "Competitive Generalized Auction", Proc. 34th Annual ACM symposium on Theory of Computing, 2002.
15. J. S. Lee, and B. K. Szymanski, "A Novel Auction Mechanism for Selling Time Sensitive E-Services", Proc. 7th International IEEE Conference on E-Commerce Technology 2005 (CEC'05), Munich, Germany, 2005.
16. J. S. Lee, and B. K. Szymanski, "Stabilizing Market via A Novel Auction based Pricing Mechanism for Short-Term Contracts for Network Services", Proc. 9th IFIP/IEEE International Symposium on Integrated Network Management (IM2005), Nice, France, 2005.
17. C.A. Johnson, "Commentary: The boom in online auctions", article by forester research, 2002, available at http://news.com.com/2009-1069-962530.html
18. H. Varian, "Economic Mechanism Design for Computerized Agents", Proc. Usenix Workshop on Electronic Commerce, New York, 1995.
19. R.T. Rust and P.K. Kannan, "E-Service: A New Paradigm for Business in the Electronic Environment", Communication of the ACM, Vol. 46, No. 6, 2003.
20. A. Tiwana and B. Ramesh, "e-Service: Problems, Opportunities, and Digital Platforms", in proceeding of the 34th Hawaii International Conference on System Science, 2001.
21. M.A. Rappa, "The utility business model and the future of computing services", IBM System Journal, Vol. 43, No. 1, 2004.
22. L.J. Zhang, H. Li and H. Lam, "Service Computing: Grid Applications for Today", IEEE IT Pro, July-August 2004, pp 5-7.

23. J. S. Lee and B. K. Szymanski, "An Analysis and Simulation of a Novel Auction-Based Pricing Mechanism for Network Services", Technical Report TR-05-02, Department of Computer Science, Rensselaer Polytechnic Institute, Jan. 2005.
24. J. S. Lee and B. K. Szymanski, "Network Service Resource Allocation via Participation Incentive Auction for Non-Cooperative Customers", submitted to *JSAC*, May 2005.

Chapter 6

A FRAMEWORK FOR SERVICE ENTERPRISE INTEGRATION: A CASE STUDY

Mark E. Dausch
GE Global Research Center, One Research Circle, Niskayuna, NY 12309

Abstract: This paper presents a case study on a company that encountered numerous challenges resulting from mergers and acquisitions of other companies as well as a new strategy to promote organic growth. To address some of these challenges, a new process, systems, and applications were developed to enable the company to shift from providing primarily products to their customers to products and services. This new process together with the resources captures information on what services are performed, why the services are performed, and how the services are performed; thus facilitating this new business model. The results from this work position the company with a sustainable competitive advantage in the global marketplace.

Key words: service enterprise integration; service model; ontology; ontological framework; data heterogeneity.

1. INTRODUCTION

Today companies have many opportunities to apply information technology to gain a competitive advantage over their customers. Much research over the last twenty years has been published on this topic. However, gaining competitive advantage may not be enough to remain competitive. With the ubiquity of the Internet, even small businesses with small IT budgets can leverage the Internet to narrow the competitive advantage that large companies with large IT budgets may have. IT alone will not prevent the competition from developing better strategies.

More recently researchers in the area of strategic information systems have redirected their work towards applying IT to gain a sustained competitive advantage. This shift focuses less on the tools to gain a competitive advantage to more on the resources and the IT capabilities within the organization to sustain the competitive advantage.[1]

As more companies are playing in the global market, the resources and IT capabilities are even more challenged and have an ever-increasing role for the company. In such companies the information system resources are typically heterogeneously distributed which also affects the resource usage, the interchange of data and information, and the interoperability amongst the various systems to enable business processes.

New approaches are dictated to promote better usage of the information systems, to address the heterogeneity of the data and information, and to facilitate the interoperability amongst the various systems to better support the business processes. Such new approaches together with IT investments to create unique resources and with the skills to manage the resources are necessary for a company to gain a sustained competitive advantage.

This work investigates a rather unique situation that addresses both issues described above, the information technology to gain a competitive advantage over their customers and the resources and IT capabilities to gain a sustained competitive advantage. This unique situation was born out of the formation of a new company from the mergers and acquisitions of several global companies.

One can image the huge number of issues when merging or acquiring other companies. The newly formed company needs to go through an assimilation phase because typically the two or more companies have different cultures, organizational structures, business processes and information systems, have competing products, and have duplicate support staff. Much of this work occurred during this first phase primarily for the company's survival.

The objectives for this work include supporting the company's new strategic direction for improving the company's competitiveness in a global market and addressing the problems associated with heterogeneous data and information, lack of appropriate data and information and outdated information systems that could not support the new initiatives.

This paper is presented as a case study. The first section provides a business profile that describes the background and history of the company, the market, the products and services, and the industries served. This sets the context for the reader. The next two sections contain a description of the problem and propose a solution to the problem. The main section discusses the approach, which makes-up a substantial portion of this paper. In the approach we provide a detailed discussion on a framework for facilitating the service enterprise integration, which is also the primary contribution from this work. The final two sections capture the results and a summary. Even though the solution was developed for a unique business situation, the approach may be generalized to solve similar problems or those of less magnitude.

2. BUSINESS PROFILE

The case study focuses on a global supplier of water, wastewater, and process system solutions. This supplier known as Water & Process Technologies is part of a conglomeration of businesses within GE Infrastructure. The business, which was founded in 1925, employs about 5500 employees worldwide with annual sales of about $1.4 billion US dollars. The headquarters is located in Trevose, PA with global offices in Heverlee, Belgium; San Pablo, Brazil; and Shanghai, China.

The company primarily provides chemicals, chemical treatments and services, and water treatment equipment while servicing many industries including beverage, chemical processing, commercial, food, general industrial, hydrocarbon processing, life sciences, medical dialysis, microelectronics, mining, pharmaceutical, power, primary metals, residential, and transportation.

Some of the major factors contributing to the issues addressed by this case study can be traced back thru the company's history. In 1925, William H. and L. Drew Betz, a father and son partnership, formed the original company in Philadelphia with three pioneering formulations for boiler feed water purification. In 1969, D. Dean Spatz founded Osmonics in Minneapolis, MN with membrane products for water purification and separation. This company will later be acquired with several other companies. In 1978, Robert Glegg founded Glegg Water Conditioning in Guelph, Ontario, Canada to manufacture equipment in the electrodeionization, filtration, membrane, and other technology areas.

In 1996 the major acquisitions began with the formation of BetzDearborn from two companies, Betz and Dearborn. This acquisition made a significant impact on Betz's market share and the number of chemical product offerings. Beginning in 1999, GE played the key role in forming the company as it is today. GE first formed GE Water by acquiring Glegg Water Conditioning, a leader in providing innovative water solutions to industrial companies worldwide. In 2002, GE acquired BetzDearborn forming GE Betz. A year later GE acquired Osmonics, Inc., which was one of the world's largest integrated manufacturers of water treatment systems and equipment for industrial, commercial, and institutional markets; thus, forming GE Osmonics.

Then in 2004, GE formed a new division within GE Infrastructure named Water & Process Technologies by merging GE Betz, GE Osmonics, and GE Water. Finally in 2005 GE Infrastructure Water & Process Technologies purchased Ionics to add to the portfolio products and services for water desalination, water recycling, and mobile water services.

The acquisitions and integrations resulted in a company characterized by different business cultures, different processes, and different business practices that would prove challenging even to the most experienced and talented managers.

The new company grew rapidly in the last five years through acquisitions and mergers. In order to sustain growth and be the market leader, the business needed to grow organically as well. However, the competitors were selling many chemical products and equipment at the same or lower prices. Traditionally the company was selling products at a premium price and providing services such as monitoring, testing, and treatment for little or no charge. The customers faced with their own market pressures had a difficult time understanding the value of the services and justifying the purchase of higher cost products. The market was slowly eroding away due to the lower cost products from the competition. The current business had to change in order for the company to survive in the long term.

Some of the other businesses within the parent company successfully grew their business by shifting from product manufacturer to a product and service provider. Companies such as GE Energy and GE Aviation now generate a significant portion of their revenues from service contracts. GE Infrastructure Water & Process Technologies followed the example of these other businesses by setting a new strategy for the company. Two key aspects of the new strategy were to grow the service sector of the business and offer service through long-term service contracts, similar to the successful business models of GE Energy and GE Aviation.

In order to sell long-term service contracts to customers who were accustomed to receiving services for little or no charge proved to be a challenging part in migrating to this new business model. The business realized that the products and services were critical to their customers' processes but somehow had to provide evidence for their customers.

Over half of the company's employees are field representatives selling products and providing services. Management recognized that the employees' knowledge about the customers, the customers' processes and problems, and treating such problems is one of the core competencies of the company. Capitalizing on these knowledge assets is critical as an enabler to the new service paradigm.

3. PROBLEM STATEMENT

The current business was built up of numerous acquisitions over the past five years. Each acquisition had its own culture, processes, and business practices. Management quickly realized that there was insufficient information to help them understand what products were used where and why. There was a lack of detailed understanding on what services are performed, why the services are performed, and how the services are performed. Without such information, the business would struggle with how to charge for services, what are the recognized and measurable benefits the services provide the customers, and what would the customers be willing to pay for such services.

The business had other problems as well. There was little organic growth due to the fact that their chemical products could be purchased from other suppliers for the same price or in many cases less. The customers did not seem to be willing to pay a premium for chemical products even though the field representatives provided services such as testing, monitoring, and treatment and possess the knowledge on how to apply chemical products to improve the customers' processes and protect the customers' assets.

Top-level management in recognizing the above issues planned for future growth by strategically shifting from a chemical product supplier to a business that provides chemical products and the knowledge to apply such products, and services so as to optimize the life-cycle costs of the customers' assets. This paradigm shift would be accomplished through long-term service contracts with their customers.

In order to accomplish such radical changes, the business would need to invest time and resources. The focus of this case study is on the insufficient information regarding product usage and performed services and developing a solution to acquire such information.

Through short surveys and polling various regional managers and field representatives, we found that most field representatives did not fill out service reports. Those that did particularly in the oil refinery industry submitted service reports only to the customers; however, the report was a non-standardized form. Some used email for delivering the reports. Some provided paper copies that were generated from Excel spreadsheets.

In summary, the business did not have standards for service reports including what information to collect, how to collect such information, how often to submit reports, and where to submit reports. The business did not have the information systems to collect, process, and manage service reports. The new service paradigm as discussed above requires collecting standardized information and managing such information so that appropriate metrics can be computed and analyses be performed. Having standardized information has benefits for the customers. The information could provide metrics on what services were performed and how the services improved or protected their assets. New services could also be developed and delivered that could monitor the customers assets and proactively detect and correct potential problems; thus offering more value to the customers.

4. PROPOSED SOLUTION

The proposed solution dictated numerous changes to the existing process. The field representatives would be asked to fill out standardized service reports and submit them electronically to a new system that would process such reports by collecting and storing the information. In order to create standardized service report forms, the field representatives would provide specific account information particular to the products and service that they sell. With such account information, the new system would automatically generate a standardize service report form.

Having a new process for collecting and managing standardize service data was critical to having the appropriate information that could provide the business with better understanding on the types of products sold, the services provided to the customers, and the value to the customers of providing such services. The appropriate information could now generate metrics and value-stories so that the costs and benefits of delivering services are measurable; thus, providing a basis for the new service-based model.

However, with any new process, there are typically implementation costs for one or more new systems, training costs, personnel changes, and such. The team was very concerned about the impact that the new process would have on the field representatives' time. Any additional task no matter how small would not be well received because their workdays were already quite full. Management was asking the field representatives to have more face time with their customers in addition to their daily tasks and the new process would require them to take time to fill out service reports on a daily or weekly basis. For this new process to be successful, management needed to provide the necessary resources but even more important, top-level management needed to communicate to the employees on how this new process was critical to the survival of the company and was aligned with the business' strategy.

5. APPROACH

The new service-based model for the business required changes to the service delivery process. This new paradigm depended on having accurate and timely data from the field representatives, which captured information on what services were performed, why the services were performed, and how the services were performed.

During the first quarter of 2004, management formed a team to design and develop the necessary systems to enable the collection and organization of service data. The team consisted of several technical experts and IT personnel. Having prior experience working as field representatives, the experts provided domain knowledge about the various industries and application areas. Since the business covered many industries and application areas, management also made available key technologists with a limited amount of time to advise and guide the team and to contribute to the knowledge-base.

One of the first tasks that the team completed was to map the existing or 'as-is' process for submitting service data. Unfortunately the process varied widely from industry to industry and in many cases there was no process for submitting service data. There was much opportunity for improvement. The team also recognized the importance of having standardized and structured data. This requirement could be attained through standardized service report forms; however, the business provides products and services to many different industries. One service report form would either be too complicated to provide comprehensive coverage or would be to simple thus having little or no benefit.

After extensive analysis, the team defined a new process or 'to-be' process that addressed the issues regarding the collection of service data and the varied industries and application area. This new process specified that a set of templates would be generated based on industry and application areas. A template would contain the necessary fields for a service report to capture the appropriate data on customer, process, systems, equipment, components, treatment, problems, solutions, and such. Since each customer account has differences, the template would be used as the basis from which a customized service report form would be generated. The customization would capture the particulars for that account.

5.1 New Process

Figure 6-1 depicts the new process. In actuality, the process has two phases, which are predominantly executed by different people. The first phase begins with capturing the knowledge from the domain experts, who work in the technical support group. These experts have practical experience working in the field but now provide support to the field representatives by helping to solve problems and answering questions. Much of the knowledge was gathered by interviewing the experts and by analyzing technical support and training manuals. This information was captured in Excel spreadsheets and contained numerous categories of process, systems, equipment, and components. The information was organized by industry and by application areas.

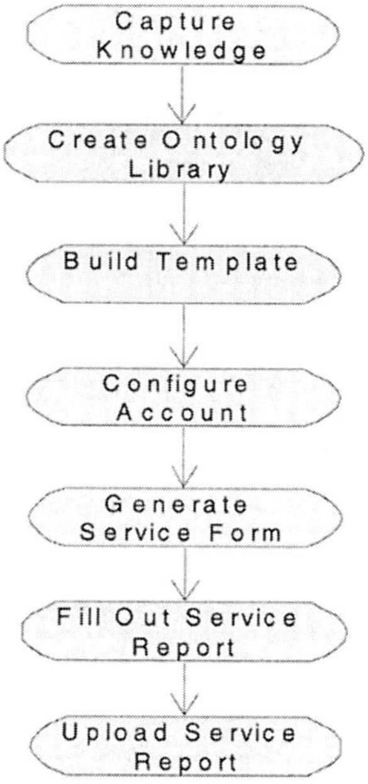

Figure 6-1: New Process

The Excel spreadsheets served as inputs for the next step, creating the ontology library. A consultant who was experienced with developing information systems and ontologies performed this step. As the ontologies were completed, they were used as the framework for building templates. The first phase culminates with the creation of templates.

The second phase begins with configuring accounts. The account representative or the field representative typically performs this task. The template provides a starting point. The representative receives a copy of the template, which may then be customized to capture the specifics of the account. This paper provides more details of templates in a later section. Once a copy of the template is customized, a service report form may be generated as needed. The field representative now has a service report form for collecting standardized data for that account. This form is filled out as part of the new process for reporting service related data. Once the data is entered in a service report, the field representative sends the report to a central repository for further processing and analysis.

In order to implement this new process with minimal impact on the level of effort by the field representative, new information systems are needed. The team determined that this approach depends on the following applications or information systems: ontology library, template generator, account configurator, an upload mechanism, and a central repository. Each one of these key components is now discussed in more detail with specifics on implementation.

5.2 Ontology

Ontology is an abstraction or model of some conceptualization or area of interest. Ontology may represent the knowledge about a particular domain or an abstraction of some real-world phenomenon. For example, ontology may provide a framework for classifying various groups of chemical compounds, DNA structures, or a boiler system in a power generation plant. Ontology provides fundamental concepts or building blocks for capturing the particular domain in a consistent and systematic manner such that there is common vocabulary of terms.

Ontology provides formal and explicit specifications that facilitate communication and sharing of knowledge amongst the user community. Since the specifications are defined as being formal and explicit, ontologies enable machine understanding.

In this approach, we developed ontologies to represent things that are important to the business such as the industries served, products sold, services delivered, things measured, observations recorded, problems encountered, and solutions provided. The ontologies consist of sets of those things and relations amongst those things. A set of somewhat related or similar things with the appropriate relations are organized into a particular ontology. All of the various ontologies are organized in an ontological library. The ontologies facilitated the development of the new business process and the resources to support the new process by providing standardized and explicit descriptions of the things critical to the business.

The business has a multidimensional organizational structure. One dimension of the structure is by industries, which represents the many market segments. Each industry has certain things that are rather unique to that industry. From the ontological modeling perspective, a logical grouping for the ontologies was by industry that aligned with the industrial areas and mimicked the business organization. This set of ontologies included ontologies for beverage, chemical processing, commercial and institutional, food, general industrial, hydrocarbon processing, life sciences, medical dialysis, microelectronics, mining & mineral processing, municipal, pharmaceutical, power generation, primary metals, residential and transportation.

A second dimension of the business' organizational structure is by application area. A cooling system is one example of an application area. The business provides specific products and services for this area and has experts, technical support and administrative personnel assigned to this area. An application area typically spans more than one industry. From the ontological modeling perspective, a second logical grouping for the ontologies was by these common application areas. This set contained ontologies for boiler systems, cooling systems, influent water treatment and wastewater treatment.

During the ontological modeling, there were important things that were identified in more than one industry and in more than one application area. To avoid defining such things in multiple ontologies, we defined a third set of ontologies, which may be used in more than one industry-based ontology and may be used in more than one application-based ontology. This set provided ontologies for measurements, electronic and mechanical things, and chemical products and treatments.

During the ontological modeling, we identified a fourth logical grouping of ontologies. This set did not represent any business specific things but provided for such things as currencies and units of measure. The International Standards were leveraged as much as possible for these ontologies. The ISO 3166 is the International Standards for geopolitical areas and country codes. This standard provided the basis for the geopolitical ontology. The currency ontology, which as based on the ISO 4217 International Standards for currency, also includes the geopolitical ontology for regions and country codes. For units of measures, the ISO 31, the International Standards for quantities and units, provided units of measure for the metric system. Since there are locations in the world that still use customary units of measure, a customary unit of measure ontology was built using definitions and symbols found in Perry's Handbook[2]. This fourth set of ontologies utilizing international standards and customary entities such as geopolitical entities, currencies, and units of measures, further facilitated the integration of data from industries and applications that span across different countries. As described above, leveraging ontologies from other ontologies promote standardization of vocabulary and semantics and reusability.

In the ontology, each entity represents some thing or concept in the domain such as a production process, a system, equipment, or a component of the equipment. An entity is modeled as a class or a frame.

Entities may have properties or attributes associated with them. A property further describes the entity of interest. For example, the storage tank in a system may have attributes representing the diameter of the tank, the length of the tank, the capacity of the tank, and the metallurgy of the tank wall. Using ontology terminology, a property or attribute is modeled as a slot on that class.

The entities may be related through associations or relations. A relation may also have properties such as the cardinality, the class-type or data-type for each end of the relation, and other such attributes. A commonly applied association relates one or more generalized classes to one or more specialized classes. The ontology terminology for this type of association that relates a generalized class to a specialized class is an "IS-A" relation. The ontologies also employ another type of association that represents the relationship concept of whole entity to its parts. This ontology terminology for this type of association is a "HAS-A" relation. The ontology engineer typically defines numerous relations when building the ontology. The ontology modeling also provides for relations from entities in one ontology to entities in other ontologies to maximize the reusability of entities. Examples on both types of relations are provided later in this writing.

The next several sections provide examples from each of the four sets of ontologies. The examples describe the important aspects of the ontologies and some usage for the entities and relations as applied to the new business process.

5.2.1 Industry-based Ontology Example

The first set of ontologies contains industry specific entities and relations. For example, an industry-based ontology such as the chemical processing consists of processes, systems, equipment, and components commonly found in such an industry. An ammonia producing plant is one type of chemical process, which would use this ontology for building the industry-based template. Figure 6-2 shows a partial diagram from the ontology for the chemical processing industry. The top level in the ontology has a general purpose Chemical Processing class. A chemical process depending on the specifics may have equipment such as gas-solid separation, liquid-solid separation, solid-solid separation, heat exchangers, and reactor catalyst systems. The industry ontologies also provide for associating measurements, costs, chemical treatment, and other data that may be of value to managing the service operations.

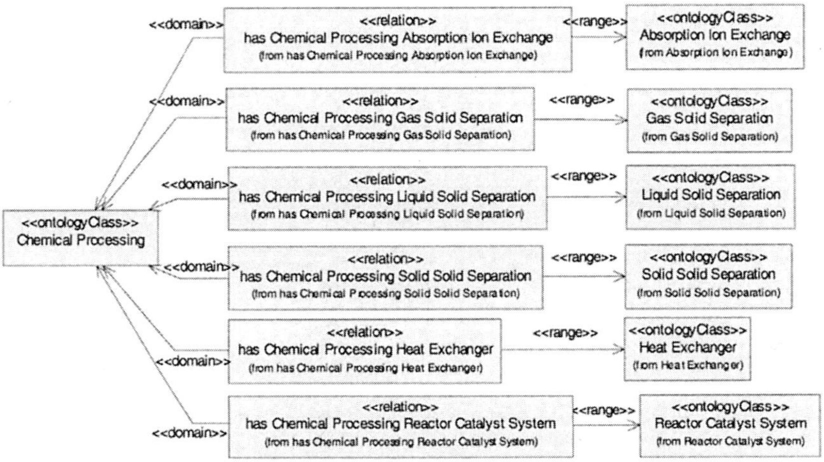

Figure 6-2: Chemical Processing Diagram

5.2.2 Application-based Ontology Example

The second set of ontologies addresses the specific entities and relations for the application areas. An application-based ontology such as for a cooling system follows a similar pattern as an industry-based ontology. Such an ontology contains processes, systems, equipment, and components. Figure 6-3 shows a partial diagram from the cooling application ontology. An Open Recirculating Cooling System class has relations to Condenser, Cooler, Cooling Hood, and Cooling Tower classes. The relations represent "HAS-A" associations. Each of these classes may be further decomposed into its component classes. The application ontologies also provide for associating measurements, costs, chemical treatment, and other data that may be of value to managing the service operations.

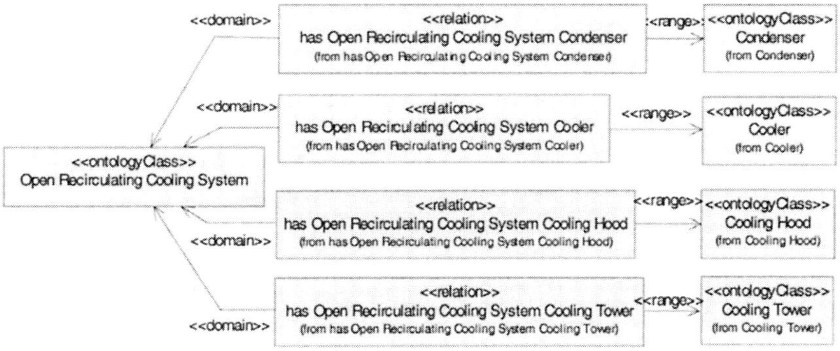

Figure 6-3: Cooling Application Ontology

As another example, heating and power generation systems employ a boiler system in a power plant to heat and circulate water as either hot water or steam. Figure 6-4 shows two specialized or types of boiler systems: fired boiler system and waste heat boiler system. An "IS-A" type relation represents the general class to specialized class association. A collection of entities with "IS-A" relations defines a taxonomy. The simple diagram shows the taxonomy with the Boiler System class as the general class and the Fire Boiler System class and the Waste Heat Boiler System class as the specialized classes. A fired boiler system contains a combustion chamber that may burn natural gas or coal with which heats the water. The other type as the class name implies utilizes waste heat from some other process as a means to recover spent energy.

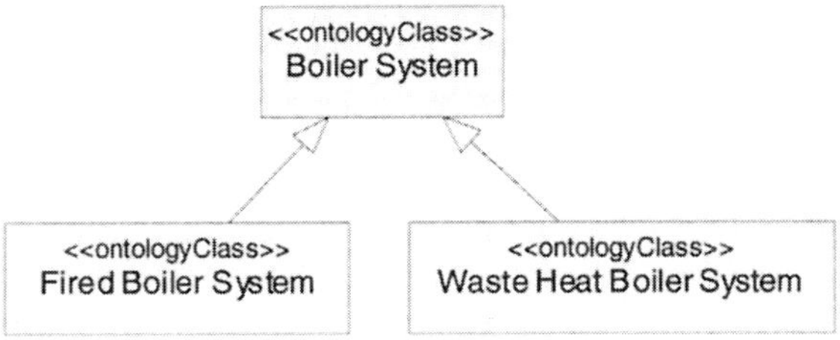

Figure 6-4: Boiler System Taxonomy

A boiler system contains many components and equipment. Figure 6-5 depicts five pieces of equipment that are common to both types of boiler systems. The ontology represents these entities as classes and these classes are associated to the general class, Boiler System. The two specialized boiler systems inherit these relations. Each of the specialized boiler systems has additional relations to equipment and component classes. This ontology has a total of twenty-three classes and one hundred and two relations.

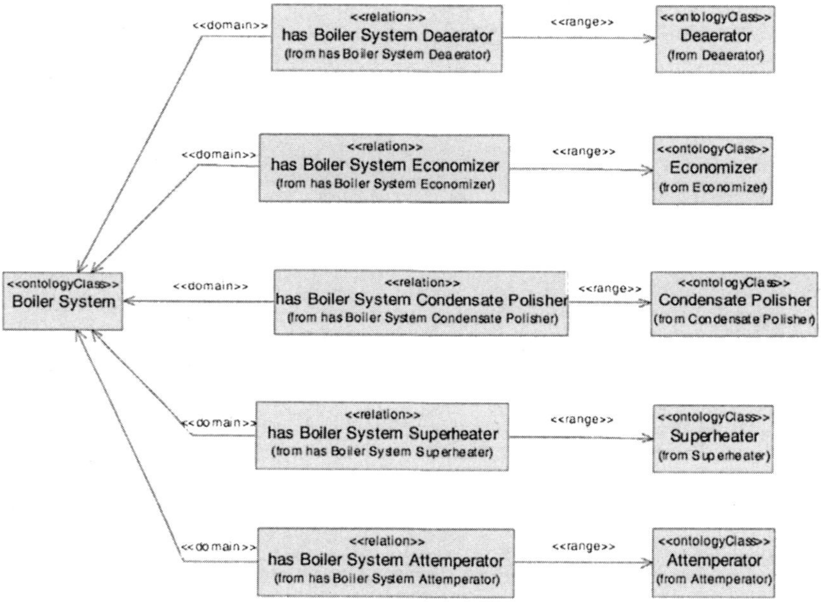

Figure 6-5: Boiler System Components

5.2.3 Common Ontology Examples

The third set of ontologies defines entities and relations that are commonly found in industry-based areas and applications. As mentioned in a prior section, this set provides for measurements, electronic and mechanical things, and chemical products and treatments. The measurement ontology defines over one hundred and thirty classes of measurements defining such things as pH, conductivity, alkalinity, concentration, total dissolved solids, corrosion rate, flow rate, pressure, temperature, and hardness. The electronic and mechanical ontology provides for equipment and components including valve, input, output, heat exchanger, pump, furnace, fan, and many others.

The example depicts an electromechanical piece of equipment called a heat exchanger. This diagram represents another example of "Has-A" relations containing the inputs and outputs for both the hot side and the cold side of a heat exchanger. It is worth noting here that even though the heat exchanger has relations to four entities. The configurator allows for more than one instance of any such entity.

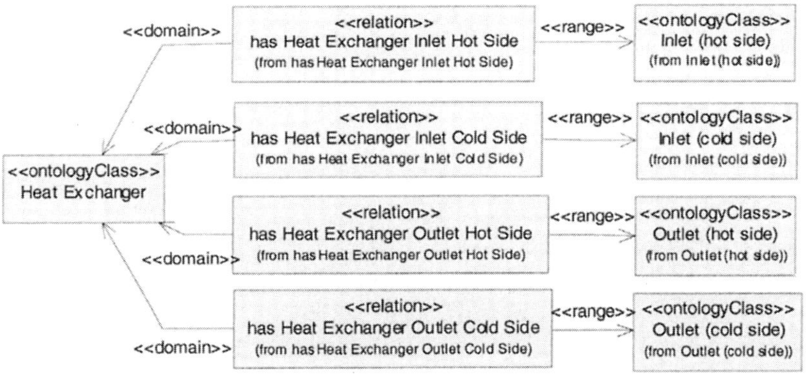

Figure 6-6 : Standards Ontology Example

The fourth set of ontologies covers the entities and relations defined in standards and by conventional practices. This set contains a geopolitical ontology, currency ontology, and quantities and units ontologies.

The geopolitical ontology leverages the International Standards ISO 3166 for country codes. The currency ontology uses the ISO 4217 for currency codes, which also includes the geopolitical ontology. The quantities and units ontologies provide for both the ISO 31 standards for quantities and units of measure and for commonly employed units of measure as found in reference books such as Perry's Handbook[2]. All physical measurements are stored in the ISO 31 standard units of measurement; however, the applications provide for converting into the preferred units of measure.

The next two diagrams are excerpts from the currency ontology. The first one shows that currency is a type of unit of measure. The second diagram depicts an instance of currency. The ontology terminology for an instance of a class is an individual. The euro is an individual of currency and is used by the European Monetary Union.

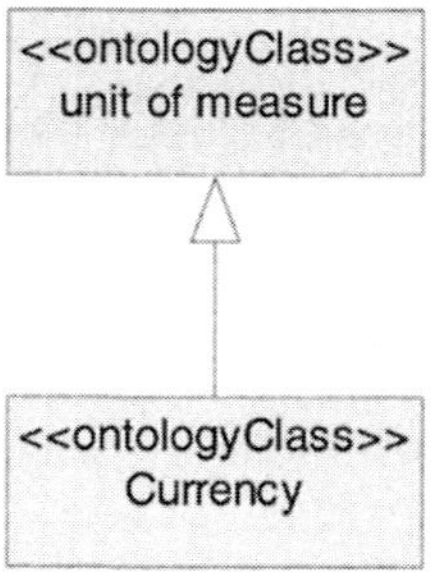

Figure 6-7: Currency Example

The geopolitical ontology defines the European Monetary Union as an individual of a geopolitical collection.

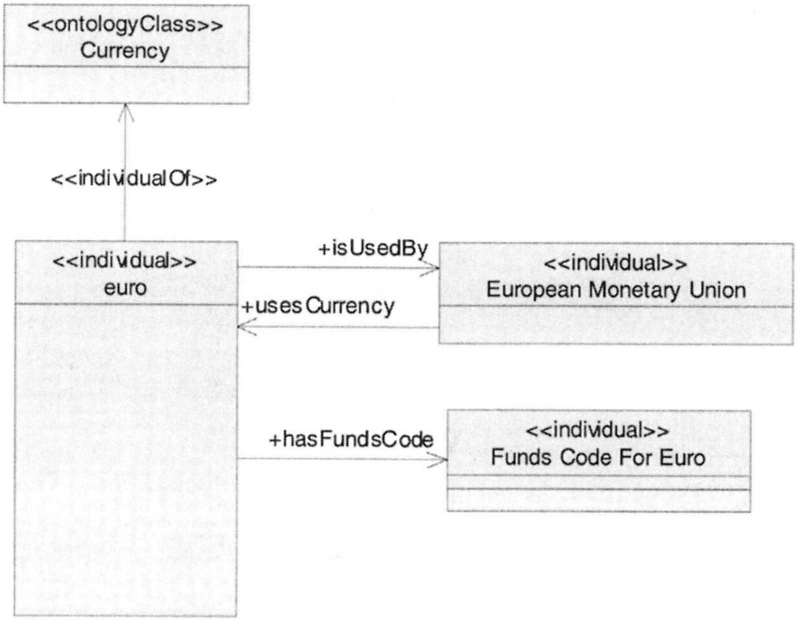

Figure 6-8: Currency Example - euro

As mentioned several times, one objective for representing the business things in ontologies is to promote the reusability of such things. Figure 6-9 depicts the dependency amongst several ontologies. The boiler ontology includes the influent water treatment ontology and electronic and mechanical ontology as well as several high-level abstract ontologies.

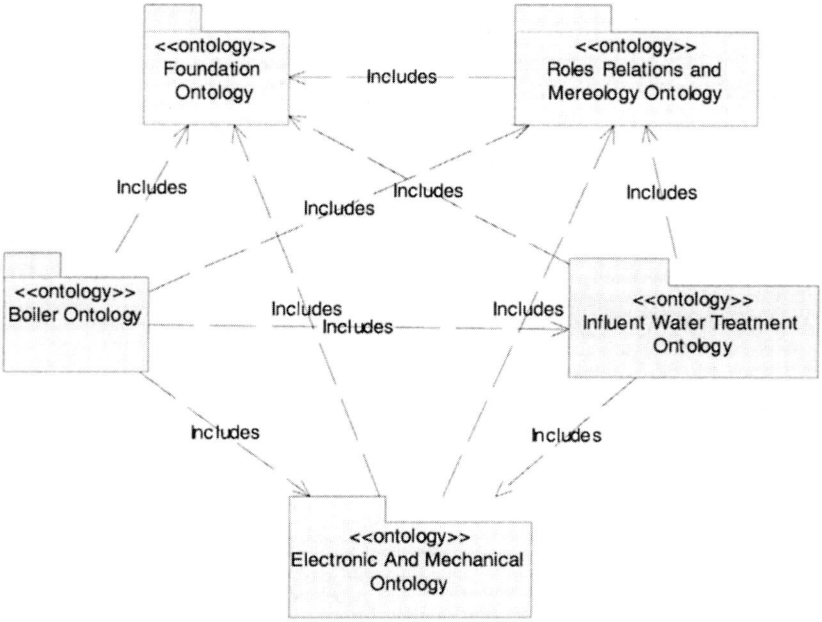

Figure 6-9: Ontology Dependencies

The four sets of ontologies represent the initial release of the ontology library. As more applications and products get developed, the ontology library will be extended to include the new entities and relations.

5.2.4 Ontology Modeling Tool and Ontology Standards

The ontology modeling team defined the following criteria or critical to quality measurements for selecting a modeling tool. Since the ontology development involved much interaction with domain experts, the tool should provide visualization of the classes, relations, and properties to facilitate communication and discussion amongst the team and the experts. Secondly, the software development team was trained on UML (Unified Modeling Language) for designing the applications so having an ontology tool that utilized UML notation was beneficial for communicating with the software development team. Thirdly, the team felt that new standards such as OWL should be employed so that future integration of new applications and commercially available software for ontologies would be supported. OWL stands for Web Ontology Language, is written in XML, and was designed to be interpreted by computers. Based on the criteria, the team selected the Visual Ontology Modeling tool from Sandpiper Software, Incorporated[3].

5.2.5 Ontology Deployment

The Visual Ontology Modeling tool provided for developing the ontology library and for generating OWL files; however, there was a lack of tools to support the interpretation and storage of the ontologies. In the first phase, the team resorted to a manual step of parsing the OWL files and creating the SQL script to load the ontologies into the relational database. The long-term goal is to eliminate this manual step by storing the ontologies directly into the database.

Once the ontologies reside in the database, the account configurator may generate templates as the basis for configuring the customer accounts as discussed in the next section.

5.3 Template

A template is currently a temporary artifact that the account configurator generates dynamically from one or more ontologies. A template consists of a group of objects and relations amongst the objects that are instantiated from classes in the industry ontology and the application ontology together with the dependant common ontologies.

An example may help clarify the concept of a template. Suppose the user is setting up an account for a boiler system. The Account Configurator, which enables this tasks, reads the boiler ontology together with the ontologies included with the boiler ontology, creates objects for each class in the boiler ontology as well as for the classes included from the other ontologies, and defines a hierarchical structure within the concept of a template to represent the objects and associations defined amongst the ontologies. The Account Configurator presents the template in web-based forms to the user as a partially configured account that allows the user to further personalize the configuration with customized names for the objects and other notations. The template provides a starting point for configuring an account.

5.4 Account Configurator

The account configurator is a web-based application that provides users with an easy to use interface for inputting the customer specific details about the account. Prior to using the application, either the system administrator or an automated process loads account information and the assignees of the account from SAP, the enterprise information system into a local repository.

To begin the configuration process, the user points the web browser to the configurator's URL and logs on. The configurator authenticates and authorizes the user against the assignee information and then under a normal situation provides a list of one or more accounts available for configuration.

The user selects the targeted corporation, division, location, and other identifying information for the specific account. The account information also contains coding for the type of account. Based on this account type, the configurator generates either the industry template or the application template.

The configurator presents the template in web pages that are organized in a hierarchical structure, which reflects the levels in the template. The user may traverse the hierarchy from the top down or the bottom up. Each web page provides a form with input fields for the user to enter specific information and details as well as pull-down lists and pick lists for more standardized data values.

When configuring an account, the user enters a name or some unique identifier for each object in the template. The name may come from the customer's process model or a nameplate that is typically found on equipment. The user may also create new objects and add them to the configuration but only objects instantiated from classes dictated by the ontology.

For instance, a particular process may consist of two heat exchangers. The template provides for one so the user is permitted by the business rules embedded within the configurator to create a second instance of the heat exchanger class to match the actual process.

Once the user configures an object, he or she may add measurements and cost parameters to that object. Using the boiler example, the field representative measures the conductivity of the feed water for the boiler. Since conductivity is a valid measurement for the boiler feed water, the user is allowed to add this field for such a measurement in the configuration.

Upon completion of the configuration, the user saves the work, which is stored in the database. This step completes the configuration process.

Some customer accounts are very large having complex processes with many systems, equipment, components, and measurements. Configuring such processes requires more time than a simpler account like for a boiler system so the configurator allows the user to save the work in progress session. At a later time, the user may return to the configurator and load the work from the previous session to add and delete objects and modify configuration information. Once the user finalizes a configuration, no more objects can be deleted only new objects may be added. This restriction prevents database corruption due to input data losing the association to a deleted object.

5.5 Service Reports

After the user finalizes the configuration, service report forms may be generated for that account. These forms are created dynamically from the information in the account's configuration. The form contains a header, which consists of customer's corporation, division, location, and such. Following the header the form has read only fields representing the identifiers for processes, systems, equipment, and components together with empty fields for entering measurements, costs, chemical treatments, and problem descriptions with solutions.

The field representative downloads the service report form to a laptop or a PDA. These forms may be accessed only by those assigned to the account or acting as a delegate for an assignee. The forms are available from an intranet web site.

Once the field representative fills out a service report form, the report may be uploaded to the same intranet web site and a copy may be optionally emailed to the customer. The service reports are stored for future retrieval, analyses, customer viewing, data mining, and other needs.

Standardized and structured data are achieved through the usage of ontologies that controls the mandatory and allowed fields in a service report form.

6. RESULTS

The first release of the ontology library has over fifteen hundred entities, relations, and individuals providing a rich and detailed representation for configuring customer accounts from five industries and four application areas. The ontology library together with the account configurator and the mechanisms for downloading and uploading service report forms enables the business to capture standardized and structured data on what services were performed, how services were performed, and why service were performed. This information facilitates the business in shifting from a product provider to a product and service provider and promotes the integration of the service business.

Out of this new system and process came another tool called Insight^{tm}, which is a "web-based data management tool designed to help customers reduce water, energy, and labor costs while improving their water and process treatment programs[4]." This global application generates a variety of management reports including high level performance reports, statistical summaries, and historical trend analysis on key performance indicators (KPI) monitored by the system. Currently there are over two hundred customers on a globally basis that utilize this application to see how well the treatment programs are working for them. Insight^{tm} is a service differentiator for the business providing customers with information and decision support that were previously unavailable or were very labor intensive to generate. The new process together with the resources to support the process enables applications like Insight^{tm} to sustain a competitive advantage.

7. CONCLUSIONS

The business faced numerous challenges with cultural differences due the mergers and acquisitions of various companies, with incompatible systems and infrastructure, and with different processes for business execution. The new process together with the resources to enable the process provided much benefit to the company in addressing these challenges. The results from this effort include standardized and structured data and information, a new process for reporting on services, and mechanisms to capture and manage service related data, information, and knowledge.

REFERENCES

1. S. Zhang and L. Huang, Comparative Study of Obtaining Competitive Advantage from Information Technology, Proceedings of the International Conference of Service Systems and Services Management (ICSSSM '05), Vol. 1, pp. 19-23, June 2005.
2. R. H. Perry and D. W. Green, Perry's Chemical Engineers' Handbook (7th Edition), (McGraw-Hill Professional, 1998).
3. Visual Ontology Modeling (VOM) tool, http://www.sandsoft.com.
4. Insighttm, http://www.gewater.com/service/service_insight.jsp.

5. M. Dausch and C. Hsu, Engineering service products: The case of mass-customising service agreements for heavy equipment industry, International Journal of Services, Technology and Management (2006), Vol. 7, No. 1, pp. 32-51.
6. M. Dausch, Strategic Product service planning for heavy industrial equipment: a reference information model, PhD Thesis of file at Rensselaer Polytechnic Institute Library (December 2002).
7. M. Dausch, Process Analysis Using Ontologies for Water & Power Management, *Presentation from Second Annual Semantic Technology Conference* (May 2006).
8. R. Mizonguchi, *Part 1: Introduction to Ontological Engineering, New Generation Computing* (Ohmsha, Ltd. and Springer-Verlag 2003), Vol. 21, No. 4, pp. 365-384.
9. R. Mizonguchi, *Part 2: Ontology development, tools, and languages, New Generation Computing* (Ohmsha, Ltd. and Springer-Verlag 2004), Vol. 22, No. 1, pp. 61-96.
10. R. Mizonguchi, *Part 3: Advanced course of ontological engineering, New Generation Computing* (Ohmsha, Ltd. and Springer-Verlag 2004), Vol. 22, No. 2, pp. 198-220.

Chapter 7

CONTINUOUS EVALUATION OF INFORMATION SYSTEM DEVELOPMENT

A Reference Model

Ming-chuan Wu

Dept. Of Information Management, Chang Jung Uni., Tainan 711, Taiwan ROC

Abstract: Continuous evaluations are commonly practiced on complex, long-term Information Technology and Systems (IT/S) projects, but in an ad hoc and nonsystematic way. The root cause lies in the lack of a comprehensive understanding about the nature of continuous evaluation and the appropriate mechanism to guide the evaluation process. As a result, the previous practices tend to be costly and often with unsatisfactory quality.

To addresses the challenges, this research combines literature review with two case studies to develop a reference evaluation model. The model consists of three dimensions: organizational goals, system components, and development stages. Each dimension provides a comprehensive framework of elements with respect to other dimensions: together these dimensions constitute a mechanism for identifying benefits in all aspects. Through validation in two different contexts, the model is showing its soundness and merit in the higher education domain, especially the military higher education. Future research promises to generalize the model for broader applications in the field of IS development, evaluation, and project management beyond higher education.

Key words: IS evaluation; IS development; project management; reference model.

1. INTRODUCTION

1.1 The need of continuous evaluation for Information Systems

Organizations continue to invest heavily in Information Technology and Systems (IT/S) in the new millennium[3]. The driving force is, of course, the deeply accepted promise that IT/S is a strategic enabler of contemporary enterprises. However, the literature does not provide sufficient scientific results for evaluating IT/S projects as strategic investments. Among the problematic issues is, for example, how to account for long-term qualitative and intangible benefits that strategic IT/S applications promise. Such unaccountability of IT/S is even more noticeable for service-oriented enterprises because of the intangible nature of services. Knowing that there is no silver bullet to address such problems, several researchers have advised that IT/S evaluations be conducted on an ongoing basis rather than in a one-shot fashion [1-7].

1.2 Current practices of continuous evaluation

From our observations, such ongoing evaluations are not rare in practice, especially for complex projects of extended duration. One such example was the Laptop Program of the Rensselaer Polytechnic Institute (RPI) [8]. The program started with a four-year pilot testing on a few designated courses in 1995-1998, followed by a decision to expand the program in 1999. After a gradual implementation for incoming freshmen from 1999 to 2002, every undergraduate is now required to have a laptop preloaded with a standard set of software applications. In the meantime, initiatives such as network construction, classroom renovation, and course redesign on the web are underway to deliver new modes of teaching.

During the time, the program was evaluated in many ways. For example, the institute formed committees composed of faculty and staff to conduct evaluations, review plans, and make suggestions for implementation during different timeframes. Its Anderson Center conducted student surveys to examine the program's impacts after implementation. Faculty forums were held to discuss whether or not the program has improved students' learning. More evaluations are reportedly underway as the program continues to advance.

Like the Laptop Program, many IT/S projects are evaluated in organizations, in various forms. Some evaluations (especially at the planning

[3] For example, see CHAOS reports from Standish Group (http://www.standishgroup.com).

and post-implementation stages) are conducted in a stand-alone and formal way (such as those reviews by the Faculty Senate); others are less formal practices and often incorporated into the development and implementation processes. However, there does not seem to be an overall plan or a measure for fleshing out all these separate evaluations into an integrated and optimized maneuver from the beginning. Continuous evaluations are commonly practiced in the field, yet with dubious quality and high cost.

First, while improving project quality is the original purpose of extending the evaluations over time, such extensions are no guarantee of improvement if the incorporation or additional measures are not systematic to assure consistency and comprehensiveness. This often happens on occasions where only project managers and their associated staffs take charge of the evaluations throughout the life cycle. They may not have the luxury of deployable resources as in the RPI case where faculty, staff, and certain agencies are involved in the evaluations. It is rather likely that the team members, with preconceptions of their previous evaluation at the planning stages, will be skeptical about the necessity of later evaluations and subconsciously ignore the practices. Or else, the preconception may, in effect, prevent the members from sensing any emerging opportunities, problems, or changes. Under such circumstances, the evaluations at the later stages are prone to produce incomplete results, inhibit adaptive changes, and generate low quality results.

Second, evaluations incur costs. The costs are certainly higher for continuous evaluations with more people involved. They would get exasperated greatly if some of the evaluations contradict each other or overlap. A general practice to avoid the above "group think" is to recruit a bigger group of various interests, professions, and distributed responsibilities for the evaluation practices, such as brainstorming ideas, soliciting feedback, conducting surveys, or even making decisions. Besides the possible difficulty in recruiting professional and committed people in many organizations, the main challenge of this approach becomes how best to use it; that is, how to extract effective performance from an ad hoc and unprepared group. Otherwise, such evaluation practices will not only consume costly resources, but also end up with no better quality than a simple work force.

The root cause of the prevailing ad hoc and nonsystematic practices lies in the lack of a comprehensive understanding of the nature of continuous evaluation on complex, long-term IT/S projects. Accordingly, no justifiable mechanism is available to guide the evaluation process. As a result, the prevailing practices are full of ineffective and inefficient use of evaluation resources. There are overdone or redundant evaluations, which result in high costs, or too little attention and work on evaluations, which jeopardizes quality.

1.3 The need of a reference model for continuous evaluation

The above analysis reflects the need for an integrated method to reduce cost and assure quality of evaluation. The literature on IT/S evaluation is filled with evaluation methods, measures, and processes, such as financial methods (i.e., ROI, NPV, Payback, etc.) and Information Economics [9, 10], to name just a few. However, they each tend to address an individual aspect of a problem separately, not the need for integration. To address the need for integration essentially requires a model that consists of a comprehensive reference of the IT/S benefits and available measurement tools, whereby evaluators can systematically refine, adjust, and measure all pertinent facets of benefit and assure the evaluation quality.

2. THE REFERENCE MODEL

To address the above problem, we first defined the requirements that the reference model ideally promises to assist in IT/S evaluation. The model was then constructed in a three dimensions based upon the defined requirements, and followed by a developed methodology for its application. The model was then validated for its soundness and applicability with two case studies in the context of the higher education institution.

2.1 Model requirements

After reviewing the literature on IS planning and evaluation, we defined how the model should promise to facilitate evaluations as follows:

1. The model should assist in ensuring system alignment with organization's goals and needs. Although system requirements may change along the way, systems development should always maintain its commitment toward the organization's goals and needs lest resources are spent on building technically sound but operationally useless functions and features. It should help detect and avoid this situation at any stage.
2. The model should enable comprehensive benefits identification and analysis at all levels, i.e., different horizontal (operations, sales, marketing, etc.) and vertical (operational, management, and strategic) functions, or any stakeholder.

3. The model should coordinate system development and evaluation tasks. That is, it should enable evaluators to make the best use of the information available from the development process. Also, the evaluation results should support the needs of development. As a result of such coordination, the costs of both activities can be minimized.
4. The model should build linkages between different evaluation tasks. Evaluation results at one stage should be a reference for those that follow. Such integration also serves to reduce costs and maintain accountability of evaluation.
5. The model should support decision making at each stage. One main purpose of evaluation is to control resources and results of development. To the largest extent, evaluations should lead to a project selection (for multiple projects) or go-no-go decision (for single project). Beyond that, they should also support numerous minor decisions such as those regarding design alternatives in the course of development and implementation.

2.2 Model Construction

Summing up the above requirements, we concluded that, at least, two categories of information are essential for the model. One is information about benefits for all organizational levels and related evaluation measures and methods. Such information should be organized in a comprehensive structure or a profile where evaluators can easily pick and choose those benefits and measures they need. On top of that, the profile should also enable evaluators to further expand its contents and grow into a knowledge base for the organization. Other information includes the needs and resources of evaluation and development/implementation at each stage, which is essential to establish coordination between the two activities.

Based upon the above requirements, the reference model was constructed with three dimensions--organizational goals, system components, and development stages, which collectively conceptualize the integrated, continuing evaluation. Each dimension is further substantiated into reference elements with profiles and matrices based upon literature results and observations from the fields. The reference elements are then used to generate a series of evaluation worksheet and action plan at different stages. Together, the conceptual model, the substantiated elements of each dimension, and the implementation templates combine a three-tiered model, as illustrated in Figure 7-1.

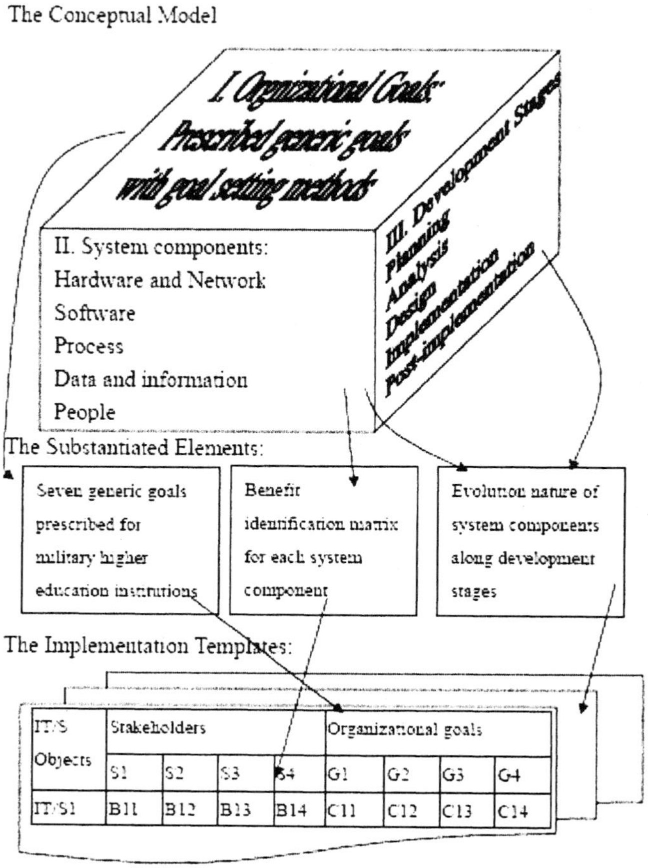

Figure 7-1. An Overview of the Reference Model

The first dimension of the model pertains to organizational goals, which capture the highest-level benefits of all systems and thus serve as a good start for benefits identification. In addition, organizational goals direct planning and help ensure system alignment. They may also serve as a common basis for comparison and selection among different projects when necessary. However, because goals are usually articulated with a high level of abstraction, they need further specification for measurement.

System components, the second dimension, serve the purpose of guiding benefits specification and identification. There are five basic mutually exclusive and collectively exhaustive elements for all systems--people, process, data, software, hardware and network. Due to their relative ease of decomposition, these components help substantiate the organizational goals into particular benefits that are more operational for direct evaluation. Each component also provides a direct planning reference to enumerate the necessary follow-up development and implementation tasks as a result of evaluation.

The third dimension pertains to the system development stages. The system development life cycle provides a natural categorization for multiple-stage evaluation. The IT/S literature has prescribed a series of generic development activities in planning, analysis, design, implementation, and post-implementation stages. At each stage, system components are continuously defined, analyzed, and designed. These activities produce more accurate information to enable refined evaluation, which, in turn, provides feedback to better understand development needs.

2.3 Substantiated Elements of the Model

2.3.1 Organizational Goals

A goal is a broad statement describing a desired future condition or achievement. Organizational goals address the key processes that support an organization's mission and vision. They set specific directions for performance of products or services to customers. All the internal processes, agencies, and other resources are organized optimally to pursue these goals. IT/S has become a key organizational asset that promises to impact all aspects of activities and resources. Thus, any investment on this asset should eventually aim to contribute to organizational goals.

Generally organizational goals should remain valid over time and be revisited at regular intervals for guiding the organization's efforts, managerial practices, and resource allocation. There are several guidelines for goal setting, such as using teamwork to establish goals through consensus, determining whether the goals support mission and vision, and examining whether the statements clearly address direction, performance, and customers' needs. Further, some well-established methods such as Balanced Scorecard [11-13] and Value Chain are useful to define organizational goals effectively. We typically consider Porter's Value Chain appropriate for setting goals because the method has been broadly applied for strategic planning and it captures a high-level process view, and may facilitate the need of impact analysis of IT/S.

According to Porter, an organization is a collection of primary and support activities that perform to design, produce, deliver, and support its product or service. All these activities can be represented by a value chain.

Every value activity consists of both physical and information processing components. The physical component includes all the physical tasks required to perform the activities. The information component encompasses the steps required to capture, manipulate, and channel the data necessary to perform the activity. All the value activities are interdependent and connected by linkages that usually require information or information flows to exploit [14, 15]. IT/S clearly has pervasive impacts on both physical and information components within the activities and the linkages among them as well. We applied the concept and identified nine technologically and strategically distinct activities for military institutes. Of them, four are primary and five belong to support categories, as illustrated in Figure 7-2.

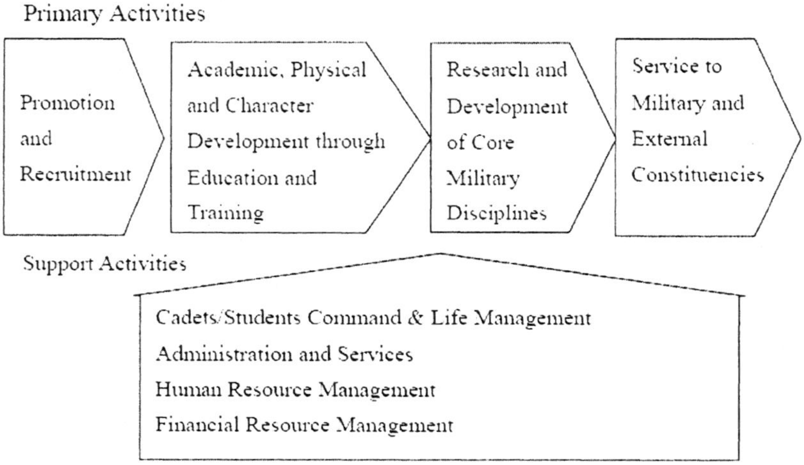

Figure 7-2. A Value Chain for Military Higher Education Institutions

1. Promotion and Recruitment: Promote institutional image and reputation, recruit cadets/students, perform application processes, and establish marketing and service channels to prospect cadets/students.
2. Academic, physical and character development through education and training: Develop and execute programs and curricula for academic learning, military training, physical training, and character development.
3. Research and development of core military disciplines: Identify core military disciplines and subject areas, setup development strategies, provide resources for research and development, and review results.
4. Service to military and external constituencies: Provide various services to external customers and constituencies. For example, provide

cadets'/students' family and working agencies with information services about their performance and life management; offer local community with opportunities to attend celebration, sport, or charity events, etc.

5. Cadets/Students Command & Life Management: Lead, command, and manage cadets/students' life, learning and other activities with consulting and mentoring services.
6. Administration and Services: Provide administration services to cadet/students, faculty, and other constituencies.
7. Human Resource Management: Recruit, develop, retain, and service military and civilian personnel.
8. Financial Resource Management: Budget planning, controlling, and financial services.
9. Procurement and Logistic Management: Procure necessary resources to maintain academic, training, athletic, administration, and life facilities and equipment.

These activities work together to render performance for sustaining an institute's existence. Yet institutes do not work for existence only, but rather strive for what they want to be in the future. Thus we surveyed several US military higher education institutes, looked into their visions and missions, further applied Porter's low cost and differentiation strategies, and prescribed seven generic goals as follows:

1. Promote reputation and recruit quality cadets/students.
2. Elevate education and training programs to develop professional military officers and leaders.
3. Enhance research and establish core military disciplines and competencies.
4. Develop a high performance team of committed personnel
5. Maintain quality military education environment with high availability and effective usage of facilities and equipments.
6. Excel in command, administration, and internal services.
7. Extend external services and expand institutional resources.

2.3.2 System Components

The second dimension of the model is adapted from Zachman's original Information System Architecture, which provides a basic framework for considering the various elements of an information system with data (what), function (how), network (where), people (who), purpose (why), and time (when) [16, 17]. This dimension consists of five components, each of which interacts with one another and addresses a key concern in a system that carries out tasks to meet certain organizational goals. Software and hardware (and network) usually enable changes in the other three components, process, data, and people, which collectively translate into benefits for organizations. Besides being a change enabling agent, software and hardware often require interval changes in order to remain functional and valuable, i.e., to upgrade its performance or to lower maintenance costs. We elaborate on the specific benefits that can typically be realized on each component. To assist benefit identification, the scope of each component is defined, all possible courses of action are reviewed, and from that, the possible respective benefits identified.

- Hardware and Network

Hardware includes those devices that accept, process, display, store and retrieve data and information. Examples range from mainframe computers, servers, and PCs, to mobile computing devices and various input and output peripherals. Network refers to the connection of material, equipment, and mechanisms that collectively permit the sharing of resources by different computing devices. In a broader sense, this category includes facilities that house the computers and network, such as labs and classrooms. Different configurations of hardware and networks provide various functionalities and create different effects even when software basically remains the same. For example, in military academies where outdoor activities are more prevalent than in civilian schools, emerging hand-held computers wirelessly networked and employing handwriting recognition capabilities may enable users to perform their jobs online without any spatial-temporal limitations.

Table 7-1. Benefits Identification from Hardware and Network Perspective

Scope	Servers, PCs, mobile computing devices, peripherals, network devices, and supporting facilities such as labs and classrooms.
Courses of action	Replace or add hardware or network equipments to upgrade performance or provide new capabilities.
Benefits	Reduced hardware maintenance costs. Enhanced system performance and capabilities in terms of reliability, portability, security, scalability, etc.

Generally, the basic purpose of computer hardware is to allow software to perform desired functions. Therefore, in most cases, benefits realized by hardware are dependent on the residing software, the performing functions, and the affected stakeholders than the hardware itself. However, there are occasions when computer hardware or networks are added or replaced without much change in software or data content. This is done in order to upgrade performance or provide new capabilities, such as increased speed, larger bandwidth, more memory and storage space, easier use of input-output devices, and increased number of users served. Another basic benefit of installing new hardware and network products is reducing the cost of maintaining the equipment that tends to become obsolete relatively quickly. The above elaboration is summarized in Table 7-1.

- Software

Software covers such aspects as computer programs and data structure, which enable data manipulation and instruction operation. Off-the-self business applications are usually purchased or leased from major vendors. Other special-purpose software is built in-house or outsourced. Regardless of where it comes from, software serves one very basic purpose, much like hardware. Occasionally software needs to be upgraded to reduce its maintenance costs. On a higher level, software is developed or purchased to enable changes of process, data, or people, and thus its benefits are more dependent on the effects of the three elements than itself. That is, its benefits are more appropriate to be realized and measured from the three components, which will be further discussed in the next three sections.

One special feature of software is its relative ease of reproduction and reusability with minimum or virtually no additional costs. When an organization develops an innovative system and turns it into a product for sale or gift, the system may become a strategic weapon and generate huge economic returns. The Sabre system developed by American Airlines is one classic case of such practices. While practices of software reusability may not bring in direct cash in non-profit organizations, it is still possible to reap much benefit. For example, organizations can transplant or tailor an in-house built system to different branches or departments to achieve the same system performance while saving the development costs and establishing a common platform. Table 7-2 summarizes the above discussion.

Table 7-2. Benefits Identification from Software Perspective

Scope	Software architecture, computer programs, data structure, and documents.
Courses of action	(Purchased off-the-self, built in-house or outsourced) Replace old software; Implement new software to replace or support processes and/or people; Upgrade performance, add functionality or capability; Reuse the software: tailor or turn into sale or gift products.
Benefits	Enabling the change of process, data, and people; Reduced software maintenance costs; Profits or other benefits from sales or reuse of software products or services.

- Process

Process depicts a broad activity concept including major functions in value chain and their decomposed sub-functions, activities, or work flows. A process can be internal or external to an organization, it can contain physical and/or information activities, and it can be decomposed into sub-processes.

Because information flows inside and between processes, information systems cast pervasive impacts on process. Internally, they may take various forms of deletion, replacing, streamlining, and other modifications of processes and create effects such as saving time, material, labor, space, and other costs of existing processes. Besides mere changes to the existing processes, information systems often reveal new processes, adding new functions, capabilities, performances, and value to users. Beyond organization walls, information systems may connect to the processes of external constituencies and enable extended enterprise integration. The above discussion is organized in Table 7-3.

Table 7-3. Benefits Identification from Process Perspective

Scope	Major functions, value chain, decomposed sub-functions, activities, or work flows.
Courses of action	Delete, replace, streamline, create, and modify internal processes. Connect and integrate processes with external constituencies
Benefits	Reduced cycle time, labor, people, material, space, and other costs compared to existing processes. Adding functions, capabilities, performances, and other values to users (internal or external).

- Data

Data component refers to raw data, information, documents, and knowledge that are processed, transferred, or disseminated by people either with or without enabling mechanisms such as software and hardware. The enabling software and hardware typically process data through manipulation, storing, retrieving, integration, transferring, sharing, warehousing, data-mining, and re-formation.

Table 7-4. Benefits Identification from Data and Information Perspective

Scope	Ranging from various data entities and documents to information and knowledge in various forms such as texts, graphics, sound, and virtual realities.
Courses of action	Generate, manipulate, store, retrieve, transfer, share, integrate, warehouse, data mine, and re-formate, disseminate, analyze, etc. Use data or information base for sale or other research.
Benefits	Better information characteristics: Timeliness (currency, frequency, synchronizibility); Content (accuracy, relevancy, personalization, customization, completeness, redundancy, level of detail); Format (medium, ordering, graphic design, comprehensibility, predictability, interactivity, security, availability, etc.); Reduced costs of processing data, information, and knowledge; Better information and decisions supports on processes such as marketing, sale, pricing, production, customer services, and administration; Knowledge or intelligence benefits generated from added value activities such as research on data or databases; Revenue from sales or benefits from turnover of data, information products, or customer base.

The basic benefit regarding data component is the change of its characteristics due to system processing. Three major categories of information characteristics are timeliness, content, and format. Making use of and improving these information characteristics generates benefits of three kinds. The first is cost savings from more efficient information processing capabilities such as manipulation, storing, retrieving, and transferring. The second is the addition of value from better information and decision supports on processes such as marketing, sales, pricing, production, customer services, and administration. The third class refers to those benefits of knowledge or intelligence generated from added value activities such as research using data or databases. Finally, similar to the software situation, reproducing data (or selling databases), information, or knowledge may also generate large value, if it is a legal practice. Table 7-4 summarizes the above argument.

- People

From a system perspective, the people component broadly refers to those involved with systems directly and indirectly. Analogous to "of the people, by the people, and for the people," this component includes system owners, developers and maintainers, and users. The three parties need to interact in equilibrium to assure a systems' performance. That is, system owners need to make the right decisions for building an operational system and allocate resources for development and maintenance. Here, users are usually employees or customers, or further extend to suppliers or strategic partners, while systems can be developed or maintained by internal IT/S staff or external vendors.

Table 7-5. Benefits Identification from People Perspective

Scope	System perspectives: system owners, developers & maintainers, users. Organizational perspective: functional divisions or horizontal layers, Value chain perspective: customers, suppliers, employees
Courses of action	Add or eliminate internal personnel; Provide education and training; Change job content, tasks, skills, and the way of working; organization structure; Eliminate external intermediates, reach external constituencies.
Benefits	Cost savings on time, labor, people, money, etc.; Individual: Improved skills, knowledge, learning, decision-making, performance, and work life (physical, emotional, and social). Groups: improved coordination, cooperation, collaboration, communication, decision-making, productivity, culture, etc. Larger market share, saving transaction costs with external parties, Improved performance, better customer services.

We organize the possible courses of action and benefits in Table 7-5. Internally, IT/S often induces reorganization of workgroups as well as hiring a new workforce of some kind and eliminating others. On the next level, IT/S may provide education and training to personnel and change job content, tasks, skills, and the way an individual employee works. Externally, emerging IT/S is often seen to eliminate external intermediates and enable direct reach to the external constituencies, such as customers and suppliers.

Table 7-6. The Evolution of System Components throughout Development Stages

	People	Data	Process	Software	Hardware and Network
Planning	General user profile, targeted user groups	Information scope, major data entities, and rules	Functional scope, business process, value chain	Application direction, OS, DBMS	General hardware and network architecture
Analysis	Detailed user profile, organization analysis, interviews	General data requirements, data entities, attributes, and rules	Analyzed functions, operations, and processes requirement	Platform, developing tools, software, architectures	More specific hardware and network architecture
Design	Organizational restructuring, job design.	Database design	Design operations, tasks, and work flows	Software specifications for process, interface, and data.	Hardware and network specifications
Implementation	Training, operation	Data and information conversion, system documentation	Implement new operations, tasks, and work flows	Program coding, testing, configuration, installation	Procurement, installation, configuration and testing
Post-implementation	Document user feedback, people related measures.	Database maintenance, transaction verification, content verification	New operations, tasks and work flows, technical support	System usage and performance verification, maintenance, correction, and improvement	Performance verification, maintenance, and upgrading.

2.3.3 Development Stages-- Planning, Analysis, Design, Implementation, and Post-implementation

The purpose of this dimension is to characterize the evolutionary nature of system development and implementation so that evaluators can better adapt any necessary changes along the entire timeframe. A basic division is to separate the system timeline based on the time of system delivery to operation, with pre-implementation and post-implementation evaluations. Normally, the former mainly relies on the evaluator's projected value of a future system, and the latter may have more realistic measurement of benefits after the system is in operation. Yet, many IT/S projects typically involve extended software development processes. They require a further categorization of the activities before implementation. System development life cycle provides a natural categorization for this purpose. IT/S literature has prescribed a series of generic development activities in planning, analysis, design, implementation, and post-implementation stages. These activities produce ever more accurate information to enable refined evaluation, which, in return, feedbacks to development and implementation needs at each consecutive stage. We organize these activities and related information according to each system component and stage in Table 7-6 for evaluation reference.

The categorization generally follows the waterfall development model, i.e., one stage after the other. Yet it does not intend to be hard-pressed for applications in other system development models such as the spiral model used by Rensselaer's Laptop Program. Rather, evaluators should judge the existing development stage and adapt the content in each system component accordingly. For projects require little software development work, the analysis, design, and development stages naturally need to be packed down into one planning stage.

2.4 Implementation of Evaluation

An evaluation worksheet followed by an action plan was further developed as templates to facilitate the evaluation process. The worksheet serves as a tool to collect, analyze, aggregate, and process all the information available at each development stage and generate a result for certain decision making, i.e., a go-no-go. Besides, on most occasions, evaluators need to come out with an action plan that identifies development and/or implementation tasks for the next stage following a go decision.

2.4.1 Benefit Evaluation Worksheet

The benefit evaluation worksheet is designed to capture benefits of all levels and provide analysis and aggregation support for evaluation at each stage. It may be easier to understand the worksheet design by considering benefits as a relation between two entities, IT objects and stakeholders, as illustrated in Figure 7-3. That is, a certain benefit must be provided by a certain IT/S object and of concern to some stakeholders. IT objects can be a system as a whole or any of its subsets such as subsystems, functions, services, data, information, hardware, networks, etc. IT objects and stakeholders consist of virtually all system components, the second dimension of the model. Since both stakeholders and IT/S objects are tangible entities with composite relations and the whole system development process is endeavored to analyze, specify, and design them, there is no difficulty for specifying them along stages. With more specific IT objects and stakeholders, related benefits can be further specified, analyzed, and adjusted as necessary at each stage.

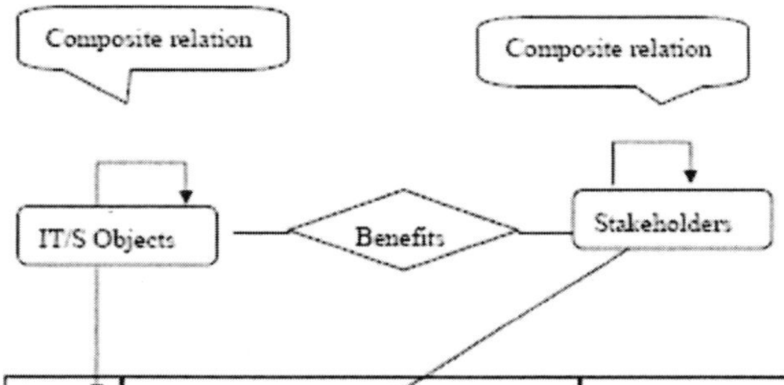

IS Objects	Stakeholders				Organizational Goals			
	S1	S2	S3	S4	G1	G2	G3	G4
IS1	B11	B12	B13	B14	C11	C12	C13	C14
IS2	B21	B22	B23	B24	C21	C22	C23	C24
IS3	B31	B32	B33	B34	C31	C32	C33	C34
IS4	B41	B42	B43	B44	C41	C42	C43	C44

Figure 7-3. Benefit Evaluation Worksheet

This relational model can be easily converted into half of the evaluation worksheet with IT objects on the rows, and stakeholders on the left half columns. The number of columns and rows are expandable as more specific IT objects and stakeholders are defined along system development timeline. The related benefits of specific IT object and stakeholders can be evaluated and put in the corresponding cells (i.e., B11 to B44 in the worksheet) with the assistance of a reference on system components.

The right half worksheet serves for evaluators to assess the contribution of each IT object to organizational goals. These goals, in a way, represent the ultimate benefits from the perspective of top management (a special body of stakeholder). While management may not be a direct user of the system, how the system impacts the institute as a whole is certainly a concern of top management. In practice, after completing the left half worksheet, the contribution level of each IT object is then assessed against each goal. The assessment on the cells under each goal column can be noted with descriptions, scores, or other numeric symbols.

Together, the worksheet provides a mechanism to view IT/S benefits on all levels in a simple yet comprehensive way. On each row, evaluators can examine how the whole system or any of its subsets impact each stakeholder and contributes to each goal. This feature supports the needs of various system planning and development decisions at different stages. For example, an evaluator can reject a system element or design when he/she does not see enough benefit for stakeholders or not much contribution to organizational goals. Besides, on each stakeholder column, evaluators can closely scrutinize benefits from user operation and system usage perspectives. This may provide a reference for planning implementation tasks and conducting post-implementation evaluations. Finally, the goal columns demonstrate a total contribution profile of a system from top management perspective. The worksheet operates such that evaluators will not "miss the forest for the trees."

2.4.2 Project Selection and Go-no-go Decision

One important purpose of IT/S evaluation is to support decision making in system planning, development, and implementation. There are at least three types of decision involved in the process. First, project selection or prioritization is often required in strategic planning where multiple projects often compete for scarce resources. Second is the go-no-go decision, which may be seen at the system planning stage or any of the later stages. Finally, various minor decisions need to be made for system design alternatives in the development process.

Essentially, all decisions depend primarily on the evaluator's judgment of various choices, which are influenced by factors such as the available courses of action, possible outcomes of the courses of action, individual preferences, and uncertainty. The model is not designed to replace these judgments, but rather, to provide a framework to help decision makers clarify and articulate decisions. The model, including the evaluation worksheet above, provides evaluators with a comprehensive view of benefits and their respective courses of action. It can support decision making with additional assessments of costs and risks.

Basically, IT/S costs can be determined from an activity or resource perspective. Generally, IT costs can be categorized into five kinds of activities: development of new IT/S, maintenance of existing IT/S, operation, end-user supports, and other planning and administration activities. A second, complementary approach is to segment the IT/S cost by mix of resources: hardware and software costs, personnel costs, costs of outside services, and other miscellaneous costs [18].

Risks may come from various sources. For example, there are risks inherent to projects due to characteristics such as project size, structure, complexity, duration, and employed technology. Other organizational and market factors, such as organizational experience with information technology, organizational culture toward change, and supply and demand changes in market, also need to be taken into account. McFarlan has proposed a Portfolio Approach to assess project risks by analyzing and scoring three risk categories: project size, organizational experience with technology, and project structure [19]. Such an approach is especially useful at the strategic planning stage. After a project is launched, risks in the above areas as well as other emerging risks should be continuously monitored, especially for long-term projects.

A spreadsheet using tools such as Scoring Model, Break-even Analysis, and other financial methods may do the job for multiple project selection or prioritization. Certainly, evaluators must be comfortable with quantification of benefits, costs, and risks in this situation. For tangible benefits and costs, any financial tool such as ROI, NPV, and Payback can be used to calculate metrics, which are then evaluated with other goals by entering scores and weighted indexes and calculating into a total score for comparison with other projects. Each project can also be evaluated by plotting its own benefit score against its projected risk. From the scattered plot diagram, an evaluator can select or rank projects with balanced consideration of benefits, cost, and risks.

Similarly in a go-no-go situation, it is easy to use a scoring model and financial methods to calculate the expected value of the project. Evaluators simply need to select a financial tool such as ROI to calculate tangible benefits and costs using the benefits evaluation worksheet. The calculated value along with intangible benefits and costs are together scored with a numeric scale. Adding the identified risk of the project, the evaluator can calculate the total expected value of this project. Usually a positive and high expected value would suggest a go decision, and a negative or low expected value would imply a termination decision or other necessary remedial measures. One should note that the risk involved in a project generally deceases as it progresses toward completion. And, especially at the later stages, costs incurred before the evaluation point should be considered "sunk costs," and be ruled out when considering project termination.

2.4.3 Action Plans for System Development and Implementation

An action plan is a by-product of evaluation. It serves a preventive and diagnostic function to chart the development and implementation activities forward. It should, on one hand, reflect the results of the evaluation, and, on the other hand, address the process needs of the following stages. The reference model includes elements for such needs. Based upon a completed benefits evaluation worksheet, evaluators can further use the elements on the second and third dimensions as the references and systematically work out a comprehensive action plan for the next stage.

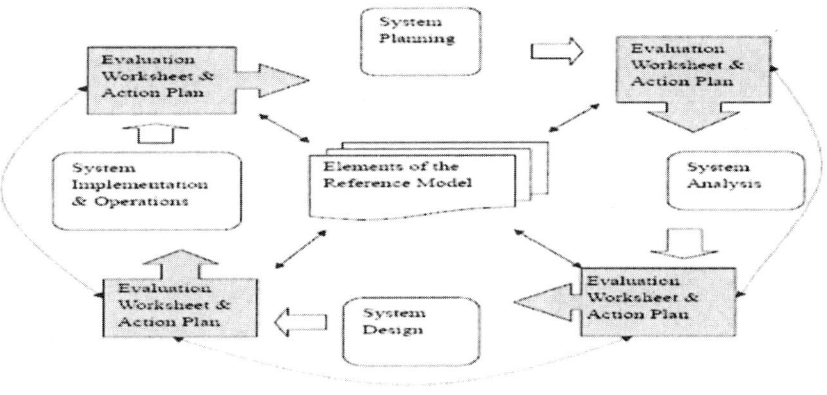

Figure 7-4. Implementation of the Evaluation along Development Stages

2.4.4 Evaluation along Development Stages

After prescribing the elements and implementation details of the model, the evaluation and development activities naturally become integrated into a continuous process, as illustrated in Figure 7-4. Evaluations take place at the milestones between each major development/implementation process. They generate the evaluation results with a benefit worksheet as the main product and an action plan as the by-product for the stage that follows. This process requires the evaluators' judgment, and it will perform more effectively with the incorporation of the prescribed elements of our model. The linkage between the evaluations at each stage (illustrated with the dotted arrows) also provides feedback and tracking capabilities. Through continuous iteration, the evaluation process can, in fact, generate insightful facts and enrich the elements of the model, which will essentially become the knowledge base of IT/S evaluation for the organization.

2.5 Model Validation

The evaluation model prescribed above has met the requirements defined before its development. It has equally served the multiple evaluation purposes, i.e., resource allocation, opportunity surfacing, quality checking and tuning, and organizational learning. Together it promises to generate better evaluation results. Such promises were validated through two case studies employing participant-observation, interviews, and documentation methods.

2.5.1 A Case Study at Taiwan Air Force Academy

From June 2000 to December 2002, we proposed and led a Campus-Wide Information System (CWIS) development project at the Taiwan Air Force Academy (TAFA) and evaluated it at different stages using the model. Through the application, the model has assisted the project team in evaluating benefits at various levels, regulating the system development alternatives in accordance with the goals and stakeholders' needs, adapting requirements and design changes, and generating an action plan for development and implementation at each stage. Overall, the model has systematically assisted evaluation by maintaining its quality while mitigating the costs and strains. The academy's management committee reflected that the model has demonstrated its value on IT/S project management and evaluation, and thus supported application on future projects to enhance accountability. An interview with US Army Academy (West Point) further confirmed that the validated institute, TAFA, resembled the US counterparts, and the model has well covered the goals and stakeholders for military institutes, and it appears to have a comprehensive structure to assist evaluations.

2.5.2 A Case Study on the RPI's Laptop Program

In the second case study, Rensselaer Polytechnic Institute was selected as the research field, a slightly different organizational setting. We looked into its Laptop Program, a long running project, to understand the nature of continuous evaluations and any respective problem. Once again, we observed the continuous nature of evaluations in a complex, long-term IT/S project. Some evaluations were conducted in a separate and formal way, and others were incorporated into development and implementation practices. Its evaluation purposes ranged from planning for approval and implementation, to diagnostic function for improved implementation. Its evaluation criteria varied from organization-level interests, to impacts on key stakeholders, and to concerns on system components.

Secondly, since it was not possible to directly apply the reference model in the program, we attempted to map the evaluation results to the model to see whether the three dimensions was in congruence with the evaluation needs. We found that the seven goals essentially matched what RPI has stated about its goals in principal, the main difference clustering around issues of areas of focus. A moderate adjustment of the goal dimension should be able to meet the institutional needs. To prove that the second dimension was also operational in this setting, we combined certain selected goals with the system components to map the benefits from the evaluation results. We easily completed an evaluation worksheet which covered all the documented benefits that RPI had evaluated in the program. Additionally, we found that the system components were useful for laying out the action plans for implementation activities. Overall, the mapping exercise validated that, with a moderate modification on the organization goals, the reference model should be applicable in the Laptop Program. The validation implies a potential generalization of the model in the broader education domain.

3. GUIDELINES OF USING THE MODEL

Though the reference model seems complex in structure with the three-tiered design, its implementation is simpler than it appears. Below are certain application guidelines.

3.1 General Guidelines

One very basic guideline is to recognize the different specification levels of application on the three tiers. Generally, the first tier comprises the three dimensions that are straightforward and easy to understand. It should work well in most generic evaluation contexts that evaluators are advised to maintain this perspective and then apply the rest in an adaptive way.

The second tier consists of elements that are further developed from the first tier. The contents are exemplified with instances and should be scalable at the disposal of an evaluator in accordance with organizational needs. For organizations that have set their goals well, there is, of course, no need to totally replace them. However, it would be always a good approach to follow the same tactic using Porter's Value Chain to review the goals. As to the benefit evaluation profile for each system component (Table 7-1 to 7-5), the contents are not exhaustive in nature. Rather, organizations should expand any possible form of benefit, and enrich this knowledge base for the time being. In the same token, Table 7-6 provides a comparative view of the evolutionary system components along the development stage. It only serves a general reference purpose for looking into the right system component at the right time. Organizations should adapt its use in different contexts, such as when using a different development approach or methodology.

The third tier is a set of modularized templates to reduce the complexity of evaluation process at each stage. With the design worksheet, evaluators can easily document and process evaluation data and make decisions accordingly. Following the same logic from the conceptual model (the first tier) and the substantiated elements (the second tier), organizations may develop their own worksheet for the same purpose. Even in many occasions where an evaluation, especially for projects of small size, only takes a simple mental process, there is certainly no need to use the template.

3.2 Criteria for Consideration of Employing the Model

Certainly, the model is not a tool suitable for all evaluation occasions. While it is appropriate to use the model in certain IT/S projects under many circumstances, it may not be suitable at all in other projects or under different circumstances. Some criteria for consideration of its application are identified and elaborated below.

3.2.1 Evolutionary Nature of the IT/S Project in Question

Like a living organism, an information system generally evolves from its initial stage through the entire life cycle. Different projects, as different species, have different evolutionary characteristics. Some quickly reach their maturity and change little after; others tend to evolve gradually and continuously. Generally, the more drastic the evolutionary nature a project possesses, the more it will require continuous evaluation, and thus the more suitable for using the reference model.

One easy way to determine the evolutionary nature of a project is to look at its five components--people, process, data, software, and hardware and network. From the external or supply side, the elements of software, hardware, and network will remain a powerful pulling force of evolution due to the continuous and drastic changes in IT. On the internal or demand side, issues related to people, process, and data components involved in a project, such as diverse user groups, uncertain requirements, and complex processes, will affect its evolutionary nature. Systems in service-oriented enterprises may obviously fall in this category. Besides, long-duration and large-scale IT/S projects tend to be more evolutionary, and vice versa.

3.2.2 Impacts of the IT/S project in Nature

The reference model, in essence, is a framework for evaluating the impacts of an IT/S project. Depending on project types and organizational settings, some impacts can be easily, directly, and immediately determined, while many others can only be realized indirectly, gradually, and even long after implementation. Some are localized in certain operational departments, while others are pervasive in organizations and tend to be strategic and intangible by nature and even provide global implications for the entire enterprise. The model should suit well regardless of the system impacts. However, IT/S projects with indirect, long-term, strategic, and pervasive impacts tend to require more attention and effort to evaluate, and thus should benefit more from using the model. IT/S projects in service-oriented enterprises obviously belong to this category.

3.2.3 Top Management Commitment to Continuous Evaluation

Another key driving force for continuous evaluation is top management commitment, which may be driven by their understanding of evaluation needs, or recognition of the strategic importance of a certain project. The model is typically useful on such occasions where top management plays a key role in evaluation, since the first dimension offers a representation of impact analysis from top management perspective with the prescribed organizational goals and respective measures.

3.2.4 Resources Available for Continuous Evaluation

The three criteria above can be recognized from a demand perspective. From a supply perspective, IT/S evaluations require various resources, such as personnel, knowledge, mechanisms, methods, and tools, which may or may not be available in every organization. In general, a collaborative approach is useful to develop consensus and ensure the completeness of evaluation. Depending on the resource availability and project's size and complexity level, the reference model may be applied with a different level of involvement. In organizations without any evaluation experience or adequate resources, the model can be used to establish a new mechanism for conducting continuous evaluations. On the other hand, the model is not aimed at replacing existing evaluation practices, or to totally reallocate the evaluation resources that have been long in position in organizations such as RPI. Rather, it can serve as a framework for integrating existing evaluation practices and resources.

4. AN ILLUSTRATIVE EXAMPLE USING THE REFERENCE MODEL

We now use the CWIS case at TAFA to illustrate the use of the model in more details[4]. A brief description of the development and evaluation process is followed by an analysis and discussion of the case in this section.

4.1 A Brief Description of the Case

As with many IT/S projects, the CWIS project encountered various problems and challenges along its course of development. Particularly, the system domain involved several different functional units, many of the processes and workflows within these divisions were complex and not yet standardized, the Academy's personnel tended to resist change, and the organizational culture was highly concerned with security. All these features increased the complexity of the project and hampered the development process. While evaluations had played an important role in managing the project and meeting these challenges, the reference model provided a framework to guide the evaluation practices along the development process.

The evaluation at the planning stage took more efforts due to the initial uncertain situation and the need for establishing convention and protocol. Its purpose was to help formulate a comprehensive plan for approval from the academy's top management and the Air Force Headquarters. The reference model was applied to analyze the projected benefits along with an overall process and required resources. We first reviewed organizational goals based upon the academy needs by examining the nine value chains that have been

[4] Due to the space limit, only key selected issues about the case are documented in this volume. For a full cover on the case, see Wu, M. "Continuous Evaluation of IS Development: A Reference Model," Doctoral thesis. Rensselaer Polytechnic Institute, 2003.

defined in the model and found that they have covered the current major activities at the academy. Each goal was then evaluated with different weights according to their importance to the academy. Next, for people component, we identified four groups of stakeholders, i.e., students, faculty, administration staff, and IT staff. For IT objects, we began with two major parts: administration system and utilities services. So far, the administration system was expected to cover human resources, enrollment, courses, and grade management, and the utilities services planned to include web service and expand email service. Though more functions and integration might be added to the project, but the exact scope and user requirements were not certain at this point. These system components and organizational goals were put into the evaluation worksheet for identifying the benefits using Table 7-1 to 7-5 as a reference. We then aggregated the benefits on the worksheet and judged their contribution level to organization goals with different scores.

In the evaluation worksheet, there were certainly more potential benefits not yet identified due to many still unknown requirements As a result, we formulated an action plan particularly for the analysis stage. Elements on Dimension II and III (Table 7-1 to 7-6) were used as a reference to point out the key tasks regarding the five system components. For example, military instructors, Professional Military Education students, and various other administration staff and several related processes were pinpointed for analysis at the next stage. Thus, we detailed a schedule for interviewing each group of users and related analysis tasks.

Evaluations at later stages followed a similar fashion, except that benefits on system components became more specific with the evaluation worksheet getting bigger. Based upon the completed evaluation worksheet after several stages, it was easy to come up with an action plan for post-implementation audit. For example, upon system implementation, system logs and data transaction was checked to understand the actual system usage. A problem reporting process was established to collect maintenance requests and complaints from paper forms, phone calls, and email. Interviews, meetings, and surveys were held and related data were collected and analyzed for taking necessary remedial measures or further improvement initiatives.

4.2 Discussion and Analysis

The TAFA case had illustrated the evolutionary nature of a typical long-term IT/S development project. The project started with an idea to simply replace an old centralized database system, and was soon expanded to incorporate a larger scope of development. The expansion was only an initial vague vision with uncertain requirements that were gradually realized through a yearlong process. A similar evolution took place within the academy's personnel too. At the early stages of development, some people were skeptical and even resistant, while others had over expectations of the initiative. There were many complaints from users concerning its implementation, yet they soon became reliant on the system and asked for further improvements and expansion of the system. As a result of such requests, the academy had to plan more initiatives for further enhancement of the system in the future.

Due to the initial skepticism and resistance among the academy's staff, it was rather difficult to redesign processes before computerizing them. Thus, benefits reaped from process redesign were limited. Yet the implemented system immediately reduced the operational costs of existing processes and maintenance costs of the previous database system. Beyond these tangible benefits, the project introduced new capabilities to the academy, such as web service, bulletin board, and online survey services, which were expected to impact faculty, staff, and students in their communication, teaching, and learning. However, as not many staff and faculty knew how to make web pages or felt they need to, these tools still required promotion, enforcement, and time to gain a widespread usage in the academy. As a result, it would take a longer time to pin down such long-term and strategic impacts while the personnel was still learning and the system itself was still evolving.

The above analysis justified that the CWIS project required continuous evaluation to best understand the project's impacts on the institute. Though the academy's top management did not fully understand the significance of continuous evaluation, they were aware of the importance of this project and ordered that the project be monitored on track toward its completion. In terms of resources, the institute's Information Center was the only agency in charge of IT/S evaluations. Yet, except for some routine checks on system usage with certain metrics such as data transaction and network volume, there was no formal mechanism to regulate the evaluation practices.

Under such circumstances, the reference model had served as a project management tool and helped establish an IT/S evaluation mechanism for the institute. Specifically, the model had helped achieve four goals.

First, the model has provided a framework for the project team to construct a comprehensive benefit profile that incorporates the perspectives of top management, system users, and system developers/maintainers. From the top management perspective, the first dimension prescribes the seven goals that the academy has endeavored to attain. The second dimension, on the other hand, helps visualize how students, faculty, staff, and other personnel interact with the system in terms of process, data, software, and hardware. Together, the two dimensions assist the project team to obtain a broad understanding about how the system and its subsystems would impact the related stakeholders and contribute to each organizational goal.

Second, the benefit profile helped identify and finalize user requirements, which tended to be unknown in the early stages and continue to change over the course of development. The issue of uncertain requirements was especially difficult in this case, because some users, who were resistant to the project, tended not to offer their requirements for the system development, while others, with over expectations for the system, would ask for unrealistic capabilities. With organizational goals and system components laid out in the framework, the model helped recognize relevant users and identify their respective process and data requirements. On the other hand, it also supported the project team to screen out certain required features that were less essential or beneficiary to the stakeholders or the academy as a whole.

Third, besides determining the users' requirements and system specifications, the model assisted in allocating resources for system development. For example, due to an overall understanding of the system components and their impacts, the project team was ready to procure additional servers and equipment in the middle of development when a certain amount of budget surplus was added to the project's disposal. The installment of the additional devices, though not included in the original system plan due to the initial budget limit, had improved the system performance and enhanced its security.

Finally, the model provided a linkage between stages and offered references for system evaluation and development practices. Information loading for evaluation at each stage was reduced by incorporating the evaluation results at the previous stage with relevant system information at the present stage. Subsequently, the model systematically provided tracing back and charting forward capabilities, which had mitigated the costs and strains of evaluating the CWIS project.

5. CONCLUSION

The research aims to pursue a better solution for evaluation on complex, long term IT/S projects. Through participant-observation, interviews, and document examination on two cases, we have revealed and constructed the real nature of continuous evaluation on complex, long-term IT/S projects. We have also analyzed the problems observed and identified the needs for a methodology to facilitate continuous evaluation in the course of system development.

Based upon the problems and needs, we have developed the three-dimensional reference evaluation model, a framework that enables continuous evaluation to be conducted in a systematic and cost-effective way. This original model adds to the previous results on project evaluation and program management. The case study on the Laptop Program has exploited the potential for a generalization of the model in the general higher education domain. Further extensions of the model to general business firms, especially to service-oriented enterprises, are also possible and favorable.

The research can strengthen further in the area of longitude case study. Validating the model on additional cases would be advantageous to its generalization to a certain extent. Future research would benefit from an extension of the model to incorporate such categories as costs and risks into a more inclusive framework. Lastly, the model is amenable to computerization, using more powerful templates or even database applications. Further integration of the model with certain CASE (computer-aided software engineering) tools is also possible. Such a computerization promises to mitigate costs and further promote continuous evaluation in the actuality.

REFERENCES

1. Keen, P.G.W., *Computer-Based Decision Aids: The Evaluation Problem.* Sloan Management Review, 1975(spring): p. 17-30.
2. Keim, R.T. and R. Janaro, *Cost/Benefit Analysis for MIS.* Journal of Systems Management, 1982(September): p. 20-25.
3. Gildersleeve, T.R., *Successful Data Processing System Analysis.* 1978, New Jersey: Prentice-Hall.
4. Peters, G., *Beyond Strategy - Benefits identification and Management of Specific IT Investment.* Journal of Information Technology, 1990(5): p. 205-214.
5. Ward, J.e.a., *Evaluation and Realisation of IS/IT Benefits: an Empirical Study of Current Practice.* European Journal of Information System, 1996. 4(4): p. 214-225.
6. Willcocks, L. and S. Lester, *The Evaluation and Management of Information Systems Investments: from Feasibility to Routine Operations*, in *Investing in Information System: Evaluation and Management*, L. Willcocks, Editor. 1996, Chapman & Hall: London. p. 15-36.
7. Remenyi, D. and M. Sherwood-Smith, *Business Benefits from Information Systems Through an Active Benefits Realization Programme.* International Journal of Project Management, 1998. 16(2): p. 81-98.
8. Roy, S., *Interactive Learning and Mobile Computing at Rensselaer*, in *Ubiquitous Computing --The Universal use of Computers on College Campuses*, D.G. Brown, Editor. 2003, Anker.
9. Parker, M.M., *Enterprise Information Analysis: Cost-Benefit Analysis and the Data-Managed System. IBM System Journal*, 1982. 21(1): p. 108-23.

10. Parker, M.M., *Strategic Transformation and Information Technology: Paradigms for Performing while Transforming*. 1996, NJ: Prentice-Hall.
11. Kaplan, R.S. and D.P. Norton, *The Balanced Scorecard - Measures that Drive Performance. Harvard Business Review*, 1992(January-February): p. 71-79.
12. Kaplan, R.S. and D.P. Norton, *Putting the Balanced Scorecard to Work. Harvard Business Review*, 1993(September-October): p. 134-47.
13. Kaplan, R.S. and D.P. Norton, *Using the Balanced Scorecard as a Strategic Management System. Harvard Business Review*, 1996(January-February): p. 75-86.
14. Porter, M., *Competitive Advantage*. 1984: Free Press.
15. Porter, M.E. and V.E. Millar, *How Information Gives you Competitive Advantage*. Harvard Business Review, 1985(July-August): p. 149-60.
16. Zachman, J.A., *A Framework for Information Systems Architecture*. IBM Systems Journal, 1987. 26(3): p. 276-292.
17. Sowa, J.F. and J.A. Zachman, *Extending and Formalizing the Framework for Information System Architecture*. IBM Systems Journal, 1992. 31(3): p. 590-615.
18. Zee, H.v.d., *Measuring the Value of Information Technology*. 2002, Hershey, PA: Idea Group Publishing. 213.
19. McFarlan, F.W., *Portfolio Approach to Information Systems. Harvard Business Review*, 1981. 59(5): p. 142-51.

Chapter 8

MODELS OF CYBERINFRASTRUCTURE-BASED ENTERPRISES AND THEIR ENGINEERING

An Evolutionary Journey

Cheng Hsu
Rensselaer Polytechnic Institute, 110 8th Street, Troy, NY 121809-3590, USA

Abstract: The object of the analysis here is to understand how to simultaneously maximize the value to customer and the economy of scale, for enterprises that rely on knowledge workers and digital production factors. Cyber-infrastructure, in this study, is defined to be the fusion of information technology and information resources, including the elements that integrate persons and the environment with the enterprises. Computerized manufacturing, e-commerce/e-business, and on-demand business/services all represent the evolution of cyber-infrastructure-based/assisted enterprises. The evolution is analyzed to be driven by a new mode of micro-economical production function: the Output-Input Fusing paradigm. In this context, the value to client/customer is acquired with on-demand co-production, and the economy of scale is achieved through concurrent co-productions with the assistance of the cyber-infrastructure. Basic principles for planning such enterprises are derived from previous results. A "thought model" for the design, administration, and processing of the new cyber-infrastructure is presented. Particular new results, including a specific design for person-environment-enterprise interaction, are proposed.

Key words: Cyber-infrastructure, Enterprise Engineering, Service Productivity, On-Demand Business/Service, Person-Centered paradigm.

1. CO-PRODUCTION IS THE SOLUTION, NOT THE PROBLEM

1.1 The Micro-Economical Production Function

The journey of natural sciences is marked by discoveries of the basic laws, elements, and structures of our universe. In a similar albeit far less definitive way, the journey of economic sciences also manifests certain basic principles that have withstood the test of time. One such principle is the pursuit of economical efficiency embodied in this micro-economical model: efficiency (E) is achieved by the quotient of output (O) over input (I); or:

$$E = O/I$$

From a person-centered perspective, E is measured in utility, or the value to the person. For firms, however, E is ultimately evaluated in terms of profit. More telling is, perhaps, the principles revealed for I and O. They define the models of enterprises and their engineering at a macro (societal) level – i.e., their implementation determines the production function of an economy. Clearly, there can be three basic paradigms for improving the production function and creating better E: O-pulling (user/demand-dominate), I-pushing (provider/supply-dominate), and O-I fusing (user-provider co-production).

The O-pulling paradigm is the historical norm [8]. That is, human economical activities are always motivated by demand and delivered on demand. We do not have much reason to believe that the force of demand today is weaker or stronger than it was in the past, or it will be in the future. However, I-pushing has become a norm, too, especially for manufactured goods since the Industrial Revolution. This mode of production thrived on its promises of affordability and availability to the customers, achieved through the ever-lowering of production costs made possible by electricity and other technological breakthroughs at the time. The innovations opened up a historical possibility to alter the micro-economical production function and pursue the economy of scale on the provider side. The then new paradigm pursued and achieved standardization of parts (e.g., bills of materials) and rationalization of processes (e.g., flow shops and job shops), and resulted in attendant enterprise engineering models. They perfected mass production and the organizations that implemented this paradigm of production [4, 15].

I-pushing can reconcile with O-pulling as long as user demands are substitutable. That is, users could trade less preferable products for more affordable ones and still satisfy their basic needs. This premise fits well with most physical products, but it is dubious when the utility is concerned with services – be it personal services such as medical care or business consulting such as enterprise processes. Consequently, the I-pushing paradigm has never really succeeded on services, thus failed the need of service economy.

1.2 The O-I Fusing Paradigm

The third paradigm, O-I fusing, stems from yet another wave of technological breakthroughs: the advent of digital chips, computers and telecommunications/networks. This mode of production places the user (persons and enterprises) alongside the provider throughout the product cycle as in a pre-Industrial Revolution O-pulling ideal, but this time with the affordability and availability of the I-pushing promises. If we employ the notion of co-production from services, then this mode is precisely co-production with economy of scale.

The paradigm first emerged in the form of computerization as a fix or extension to the I-pushing mode, i.e., a pursuit of automation with flexibility, so as to further lower the cost and better accommodate the demand [6]. The notions of agile manufacturing and mass-customization reflect this initial understanding of O-I fusing; both of which seek to make standardization flexible by using informatics. Then, the pursuit became a fundamental shifting of paradigms prompted by the New Economy of e-commerce/e-business [3, 5, 11] and on-demand business/services. The new vision, riding on the new waves of technological innovations, calls for bringing the illusive productivity gains into the service sector, or even reconcile the models of service enterprises with those of manufacturing.

To fully realize the vision, the field needs more specifics to substantiate the new paradigm. For instance, automation implies embedded intelligence, and flexibility the ability to reconfigure. When they are put together, the implication is automatic reconfiguration using the intelligence embedded in the "system", the "environment", or the "infrastructure" (in the sense of ubiquitous, pervasive, and mobile computing). These required results need to be developed using new technology. If electricity has enabled the I-pushing paradigm, do we have sufficient technological innovations to fully enable an O-I fusing paradigm? Many would agree that the answer is affirmative, and is found in the notion of Cyber-Infrastructure. Many would even assert that the O-I fusing paradigm is becoming a reality in certain segments of the economy since 1980's.

1.3 The Cyber-Infrastructure

Intuitively, for the purpose of this study, we consider cyber-infrastructure to be the fusion of information technology and information resources at a societal level. It connects enterprises with their external constituencies, along their respective demand chains and supply chains. The field does not offer a definitive, scientific model of cyber-infrastructure, but many would describe it as a digital nervous system of the society, consisting of wired and wireless networks, computing hardware and devices, digital data and knowledge resources, computing software, and digital user interface mechanism (the phrase "digital nervous system" was first coined by Mr. Bill Gates). The societal cyber-infrastructure connects all persons and all organizations, and adds a digital dimension to all traditional infrastructures (e.g., a layer of wireless sensor networks on highways and terrains as well as shop floors; a transponder-transceiver chip on every vehicle, cargo, and workstation; and a network of (wireless) chips carried by all persons to go about their daily lives). It may include embedded analytics and databases at all nodes, as well as afford two-way communication capabilities among all nodes and between physical elements and human users. A lot of this definition is still a vision, but a lot else have already been realized since the 1960's when computers were first widely employed in industry and commerce.

The above description could be organized into a "totem pole" of cyber-infrastructure elements. At the bottom is the layer of networks and telecommunications elements. Above it is a layer of computers and other digital devices, including transponder-transceiver systems, person-carried chips, and environmental sensor networks. The third layer from below signifies digital information resources, ranging from data to knowledge and basic algorithms. The layer above the information resources is process resources made of application software programs and workflow controls. The fifth and highest layer is users and user interfaces. The totem pole describes a comprehensive environment of enterprising.

We also consider three classes of deployment of cyber-infrastructure: enterprise, environment, and person. Enterprise cyber-infrastructure refers primarily to the enterprise information technology and systems that have been widely employed by firms. This class continues to evolve, develop, and perfect. The notion of environmental cyber-infrastructure goes beyond the Internet and telecommunications satellites to include a possible digital dimension added to the physical environment. In a similar way, the personal cyber-infrastructure includes possible new technology that provides embedded or automated digital devices to persons and mobile objects.

1.4 Service Enterprises

Service products typically require co-production – i.e., on-the-spot participation of the user in the production of the service by the provider, such as consultation and the transactions of enterprise processes. By definition, the provision of this type of service must be individual, on-demand, and real-time; and hence the production processes involved must be personalized or customized. These characteristics, among other things, make standardization difficult – e.g., how to define the standard parts and the bills-of-materials for knowledge-based, perishable products? The only success of mass production in the realm of personal services is arguably the school model of education. Even here, the mode of production still differs fundamentally from that of manufacturing (e.g., the real-time, individual counseling to students). In general, the field needs to figure out what is, and how to achieve, the economy of scale of services to boost productivity.

The new technology, i.e., cyber-infrastructure, may have an answer to the problem. With the assistance of cyber-infrastructure, the user-provider co-production nature and the reliance on knowledge may become a solution for achieving the economy of scale, rather than a root cause of the failure of the I-pushing paradigm. When the products are characterized by digital production factors – which are re-usable (not consumed); and engineered by knowledge workers, who can collaborate with the users; the cyber-infrastructure that connects and organizes them all becomes the rendition of the enterprise's co-production function. The enterprise succeeds or fails on its ability to share these re-usable factors. Therefore, the cyber-infrastructure promises to be the object on which an enterprise achieves economy of scale. Cyber-infrastructure-based service enterprises in the O-I fusing paradigm could, and perhaps should, focus on pursuing co-production and achieving the economy of scale through sharing the cyber-infrastructure for all co-productions. This mode does not require standard bills-of-materials, but virtual configurations of the cyber-infrastructure on demand.

If co-production is not the problem, but the solution, then the question is how to enable it. Since large scale co-production is enabled by cyber-infrastructure, the proper way to achieve economy of scale has to be through large scale sharing of the cyber-infrastructure among co-productions, not through more I-pushing standardization. Recent results in the field, ranging from computerized manufacturing (e.g., flexible manufacturing systems) to e-commerce/e-business (e.g., the ISP and ASP models), have illustrated this point. We discuss these results in Sections 3 and 4, respectively.

We submit that co-production is the ideal of the O-I fusing paradigm. It could achieve economy of scale for enterprises using cyber-infrastructure (beyond computerization). Cyber-infrastructure-based/assisted enterprises implement the O-I fusing paradigm and, if e-commerce/e-business is any indication, up-lift the micro-economical production function for our society.

We discuss below how cyber-infrastructure-based/assisted enterprises can achieve economy of scale with co-production. Section 2 derives some principles of cyber-infrastructure-based/assisted enterprises from the lessons of computerized manufacturing and e-commerce/e-business. Section 3, then, summarizes how these principles are working for manufacturing, in a transition from I-pushing to O-I fusion. Section 4 discusses some new results required to consummate the transition for services. First, a "thought model" for achieving economy of scale using cyber-infrastructure is presented. The model features a "three-schema cyber-infrastructure" concept to support virtual configurations. Some of the best practices of e-commerce/e-business are summarized in this context, along with a suggested research agenda to develop the new model. Section 5 proposes a particular Subject-Environment Interaction Model to make the cyber-infrastructure itself an active partner of enterprise engineering, and thereby achieve automatic re-configuration of co-productions. A discussion, in Section 6, of possible future directions of the evolution concludes the chapter.

2. PRINCIPLES OF CYBER-INFRASTRUCTURE-BASED/ASSISTED ENTERPRISES

Concepts such as "computer-based", "IT-enabled", and "Internet-based" are harbingers of the notion of "cyber-infrastructure-based/assisted". As stated in Section 1, cyber-infrastructure is defined as the fusion of the common information technology and information resources for the society as well as for individual enterprises. Therefore, although the concept of cyber-infrastructure-based/assisted enterprises is newly formulated in this chapter, it is not a discrete change but rather represents an extension of the previous concepts, and embodies the lessons of their practices in the field.

2.1 The Principle of Transaction Cost and Cycle Time Reduction

The value of investment on Information Technology is not always clear. For example, the so-called "productivity paradox" of late 1990's and early 2000's shows the difficulty of properly accounting for the contributions of

IT to firms – or, more broadly, the micro-economical production function for the society. Firms tend to rely on such measures as Return on Investment (ROI) to evaluate their IT projects, although it is well known that ROI does not account well for intangible benefits, which happen to be crucial contributions of IT and Information Systems.

A broader and more appropriate view is found in the concept of organizational transaction cost [27], which examines the whole enterprise and accounts for both tangible (e.g., savings on labor) and intangible (e.g., effectiveness) returns. This concept corroborates with the well-established premise that an organization is brought into being to process information (transactions) for making the right decisions and taking the right actions to accomplish the organization's goals [9]. The interesting point is, while the notion of organizational information processing could be abstract and measurable only in theoretical terms, it becomes concrete for cyber-infrastructure-based enterprises. That is, if the cyber-infrastructure is brought into being to implement the organization, its processing is the organizational information processing. Therefore, from the productivity perspective, the value of cyber-infrastructure is manifested in its contributions to the organizational transaction cost for the enterprise. Furthermore, we submit that the contributions are measurable in terms of the reduction to the individual process transaction costs and the reduction to the total cycle time.

Cycle time is evidently measurable, such as the time to market for new product development and the throughput (service or physical) of a process. It is related to transaction cost but is not necessarily reducible to it. In particular, if a cycle consists only of sequential processes, then the cycle time is determined by the sum of the process transaction costs. However, if it is not, then the total cycle time could be more a function of the sequences of processes, than the individual transaction costs. Naturally, engineering the arrangements of component processes determines the total cycle time in the general case. In addition, automation, simplification and consolidation of processes could also reduce total cycle time. They, especially automation, are commonly associated with cost reduction – the tangible benefits.

However, transaction cost appears to be intangible in the general case since organizational tasks and processes outside shop floors tend to be non-definitive. This non-definitiveness includes service co-production. Albeit not as concrete as time and money, transaction cost is still measurable in this case, at least in terms of utility functions and overall performance. Often, it may even be measured directly through the evaluation of workload and workflow involved in these tasks and processes.

For example, how much transaction cost has paper currency saved the society over bartering? One could answer this question by asking how much it costs one to return the bottles and collect the refund at a supermarket, or how much they would be discounted if one barters them for groceries at a corner store. The transaction cost of a particular job to the person performing it could be assessed by how much the person is willing to pay others to do it for her/him – such as hiring an agent or a broker. The value of the Internet can be substantiated case by case; for instance, how much time (effort) it takes us to collect information about colleges without using the Internet? In this case, the total sales of all college data books prior to the Internet indicates an upper bound of the fungible value of the Internet on the reduction of the transaction cost for doing the job. In general, the so-called "red tapes" are precisely transaction costs, which could be so high as to become an inhibitor for undertaking an enterprise. As an illustration, if certain tax breaks are required to attract a direct foreign investment, then the value of the breaks could reflect the cost of the red tapes perceived. Finally, to show one more example, an organization could quantify the minimum value of a global database query system by compiling the time its employees spend on the phone and meetings that could have been saved by the system. In one word, "convenience" succinctly describes the nature of transaction cost. Transaction cost and cycle time together spell productivity.

We submit that the value of cyber-infrastructure investment should be measured in terms of reduction of transaction cost and cycle time. The traditional ROI could be incorporated in this new, extended measure. More fundamentally, we submit that the economy of cyber-infrastructure-based enterprises on productivity is the reduction of transaction cost and cycle time. The challenge is, therefore, how to achieve the scale factor in a cyber-infrastructure-based enterprise. The following principles explore this question. In particular, the next two achieve the digital scale advantage.

2.2 The Principle of Digital Connection and Sharing

Digitization is a premise of cyber-infrastructure-based enterprises. That is, these enterprises turn their information resources into digital, their processing digital, and their communication channels digital. However, the unique power of digitization is not just tapping into the computing power of IT – i.e., digitization is not just computerization. The really unprecedented promise of digitization is the ability to connect and share: the potential that all digital elements in the world could be connected – fused, indeed – through cyber-infrastructure and be shared as a whole by any, with infinitely many possible ways of utilization. Adam Smith's "invisible hand" promises to be visible in the cyber-dimension of the economy.

Digital camera and e-mail provide two ready examples of the power of connection. Camera for camera, the traditional optical pictures still enjoy clear advantages over their digital competitors. However, digital cameras win over the market because their pictures are digital resources that can be connected with the users' other digital resources. Users can email, edit, and publish them as they do their ordinary files on the computer; and they can integrate them with these files, as well. The fax machines lost to email as a favored means of written communication for the same reason. They are an isolated tool that cannot fuse with others, while email is open and scalable in its connection and coupling with other digital resources. More broadly, the history of Information Systems is one of integration of digital resources for their users. Needless to say, the Internet offers the most conspicuous exhibit of the power of this principle.

One might mention informally the "small world phenomenon" (due to Stanley Milgram [2]). This interesting postulate suggests that two random persons in the society are connected with no more than six intermediary acquaintances (called six degrees of separation – which could be conversely called six degrees of connection). For example, if one knows someone who knows President Bill Clinton, then s/he has one-degree connection with Mr. Clinton; and anyone who knows her/him has two degree connection with the President. With the Internet, along with search engines and email, one could argue that the small world is crashing into one where everyone is poised to connect with everyone else in zero degree through the societal cyber-infrastructure. The saving of the intermediaries spells reduction in societal transaction cost. Therefore, connection represents reduction of transaction cost (vis-à-vis the costs of connection).

We submit that an enterprise should integrate itself through digital connection for all its internal and external constituencies. All enterprise resources, especially databases, should be connected and made sharable; and ultimately, all that the cyber-infrastructure can reach should connect, including the persons in the extended enterprise. This principle reduces transaction cost. It is especially important for co-production, where the users need to share the production resources and facility with the providers, in a manner of enterprise collaboration.

2.3 The Principle of Concurrent Processes and Co-Productions

If connection is reduction of transaction cost, then concurrent processes are reduction of cycle time. With the cyber-infrastructure connecting the whole (extended) enterprise, enterprise processes become the particular uses of the cyber-infrastructure to accomplish particular tasks. The use, and hence the process, manifests a particular virtual configuration (path of usage) of certain elements of the cyber-infrastructure. The economy of scale principle suggests that the cyber-infrastructure should be shared by as many users, processes, and products as possible. Therefore, the moral here is to make all processes from all products – be it on-demand, custom, or pro forma – concurrent users of the cyber-infrastructure, for as much as they can be conducted concurrently and as long as the cyber-infrastructure can support all the virtual configurations required. A reference point is the enterprise databases. The same database infrastructure drives all virtual configurations of the data resources (e.g., views) to allow all users running their processes (e.g., global queries and applications) against it, concurrently.

This principle has a humble but intuitive illustration of its cycle time reduction nature. If, for example, a job requires 1000 man-hours to complete, then it takes only one hour to finish if 1000 men work on it simultaneously. The sophistication comes when one considers the reality of how to make all 1000 men working at the same time on the same job. Resources availability could be a bottleneck and sequencing of work could be another. Also, there is the need for coordination and synchronization. Computer science offers some basic answer at the algorithmic level, and human ingenuity provides many intriguing ideas in various domains (such as the distributed data processing in the SETI project [21]). However, the most rigorous results at the enterprise engineering level come from manufacturing.

Since 1980's, the field has established substantive models, technology, and systems under such visions as Computer-Integrated Manufacturing, Concurrent Engineering, and Agile Manufacturing. They revealed particular ways to allow for parallel manufacturing control, distributed engineering design, and simultaneous execution of product life cycle tasks. Most of all, they developed a basic concept, that of virtual team, for concurrent undertaking of enterprise processes using cyber-infrastructure. For example, the simultaneous engineering models, referred to as Design-for-X, with X being anything ranging from manufacturability to serviceability, connect tasks and processes at the later stages of a product development life cycle with the earlier ones, and executes them through virtual teams. These teams configure persons and resources from different stages without having to physically co-locate them. The team method turns sequential processes into concurrent by interweaving the detailed steps and tasks of each process with those of others, with the support of a common cyber-infrastructure.

For enterprises that rely on knowledge workers and digital resources, cyber-infrastructure could generalize the concept of virtual teams into one that includes the users and other external constituencies, along the supply chain and the demand chain, with unlimited possibilities. Teams could readily implement co-production for any cyber-infrastructure-based enterprises without changing fundamentally their internal production systems every time this mode is attempted. Therefore, an application service provider or on-demand enterprising provider could run millions of co-productions against its cyber-infrastructure. All processes of the co-productions could use different, virtual configurations of the cyber-infrastructure. Therefore, the economy of scale is achieved in this mode.

We submit that concurrent processes achieve the scale advantage made possible by digital connection and sharing. They should be designed with the concept of virtual teams for, possibly, co-production; and be implemented with concurrent virtual configurations of the enterprise cyber-infrastructure.

2.4 The Principle of Openness, Scalability, and Re-Configurability

Cyber-infrastructure is societal in nature. An enterprise cannot confine itself to proprietary technologies when using cyber-infrastructure. Instead, it has to leverage what is available in the society in order to, at least, work with its external constituencies. Furthermore, one physical cyber-infrastructure can support many different uses and could appear differently to different users if necessary. The concept of virtual teams and virtual configurations describe this virtual nature of cyber-infrastructure. Therefore, an enterprise cyber-infrastructure is inherently dynamic in almost every aspect.

It follows that the enterprise cyber-infrastructure has to be open to different technologies and proprietary controls. This call leads to the open source ideal; but could also use common standards as an open connectivity solution for proprietary technologies. Next, the cyber-infrastructure has to be able to expand continuously, without requiring reconstruction or causing major disruption. Such a requirement could arise easily from innovations in a firm's business vision. Finally, the cyber-infrastructure has to support smooth re-configuration and restructuring of its physical elements, in order to adapt to their changing usage patterns by the virtual configurations. This adjustment optimizes the overall performance of the cyber-infrastructure.

We submit that cyber-infrastructure-based enterprises need to be prepared to connect with any part of the society and deal with perpetuating transient states of their business. The IT revolution since the 1990's shows that the ever-evolving societal cyber-infrastructure brings about ever-deepening changes to all corners of the economy.

2.5 The Principle of Cyber-Infrastructure Assistance

Cyber-infrastructure possesses information resources (see Section 1); thus it is capable of being intelligent to assist the user in a responsive or even proactive way. This capacity should be exploited. In a broader sense, the history of the man-machine system evolution is one of "downloading" the burden of mundane operations and analytics, along with their attendant data tasks (gathering, storage, and processing), from the man to the machine. Examples include CATSCAN, Computer-Aided Engineering, Computer-Aided Manufacturing, Computer-Based Information System, and other models of the application of computers to human jobs. This down-loading defines fundamentally the profitable relationship between the enterprise and the cyber-infrastructure, too. (Otherwise, why bother?)

However, as the notion of machine scales up from computer to cyber-infrastructure and the man to (extended) enterprise, the man seems to humble himself into being lost in his reliance on the cyber-infrastructure; and forget that the latter is meant to be an active servant to the users in cyber-infrastructure-based enterprises. For this purpose, we might stress that the definition of cyber-infrastructure allows it to work in the background to assist the users, either automatically by itself or on the users' command. A successful cyber-infrastructure-based enterprise is poised to do better by exploiting these promises and developing embedded intelligence to support the users. For example, the cyber-infrastructure could provide automatic sensing, monitoring, and adaptive control to the enterprise processes, real-time and online. Therefore, this principle could also be called the proactive digital nervous system principle, in the spirit of self-organization [17].

We submit that a cyber-infrastructure-based enterprise should strive to become cyber-infrastructure-ASSISTED, with the ability of automatic re-configuration. That is, the cyber-infrastructure should be conceived and constructed in an end user-oriented manner. In a co-production context, the user (person or enterprise process) assumes the role of the man of the man-machine system, with the cyber-infrastructure the role of the machine. The assistance automates certain enterprise processes and virtual configurations.

2.6 The Principle of Person-Centered Service

The co-production concept is further extended into person-centered service. This notion is self-evident for personal service products. However, it is equally fundamental to all service enterprises, including the services provided to manufacturing and other physical product firms. That is, when the co-production is concerned about client enterprise processes, the users of the processes immediate fit the persons' position. Moreover, the consulting in this case will also consider the demand chain of the client when planning and designing the client processes. Therefore, ultimately, the entire chain of production is a service to the persons at the center. The distinct value of this principle is to place the client/customer of a co-production mode in a position of control: the user can pull some control levers and command the cyber-infrastructure to make the enterprise produce the product demanded. The principle further indicates that new societal value chains may emerge to provide services for effecting "enterprise of enterprises"; such as the case when cyber-infrastructure-assisted enterprises recursively expand up along the demand chain to service the ultimate users: the persons.

Conceptually, this principle leads to a man-meta-enterprise thought model where the societal cyber-infrastructure connects the economy into a virtual meta-enterprise (with many renditions) for the persons to command. The virtual meta-enterprise serves as the one-stop provider of a person-centered economy, providing everything that the person requires in going about his/her live. The service here will be the provision of the virtual meta-enterprise demanded and the (virtual) configuration of the societal cyber-infrastructure required. The notion of a person-commanded, cyber-infrastructure-assisted meta-enterprise could arguably describe an ultimate service of the O-I fusing paradigm.

In retrospect, e-commerce has revived the notion of person-centered services for the first time since Industrial Revolution. Personalization is now an iron rule for destination Web sites and personal communications – e.g., the practice of "My Yahoo!" and the like. The personalized services not only prove, once again, the power of O-pulling, they also show that cyber-infrastructure is indeed an ideal tool for personalization. One could expect that personalization of products on-demand is inevitable for cyber-infrastructure-based/assisted enterprises. This is true for any personal service, the service of physical products, the service of providing other enterprises' products to the persons, and the service of enterprising enterprises.

We submit that personalization of the product, on-demand, will become the norm for cyber-infrastructure-based (better yet, assisted) enterprises. The competition will be the continuing push of the envelope to bring about more and better cyber-infrastructures and more and better assistance through the cyber-infrastructure to enable on-demand enterprising. Clearly, protection of privacy and societal integrity and security must accompany personalization.

3. MODELS OF ENTERPRISE INTEGRATION AND COLLABORATION

The O-I fusing paradigm (see Section 1) is taking shape by virtue of the evolution of cyber-infrastructure and cyber-infrastructure-based enterprises (see Section 2). The evolution has thus far revealed some general approaches to implementing the paradigm for, especially, manufacturing. We summarize these general approaches into the conceptual models of enterprise integration and enterprise collaboration. These models are made possible by certain particular technologies for manufacturing; which we refer to as the manufacturing informatics. These results are briefly discussed below.

3.1 The Model of Enterprise Integration

This model develops an enterprise digital nervous system using cyber-infrastructure, and thereby transforms the enterprise from operating in an I-pushing paradigm towards one pursuing an O-I fusing model. Because the focus of many applications in the field is digital connection, we refer to this focus as enterprise integration (through cyber-infrastructure).

- **The Objective:** Reduce the Transaction Cost and the Cycle Time of the Enterprise (while satisfying the users' demands – the O-I fusing ideal).
- **The Means/Decision Variables:** The Design of the Cyber-Infrastructure, including its elements, configuration, and application.
- **Enterprise Engineering Principles:**

- Digitize information resources (data and knowledge), communication channels (persons and machines), and process resources (control and workflow).
- Connect digital resources to users and tasks, and thereby construct a digital nervous system.
- Develop embedded or automated capabilities in real-time analytics and data processing to enhance the performance of persons and machines in the enterprise, using cyber-infrastructure.
- Develop either global or peer-to-peer administration capability to enable the cyber-infrastructure to support sharing of digital resources among distributed persons and machines.
- Simplify enterprise processes by using the new cyber-infrastructure (through consolidating sub-tasks and/or sharing results).
- Convert sequential enterprise processes into concurrent by using the new cyber-infrastructure (through interweaving sub-tasks and/or sharing resources).

- Employ the concepts of teams and virtual organizations, the flexible machinery, and the automated control systems to make the enterprise and its facility agile.

- **Constraints:** The availability of the open, scalable, and re-configurable technologies; an industrial standard for inter-operation; and the costs.

The next model, collaboration, applies the above to extended enterprises along its supply/demand chain. These two models share common logic.

3.2 The Model of Enterprise Collaboration

For the purpose of enterprise engineering, one could argue that the fundamental difference between integration and collaboration is proprietary control. Collaboration, without the control, not only is always applied to extended enterprises, but it is especially applied to virtual organizations. Thus, for instance, if a prime manufacturer actually controls its suppliers, through stock-holding or some other long-term bonding arrangements, then the extended enterprise could actually integrate rather than just collaborate.

- **The Objective:** Reduce the Transaction Cost and the Cycle Time of the Community of the Collaborating Enterprises.
- **The Means/Decision Variables:** The Mechanism and Boundaries of Collaboration; Methods of the Connection of the Cyber-Infrastructures; and Design of the Connection, including the elements, configuration, and application, and the resultant federation of the cyber-infrastructures.
- **Enterprise Engineering Principles:**
- Make digitize information resources (data and knowledge), communication channels (persons and machines), and process resources (control and workflow) compatible, either directly or through some intermediary design (e.g., middle-ware).
- Create an inter-operable proxy for each enterprise cyber-infrastructure, for connection with other enterprise proxies, and thereby construct a community cyber-structure for the collaborating extended enterprise.
- Connect digital resources in the connection (of proxies) to users and tasks, and thereby construct a virtual digital nervous system for the community.
- Develop either global or peer-to-peer administration capability to enable the virtual cyber-infra-structure to support sharing of digital resources among distributed persons and machines of the community.

- Simplify extended enterprise processes by using the new extended cyber-infrastructure (through consolidating sub-tasks and/or sharing results, along, e.g., the supply chain).
- Convert sequential extended enterprise processes into concurrent by using the new extended cyber-infrastructure (through interweaving sub-tasks and/or sharing resources).
- Employ the concepts of teams and virtual organizations, the flexible machinery, and the automated control systems along demand chain and supply chain, to make the community and its facilities agile.

• **Constraints:** The availability of the open, scalable, and re-configurable technologies; an industrial standard for inter-operation; and the costs.

The enterprise value chain could serve as guidance for identifying the candidates for process-level collaboration for the extended enterprise. At the level of strategic vision, the Person-Centered Service Principle of Section 2 could promote identification of possible opportunities of collaboration.

3.3 Manufacturing Informatics

The above models describe some of the past and emerging practices in computerized manufacturing, including supply chain management. Much of the manufacturing cyber-infrastructure required has already been proven in the field. We summarize some of the representative results below.

• **Standardization**
- Computer-Aided Design/Engineering (parts)
- Bill-of-Materials (product)
- Product Data Management (parts database)
- Computer-Aided Process Planning (generic machining control process)
- Computer-Aided Manufacturing (workstation)

• **Rationalization -** Industrial Engineering
- Work and Workflow Design
- Facility and Factory Layout Design
- Scheduling and Production/Inventory Control
- Quality Control/Statistical Process Control
- MRP/MRP II/ERP: manufacturing enterprise resources planning

• **Flexibility**
- SCADA: automated factory data collection (monitoring)
- AGV-MHS: flexible material handling and layout (facility)
- Flexible Manufacturing Systems (cells)
- Manufacturing Execution Systems (shop floor control)
- Computer-Integrated Manufacturing (factory)

- **Extended Enterprise**
  - Concurrent Engineering (distributed design)
  - Simultaneous Engineering/Design for X (design-production collaboration)
  - Agile Manufacturing (team)
  - Product Lifecycle Management (design-production-service collaboration)
  - Supply Chain Integration/Management (prime-supplier collaboration)
- **Standards**
  - STEP (and PDES, etc.) (international/US, for CAD-CAM-CAPP)
  - ESPRIT/CIMOSA (European, for CIM)
  - Society of Manufacturing Engineers models (US, for flexibility)
  - IEEE (international/US, for hardware and others)
  - ISO/OSI (international, for networking and software)

The above list is by no means complete. They represent the technological innovations that transition from the I-pushing paradigm into the O-I fusing domain. It is the co-production dimension that they miss, that requires new fundamental results. The O-I fusing paradigm is evidenced in certain emerging technologies that continue the previous progress in the directions of, e.g., mass-customization and enterprise collaboration. They include the core product models and other standards to enhance STEP (ISO 10303) [22] and other industrial specifications; the reference models and ontology for supply chains [16, 20]; and process description languages and process libraries to automate process planning [7]. An obvious direction for future development is to make the previous deterministic results adaptive to changes, such as making the manufacturing process specifications stochastic. An approach envisioned herein is to incorporate the concept of "tolerance" into process design. In this sense, automated data sensing, monitoring, and analytics can be embedded into machines that execute the processes, and thereby adjust the processes. Such a concept is referred to as the Manufacturing Process Informatics (by Dr. Mark Dausch and the author).

We submit that cyber-infrastructure-based service enterprises should consider the proven practices in manufacturing, including the above models of integration and collaboration and the manufacturing informatics, to the extent applicable. The best example of cyber-infrastructure-based enterprises thus far is e-commerce/e-business, which shows the extent to which manufacturing informatics may apply to service.

4. SERVICE INFORMATICS: ACHIVING THE ECONOMY OF SCALE FOR SERVICE

The premise here is that the economy of scale is a relevant ideal to service enterprises. However, this ideal is not achieved by standardization, such as figuring out the bills-of-materials, for service products that are inherently personal, custom, and on-demand. Rather, it is achieved through concurrent co-productions of service using concurrent virtual configurations of the cyber-infrastructure, in a model of cyber-infrastructure-assisted enterprises. In other words, the previous notion of concurrent processes is extended to include concurrent co-productions using on-demand processes executed through virtual configurations of resources, with the embedded assistance of the cyber-infrastructure itself. Such a conceptual model is discussed first, followed by a summary of previous and emerging technologies that support this vision, and concluded in a general analysis of the requirements for new results.

4.1 The Thought Model of Concurrent Co-Productions

Again, we invoke the model of databases as a reference point [25]. Formally speaking, the enterprise database model defines a three-schema logic consisting of the internal schema (defining the access methods of the physical data storage), the conceptual schema (defining the logical data objects and their semantics for the enterprise as a whole), and the external schemas (defining the virtual data objects and semantics that individual classes of users and/or applications use). The external schemas are derived from the conceptual schema and do not determine the underlying physical data structures; therefore, they can be added, dropped, or modified online without affecting the underlying database. The conceptual schema, on the other hand, determines the internal schema and hence the physical data structures used. It represents the real database. This three-schema model can and has been extended to administer distributed databases, where the conceptual schema is generalized into some (federated) global or common schema, with the external schemas accommodating the conceptual schemas of local databases. Depending on the design and requirements, the global or common schema could be explicit – i.e., actually serving as the schema for a central synchronization mechanism. But, it could also be implicit, taking the form of some ontology and/or middleware to facilitate peer-to-peer interchange of data. The latter is particularly popular for Internet databases.

The enterprise database model sheds light on a possible conceptual model of the new cyber-infrastructure at an enterprise level. A key concept to this thought model is the formulation of the co-production of service – be it a consulting, a process, or an enterprising – to be a concurrent use of the cyber-infrastructure (e.g., running a client company's payroll processes). This use is then compared to the use of a database, such as a particular query job for an end user or a data processing job for an application program. Therefore, the co-production is a session (e.g., payrolls) of the running of the cyber-infrastructure, rather than being a structure of it (e.g., a dedicated payroll EDI/network). Each co-production can be unique, in terms of the processes involved and the (virtual) configuration of resources required; but they will be supported by the cyber-infrastructure as sessions. The processes involved and production factors used in the co-production do not have to be repetitive, nor standardized. The economy of scale comes from the concurrent co-productions performed on the same cyber-infrastructure – or, simply, the sharing of digital resources. The economy will come primarily in the form of transaction cost and cycle time reduction (see Section 2).

The technology required will center first on the acquisition of an open, scalable, and re-configurable cyber-infrastructure for the enterprise. Next, person-centered "control levers" must be afforded to the users, including both the client/customer and the producer of the co-production, to enable virtual configurations of the cyber-infrastructure for individual co-production sessions, ideally with the assistance of the cyber-infrastructure itself. That is, the cyber-infrastructure should be able to customize its jobs (e.g., helpdesk processes, customer relations processes, and payrolls) for the particular sessions on the users' command, in a manner in which the cyber-infrastructure appears to be custom designed just for the particular co-production at hand. The processes can be one-of-a-kind since they are realized in the on-demand employment of the cyber-infrastructure, or, the virtual configurations commanded. If a co-production process is compared to a database query/application, then the virtual configurations are compared to database views. This model of cyber-infrastructure affords both large scale construction and on-demand flexibility for individual service products.

Albeit in an initial state of development, the above thought model actually describes many e-commerce/e-business enterprises. A prime case is the ISP (Internet Service Provider) and ICP (Internet Content Provider) models. They, along with Portals and Search Engines, have thrived on sharing their digital resources among customized (virtual/non-consuming) uses – or, concurrent co-productions using the same cyber-infrastructure. Although their service products are not nearly as complicated as enterprise processes and professional consulting, as we envisioned above for cyber-infrastructure-based/assisted enterprises, they are still telling precedents.

We submit that the above three-schema cyber-infrastructure model will reduce the challenge of service productivity to cyber-infrastructure design, rather than to standardization of co-productions and their production factors (e.g., the processes and the knowledge workers). The former can stand on the shoulder of the giant of the science, engineering, and management results; while the latter may be intractable, and inappropriate, too.

4.2 Service Informatics for Co-Production

As discussed in Section 3, although service enterprises can and have employed a lot of the cyber-infrastructure results developed in the field of manufacturing, they also need to develop new results that handle the co-production aspects of service products. That is, when a service product is user dependent and time dependent, and the user is a participant of the production using knowledge workers, then the enterprise needs to develop cyber-infrastructure-based/assisted concurrent co-production to achieve economy of scale. This concept is supported in some proven practices of e-commerce/e-business, with some proven results of the service informatics required, as discussed below.

4.2.1 Application Service Provider

One can argue that the ASP (application service provider) model is a harbinger of On-Demand Business/Services (see below). Although the ASP model is practiced primarily on the basis of leasing some common application software to different clients and/or running some pro forma operations (e.g., payrolls processing) for them based on the software, it nevertheless features co-production. Often, the application requires running the software at the client sites, involves client-side computing, or entails some co-production enterprise processes. Well-known examples include online ticketing services for airlines and many other B2C (business-to-customer) e-commerce services. The ASP model is also widely found in B2B (business-to-business) services where firms outsource certain administrative operations to some online specialist businesses, such as payrolls. The ASP firms are cyber-infrastructure-based enterprises that achieve economy of scale by running (massive) concurrent co-productions on their common, sharable, but non-consumed digital resources.

The ASP cyber-infrastructure features strong server-side computing. When client-side computing is also significantly involved, additional results for coordinating the service side and the client side computing also become important. In many ways [24], the ASP model shares the same technical characteristics with those of the ISP/ICP models. The co-production features are typically built in the user interface, application maintenance, and software support aspects of the cyber-infrastructure.

4.2.2 Exchange and Marketplace

Another signature e-commerce/e-business practice is the Exchange model; of which Marketplace is another name. An exchange either connects person-to-person or business-to-business, or both. In a broad sense, the practices of blogs, MSN zones, and many other peer-to-peer sites can be considered P2P exchanges. In the business world, all supply chains, B2B sites, and B2C sites have the potential to consolidate and turn into exchanges. The Exchange model – beyond the stock and commodity exchanges – was touted widely as the future of the New Economy, only to find itself rapidly fell out of favor afterwards. However, this concept and its technical results are basic to the economy, regardless of whether it is in vogue at the time.

The economical promises of the Exchange model are pretty much every thing that we have discussed: consolidation of processes, removal of duplicates, sharing of resources, concurrent co-productions, and so on, to reduce the transaction cost and cycle time. With sufficient participation, a successful exchange archives the economy of scale not only for the exchange provider, but more importantly also for the sellers and buyers in the market. Both of them gain through the access to the market at large and the availability of near perfect information on the market for their decision making. In the ideal case, an exchange mimics the economy itself and reveals Adam Smith's invisible hand for that particular space. Stock and commodity exchanges have demonstrated this promise.

The exchange cyber-infrastructure features user side computing and middleware [19]. The server side could be relatively moderate compared to the ISP, ICP, and ASP. A typical design for exchanges is to develop proxies to represent the market at the user sites [10]. These proxies use a global design (including data models and languages) neutral to the local sites to facilitate both the inter-operation between the user sites and the exchange site, and the interaction among user sites in a peer-to-peer mode.

4.2.3 On-Demand Business/Service and Emerging Results

The phrase "on-demand business" is credited to IBM. However, for the purpose of this research, On-Demand Business and On-Demand Service are considered generally to be a concept of providing services and enterprise processes to firms, on-demand, using cyber-infrastructure. The providers will practice this model on themselves, as well – i.e., providing on-demand enterprise processes to their own need. If the previous e-commerce/e-business practices illustrate cyber-infrastructure-based enterprises, then on-demand business/service providers are expected to exemplify cyber-infrastructure-assisted enterprises; since the capability of automatic re-configuration is implied in the notion of on-demand.

The required cyber-infrastructure will combine three categories of results: manufacturing informatics for the enterprise processes amenable to the I-pushing paradigm; service informatics for the ASP and Exchange level co-production; and emerging new results for more complicated co-production. The third category represents an evolving effort; however, some of the current results are listed below, which contribute to user side computing, the middleware, and the inter-operation in a peer-to-peer mode.

- Open Source Technology (community-sanctioned software such as Web Services, ebXML, JAVA, PostgreSQL, RubyRails, and the like)
- Industry Standards and consortia (e.g., UN/Oasis)
- Internet databases: ontology, Semantic Web, XQuery, and the like.
- Agent-based approaches to software design.
- Results under the labels of Ubiquitous, Pervasive, and Mobile Computing
- High performance computing (including collaborative/grid computing)

We submit that significant results are already available to enable some significant cyber-infrastructure-assisted service enterprises. The enterprise engineering effort required is primarily the vision and design of the cyber-infrastructure. We postulate that the requirements for future research and development in the field may be identified from the three-schema thought model of cyber-infrastructure discussed in Section 4.1.

4.3 New Research: an agenda

In general, new results required will fall into three basic categories: basic elements of the cyber-infrastructure (the totem pole), design and administration of the cyber-infrastructure (the three-schema model), and application of the cyber-infrastructure (engineering of on-demand enterprise processes). All research will promote the O-I fusing paradigm.

4.3.1 Development and Integration of Enterprise, Personal, and Environmental Cyber-Infrastructures

The first category will cover all three classes of deployment: the enterprise, the person (and other moving objects concerned), and the environment – see Section 1. Practically, all previous results of cyber-infrastructure available in the field, including the manufacturing informatics and the service informatics discussed above, belong to the enterprise class and promise to continue progressing along the current lines. Therefore, the other two classes will be a focus of new development. These new results will be fully integrated with the enterprise cyber-infrastructure results to enable extended enterprises and connect the economy in unprecedented ways. A possible scenario will envision a supply chain to be an extended enterprise that controls its freight on the public transportation infrastructure (e.g., trucks on highways), as it does the parts on the material handling systems within their factories. An integrated, cyber-infrastructure-assisted supply chain can therefore display the status of its overall production at any components of the chain in a manner of a global control panel, and command re-configuration of the processes anywhere - either at will, based on the real-time online intelligence of the cyber-infrastructure, or conducted automatically by the cyber-infrastructure itself.

The field is full of endeavors for developing personal and environmental cyber-infrastructures. Examples include the wireless sensor networks deployed in the environment to monitor animal migration as well as seismic conditions. Person-carried bio-chips are popular in many popular scientific writings. In some specific applications, such as intelligent transportation systems and inventory control, person-carried and mobile object-carried RFID chips are connected to enterprise cyber-infrastructures. However, we submit that much more will emerge, bringing both new elements and their comprehensive integration for the whole economy.

4.3.2 The Cyber-Infrastructure Model: integrated design, administration, and processing

The second categories will formalize the three-schema cyber-infrastructure model discussed in Section 4.1. The key driver here will be the recognition of the cyber-infrastructure as the digital equivalent of the (physical) organization itself. This recognition will open up the field and develop the models and techniques required. An analogy here is, again, the development of the data models, database designs, database management systems, and database applications. One would expect design-focused investigations to develop particular architectures and guide the construction of the cyber-infrastructure. For the administration tasks, the field needs three classes of results: that enable openness, scalability, and re-configurability for the cyber-infrastructure; that enable the cyber-infrastructure to provide assistance; and that provide virtual configurations and support user interface/interaction with the cyber-infrastructure. Together, they may constitute a formal model and the attendant management system for the envisioned cyber-infrastructure. The processing of the cyber-infrastructure, including the provision of virtual configurations, will be carried out through the (distributed) cyber-infrastructure management system. Person-centered control levers (user-cyber-infrastructure interaction) will be required.

4.3.3 Enterprise Engineering Using the Cyber-Infrastructure

A new field of enterprise system engineering will rise from on-demand co-productions if they are achieved through using custom enterprise processes running on virtual configurations of the cyber-infrastructure. The analogy here is system analysis and software engineering for developing information systems. Since the cyber-infrastructure is by definition distributed, the enterprise systems and their engineering will be, too. Therefore, a central theme of the engineering will be the employment and deployment of the built-in assistance provided by the cyber-infrastructure, throughout the enterprise. The products and their enterprise processes will be developed on a basis of automatic re-configuration. This principle means that the service products themselves may become automatically re-configurable by using built-in support of the cyber-infrastructure, along with their enterprise processes of co-production. In a way, one could envision certain classes of physical products be designed and produced in a re-configurable way using the built-in assistance of the cyber-infrastructure that they employ. In general, the more cyber-infrastructure elements the physical products include in their design and use, the more likely they can become automatically re-configurable by the assistance of the cyber-infrastructure.

We submit that the above new results will help enable the concept of cyber-infrastructure-assisted enterprises and implement the O-I fusing paradigm. Conversely, if the concept describes the direction of evolution of the micro-economical production function for our society, and captures the essence of the new economy of scale for, especially, the service sector, then the above new results should be brought into being.

5. SUBJECT-ENVIRONMENT INTERACTION: MAKING THE ENVIRONMENT A PARTNER

To help reduce the research agenda in Section 4.3 to practice, we propose some particular solution approaches using current technology. These results help integrate the personal and environmental cyber-infrastructures into enterprises, and thereby develop the environment into an active partner of the digital nervous system that possesses intelligence. This intelligence, downloaded from the users (the subjects), represents a key ingredient of the vision of cyber-infrastructure assistance. At the center of these new results is a new model of user-environment interaction, on the basis of a digital dimension added to the environment.

5.1 A Digital Layer onto the Physical Infrastructure

This goal is not out of ordinary. A recent study (2003-2006) at the State of New York under the auspices of the U.S. Federal Highway Administration includes a vision of turning the I-87 corridor (from the border of Montreal, Canada to New York City, New York) into a "Smart Highway" that supports regional economical growth as well as improves highway maintenance and transportation. Among the possibilities considered, massive wireless sensor networks could be deployed along the highway and exchange data with the vehicles and freight cargos that carry next generation RFID (capable of light data processing). When the real-time feed of data from the sensors are also connected to enterprise databases at the freight companies, government agencies, and all other concerned parties, the Smart Highway would become an integral part of a Homeland Security monitoring system for the U.S.; or a supply chain management system for any cargo owners or users; or an extended Just-in-Time system for any trucking companies; or a control mechanism for any intelligent transportation systems...; or, simply, it would become a digital nervous system for many possible extended enterprises.

With this possibility of a digital dimension added on top of traditional infrastructure and space, we consider below a new model of subject-environment interaction. The notion of subject here refers to persons and mobile objects concerned that need interaction with the environment.

5.2 The Subject-Environment Interaction Model

The key concept here is to make the environment "intelligent" – or, downloading some basic analytics from the subjects to the environment to perform for the subject. This is also a "co-production" partnership between the subject and the environment. This partnership is new to the field. For instance, mobile robots may use pre-placed physical marks on their environs to help them navigate. However, these marks are "dumb" in the sense that they do not possess adaptive knowledge and decision-making analytics. Cruise missiles and Unmanned Aerial Vehicles also use similarly "dumb" sensors on the ground to augment their topographical databases during navigation. These practices, nonetheless, show the value of involving the environment into the guidance regime. A logical next phase in this direction is to make these sensors "intelligent" - capable of decision-making, and thereby make the environment an intelligent partner of the navigation.

In this vision, intelligent sensors and wireless sensor networks are optimally deployed to the environment and connected remotely with enterprise databases to form a (massively) distributed information and decision system. The sensors and wireless sensor networks serve as the local information units that interact directly with the on-board control models of the subjects. The databases - the global information units - provide contextual knowledge to the local units and facilitate data fusion and adaptation of control knowledge at these devices. Together, the sensors and databases form a local-global decision model that makes the environment intelligent. The real-time interaction constitutes a collective decision process that continuously adapts itself during the entire journey of the subjects.

As such, sensors and wireless sensor networks are also decision-makers in the process; sometimes they just assist the subjects in the navigation but sometimes they also direct. We refer to this new design the Subject-Environment Interaction (SEI) model, so as to contrast to the traditional model that we call Subject Self-Reliance. A major property of this new model is that the interaction may draw from enterprise information – such as the global patterns and requirements of the subjects, and use the information to better integrate the subjects with enterprise operations.

For example, under the new SEI regime, the factory control systems could route its Automated Guided Vehicles (AGV) according to the real-time conditions on the shop floor, and integrate the AGV into the Manufacturing Execution System for Just-in-Time production control. The subject-environment interaction in this example would be comparable to an intelligent transportation system in a city that uses multimedia sensors and computerized signs to remotely control the traffic of vehicles and pedestrians on streets, while taking into consideration the control information from other government agencies (databases). The difference would be automated control (AGV-SEI) vs. human-decision-making (transportation). The former exhibits an automatic re-configurability capability.

The same idea could be employed in different contexts for a wide range of applications. For example, a homeland security system could remotely adapt its wireless sensor networks' monitoring rules based on the real-time instructions or decision information provided by its enterprise databases, which fuse data for the entire system. Similarly, exploration projects could drop wireless sensor networks that possess the necessary environment-sensing capabilities to remote regions. These intelligent sensor networks would constitute a "live" map of the region and work with the exploring robots to jointly negotiate the alien terrains.

The SEI approach requires new results to perform the following tasks: making real-time decisions at the local level, inter-operating between sensors and enterprise databases, and globally configuring the logical and information capabilities on sensors and wireless sensor networks in an open, scalable, and adaptive way. Some aspects of the problem are physical, such as the limited computing power, energy supply, and sensing capabilities on which the above tasks rely. These issues are expected to vanish soon as the technology and materials continue to progress rapidly. However, other aspects of the problem are simply not satisfied in a few areas.

From local to global, the first requirement encountered is Efficient Computing for the new sensors and wireless sensor networks. The need is to afford the sensor nodes an operating system, with sufficient on-board metadata, that supports re-programmable embedded analytics and light database processing, to make them capable of gathering decision data from other sources and process them. Next, new Data Fusion and Information Integration results are required to make a cohesive digital nervous system out of the massive collection of sensors and wireless sensor networks and enterprise databases. Finally, the design and optimization of the digital nervous system need new System Modeling and Placement results to determine the location of local units, and the configuration of the different classes of capabilities at local and global nodes. These requirements and their solution approaches are discussed below.

5.3 The Basic Components of the Model

Environment: networked (multimedia) sensors and wireless sensor networks, including the gateways and other infrastructure; they are responsible for sensing the environment, monitoring the moving objects concerned, and directing the subjects as required.

Subject: chip-based RFID (radio frequency identification) and (personal) computer-based control systems on-board the automated guided mobile objects; they are responsible for performing primary navigation (the subject of movement).

Context of Interaction: enterprise databases, including SEI-specific systems and related application systems; they are responsible for facilitating data fusion among sensors and sensor networks, information integration between the environment and the subjects, and bi-directional management of the local metadata on-board environment and subjects.

The information processing capabilities for each class include the following:

Sensor Nodes and RFID chips: implementing on-board processors with at least a few mega-bytes of memory sufficient for creating and processing a (light) main memory database.

Central Nodes and Subject Databases: PC-class machines with full range of analytical programming and database management capabilities.

Enterprise Databases: multiple-user and multiple-application environment, with full-fledged middleware to support common schema and system integration.

Given these capabilities, the concept of Subject-Environment Interaction is reduced to an automated guidance model that joins the subjects with the environment through the above distributed information units in making real-time navigation decisions. Therefore, the analytic nature of the SEI concept is the optimal distribution of the information units (including the location and connection of the sensors and sensor networks, the allocation of metadata and other decision capabilities to them, and the development of these capabilities) and their real-time processing (local execution with certain global synergism).

We define a global model of collaboration for the distributed real-time decision-making under the SEI regime:

Autonomous local nodes: any nodes of sensors, wireless sensors, chip-based RFIDs, and subject databases could be structured and controlled by different authorities, and processed under indigenous systems without constant support from the enterprise databases.

Global nodes: any application databases could be connected to any SEI nodes through at least one global node, which is a dedicated SEI enterprise database providing and maintaining global metadata (e.g., common schema and contextual knowledge) and administering global database queries.

The above components constitute the cyber-infrastructure of the SEI model. The cyber-infrastructure, to which individual information units subscribe, embodies the wholeness and achieves the global cohesiveness of the distributed local executions. The embedded metadata at local nodes that the global model maintains achieve common purpose for the SEI nodes community. At the real-time behavior level, global optimality is replaced by local feasibility, compensated by continuous adaptation.

5.4 Efficient Computing Design for Sensors, Sensor Networks, and Chip-Based RFID

Sensors, wireless sensor networks, and (chip-based) RFID belong to the same class of mobile data processing technology. Sensors and wireless sensor networks perform both transponder and transceiver roles, while RFID is conventionally considered mainly from the perspective of transponders and lacks computing capacity. However, both technologies can be considered together from the perspective of chip-based data processing, and benefit from the same design of Efficient Computing.

A wireless sensor network is a multi-hop self-configuring wireless network consisting of many sensor nodes, each of which performs sensing, computation and communication. The sensing component can be Seismic, Magnetic, Thermal, Visual Spectrum, Infrared, Acoustic or Radar. The computation component can include data analysis such as beam forming or aggregation of related data. It can also include routing computation overhead. The communication component involves radio frequency transmission and reception between multiple nodes within the transmission vicinity. A sensor network could have a central node (and/or gateway sensors) to provide necessary computing and communicating capacity to supplement the distributed processing taking place at sensor nodes. These nodes have more permanent power supply. For the purpose of this research, they are considered as belonging to the PC-class of information units.

The proposed SEI model envisions a two-way inter-operation between these "leaf nodes" of the digital nervous system and the enterprise databases. That is, the system will feature direct feeding of real time sensor data into enterprise databases on the one hand, and adaptive control of sensor networks based on new information from enterprise databases, on the other. This two-way inter-operation promises to make sensors a system of distributed information units capable of real-time decision-making. However, it also means that new efficient computing results need to be applied to support the heightened on-board computing and to limit the burden on communication. Also included in the new capabilities will be filtering and signal processing to handle noise at the sources of raw data, with the assistance of the global data and knowledge at the central nodes and the enterprise databases. The proposed research will draw from previous results [1] to design new thin operating systems that also embed metadata (knowledge) and analytics, manage databases, and execute decision tasks.

5.5 Data Fusion and Information Integration

This task realizes the synergism of the cyber-infrastructure-assisted enterprises. Therefore, its analytic nature is the development of a global regime to integrate the data from sensors, wireless sensor networks, and subject databases (on-board RFID-control systems) with the enterprise databases. The suggested approach is to focus on metadata technology, including developing an open and scalable common schema/ontology for the interaction, coupled with distributed metadata at local nodes.

The most pertinent metadata results come from the field of global database query and multiple databases inter-operation. Although these results assume certain conditions that do not exist in the SEI model, they could be modified and extended to achieve the required data fusion and information integration. The modifications and extensions are concerned with two fundamental conditions of the distributed model: collaboration of all information units and light database processing capabilities at sensors.

The field of multiple, heterogeneous, and autonomous databases have provided many metadata methods to help reconcile different data models when no one authority can practically impose a single, comprehensive data semantic standard. However, these results do not offer sufficient simplicity to work effectively in large-scale environments such as the SEI model of cyber-infrastructure-assisted enterprises. In fact, industrial experiences (e.g., the E-Engineering effort at GE and the ebXML Registry Information Model at Oasis [26]) show that an open and scalable common schema would not be feasible unless it is based on some sound ontology. Sound ontology, however, is evasive. Common practices in the field tend to base ontology on domain knowledge; that is, the ontology would enumerate all possibilities and/or requirements of the "concepts" of the application domain. Domain knowledge is a moving target at best.

In academia, a popular approach is to base database ontology on some class of linguistics [16, 23]. An alternative is to base ontology on the information modeling concepts and constructs that systems use, and employ directly these generic elements to structure a repository of enterprise metadata. The Metadatabase model, due to this author, is an example. We submit that the Metadatabase results could form a basis for developing the open and scalable common schema required. The previous Metadatabase-supported global query processing methods also provide a starting point for the execution of data fusion and information integration. The major new effort required will be the development of the new distributed metadata methods to empower local nodes at the efficient computing level [12-14].

5.6 System Modeling and Placement of the Information Units in the Cyber-Infrastructure

Any sensors and wireless sensor networks face a location-connection problem: how many gateway sensors (and/or central nodes) to use, and where to place them in order to optimize the communication of the sensors subject to fixed power supply and other constraints of the network? This problem would have to be solved continuously, in an automatic re-configuration manner if possible. Similar system-optimization problems exist. For the SEI model, the optimal assignment of decision capabilities to the information units for particular applications is also required. For instance, embedded analytics and metadata could be added or removed to activate, de-activate, or modify the functions of particular sensors, either on command or by self-adaptation – i.e., automatic re-configuration. These issues call for new engineering methods and techniques to perform the design and evaluation of SEI systems.

The analytical nature of the (automatically re-configurable) distributed SEI systems may be described by the Artificial Neural Networks (ANN). However, the traditional ANN approach faces difficulties when applied to large-scale systems – i.e., neural network models not only entail voluminous computing in their simulation, but also require considerable training data (prior history) to operate. Neither condition is favorable to cyber-infrastructure-assisted enterprises. To facilitate these problems, we propose to aggregate the basic neurons of the ANN into some prototypical modules representing the fundamental functions germane to the SEI model. An analogy is the aggregation of basic electronic elements such as gates for Integrated Circuit design. The ANN literature includes such efforts, too [18]. For the SEI model, these aggregate constructs will be the basic modeling blocks to represent the cyber-infrastructure. The development needs to determine a complete set of the functions as well as to develop the aggregate constructs; both of which will be conducted in the future research.

We submit that new aggregate ANN constructs could be developed from previous results in the field. On this basis, a modeling methodology could also be formulated to guide the general application of the new constructs and evaluate their inherent benefits. Intuitively, this approach promises to reduce the complexity of modeling and simulation (training), in proportion to the sophistication of the aggregation itself. In fact, as the aggregate constructs increase the order of their standard representation, one could expect them to decrease the size of the ANN models (as measured by the number of these modules), and hence the attendant modeling effort, by more orders of magnitude. This situation is comparable to chip design, where aggregate constructs of "pre-fabricated" gates and other IC elements are commonly used to make the design tasks attainable as the logical size of the chips continue to grow exponentially.

In conclusion, the above SEI model represents a concrete approach to develop some new results to enable cyber-infrastructure-assisted enterprises. These results extend enterprise cyber-infrastructures with personal and environmental components and capabilities. The extension, in turn, makes it possible to design person-centered, cyber-infrastructure-assisted, and even automatically reconfigurable co-productions for enterprises.

6. FUTURE OUTLOOK

The above vision is centered on a cyber-infrastructure that fuses information technology with information resources to connect persons, enterprises, and even the environment for our society. It further uplifts the micro-economical production function through the O-I fusing paradigm of production. Enterprises use it to achieve economy of scale for service, as well as for personalization of physical products. In this vision, persons are propositioned to be at the center of the economy through co-productions with various enterprises; as enabled by the cyber-infrastructure. If this vision makes sense, then it could be extended to describe the possible next steps of the evolutionary journey of cyber-infrastructure-based/assisted enterprises.

The outlook may start with Figure 8-1, (adopted from [11]) which shows a person-meta-enterprise interaction through the societal cyber-infrastructure referred to as the "Personal Wizard Architecture". The notion of "person" here could be replaced by "family", "team", or even "enterprise" as the subject of concern.

Figure 8-1 A Virtual Configuration of the Societal Cyber-Infrastructure for a Particular Person.

The central node of the Personal Wizard Architecture is the person in command, and all other nodes are enterprises. Some of the enterprises provide the cyber-infrastructure (such as those depicted in the inner-most concentric orbits). Some provide products (the outer-most orbits). The others provide services that enable the Personal Wizard Architecture and/or the meta-enterprises (the middle orbits) – such as On-demand business/service.

From the perspective of supply chain, an enterprise could be conceived at the central node and command through its own virtual "Enterprise Wizard Architecture". However, all enterprise wizard architectures ultimately lead to persons if following the demand chain. Thus, the person-centered rendition of the virtual configuration of societal cyber-infrastructure fits the O-I fusing paradigm best. In theory, the economy has as many such personal wizard architectures as it has persons; and each is a virtual configuration of the societal cyber-infrastructure. Needless to say, these virtual configurations run concurrently on the same cyber-infrastructure and tap (use, not consume) into the same digital resources.

We submit that enterprises should explore the opportunities that the societal cyber-infrastructure presents, along these orbits or across them. Consolidation will occur along societal value chains. The principles discussed in Section 2, and the models of integration and collaboration in Section 3, could be applicable to the economy as a whole – i.e., the economy could be considered as a societal virtual enterprise. To the extent that this notion is relevant, a top-down recursive application of the principles and the models from the whole economy down to industries and enterprises could shed light on future evolution of cyber-infrastructure-based/assisted enterprises. Conversely, a bottom up pursuit to apply them to extended enterprises could reveal possible business strategies. In any case, an O-I fusing paradigm using cyber-infrastructure is a reality in our economy now.

ACKNOWLEDGEMENT

The author wishes to express his gratitude to Dr. Thomas R. Willemain, for his review of the manuscript. His comments made the chapter better.

REFERENCES

1. I.F. Akyildiz, W. Su, Y. Sankarasubramaniam, and E. Cayirci, "Wireless Sensor Networks: a Survey," Computer Networks, vol. 38, 2002, pp. 393-422.

2. Thomas Blass, The Man Who Shocked the World: The Life and Legacy of Stanley Milgram, Basic Books, New York, 2004.

3. S.P. Bradley, J.A. Hausman, and R.L. Nolan, eds., Globalization, Technology, and Competition: the fusion of computers and telecommunications in the 1990's, Harvard Business Press, 1993.

4. Charnes and W. W. Cooper, Management Models and Industrial Applications of Linear Programming, Vol. I and Vol. II, John Wiley, 1961.

5. S. H. Clearwater (ed.), Market-Based Control: A Paradigm for Distributed Resource Allocation, World Scientific Publishing, River Edge, N.J., 1996.

6. R.C Dorf and A. Kusiak, Handbook of Design, Manufacturing, and Automation, Wiley-Interscience, 1994.

7. S.J. Fenves, R.D. Sriram, E. Subrahmanian, and S. Rachuri, "Product Information Exchange: Practices and Standards," Transactions of the ASME, Vol. 5, Sept. 2005, pp. 238 – 246.

8. Milton Friedman, Price Theory, Aldine Publishing Co., Chicago, 1976,

9. Jay G. Galbraith, Organization Design, Addison-Wesley, 1977.

10. R. Glushko, J. Tenenbaum, and B. Meltzer, "An XML Framework for Agent-based E-commerce," Communications of the ACM, vol. 42, no. 3, 1999, pp. 106-114.

11. C. Hsu and S. Pant, Innovative Planning for Electronic Commerce and Internet Enterprises, Kluwer Academic Publishers, Boston, 2000.

12. C. Hsu, M. Bouziane, L. Rattner and L. Yee, "Information Resources Management in Heterogeneous Distributed Environments: A Metadatabase Approach," IEEE Transactions on Software Engineering, vol. 17, no. 6, 1991, pp 604-625.

13. Cheng Hsu, Enterprise Integration and Modeling: the Metadatabase Approach, Kluwer Academic Publishers, Boston, 1996.

14. C. Hsu, D. Levermore, C, Carothers, and G. Babin, "On-Demand Information Exchange Using Enterprise Databases, Wireless Sensor Networks, and RFID Chips", IEEE Transactions on Systems, Man, and Cybernetics, forthcoming.

15. Yuji Ijiri, ed. Creative and Innovative Approaches to the Science of Management, Quorum Books, New York, 1993.

16. Y. Kalfoglou and M. Schorlemmer, "Ontology Mapping: the State of the Art," The Knowledge Engineering Review, vol. 18, no. 1, 2003, pp. 1 – 31.

17. Stuart A. Kauffman, The Origins of Order: Self-Organization and Selection in Evolution, Oxford University Press, Cambridge, UK, 1993.

18. R. Kozma and W.J. Freeman, "Basic Principles of the KIV Model and Its Application to the Navigation Problem," Journal of the Integrative Neuroscience, vol. 2, no. 1, 2003.

19. K. Kurbel, L. Loutchko, "Towards Multi-Agent Electronic Marketplaces: What is There and What is Missing?" The Knowledge Engineering Review, vol. 18, no. 1, 2003, pp. 33-46.

20. D. Levermore and C. Hsu, Enterprise Collaboration: On-Demand Information Exchange for Extended Enterprises, Springer, Boston, 2006.

21. SETI@Home, http://setiathome.berkeley.edu.

22. STEP ISO10303, www.steptools.com/library/standard/.

23. J.F. Sowa, Conceptual Structures: Information Processing in Mind and Machine, Addison Wesley, Readings, MA 1984.

24. L. Tao, "Shifting Paradigms with the Application Service Provider Model," IEEE Computer, vol. 34, no. 10, 2001, pp. 32-39.

25. Jeffrey D. Ullman, Principles of Database and Knowledge-Based Systems, Vol. I and Vol. II, Computer Science Press, 1988.

26. UN/CEFACT, United Nations Center for Trade Facilitation and Electronic Business, Core Components Technical Specification, version 2.01, November 15, 2003.

27. Oliver E. Williamson, The Economic Institutions of Capitalism, The Free Press, 1985.

INDEX

Printed in the United States of America